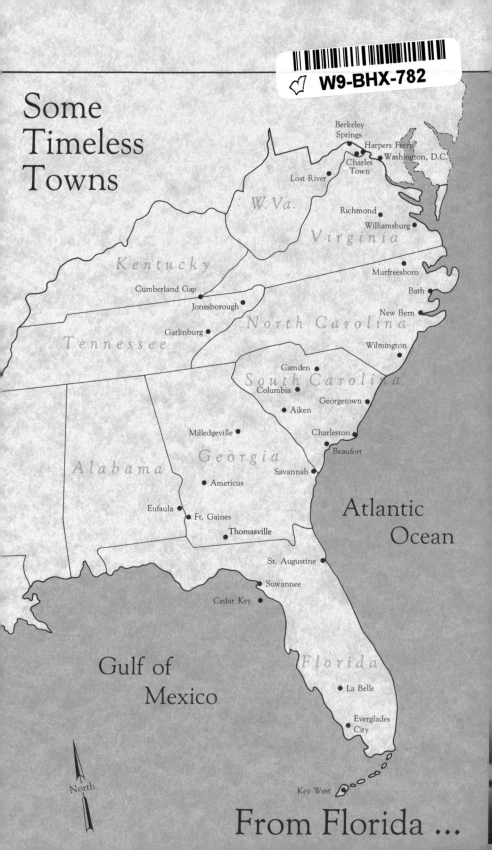

Some
Timeless
Towns

W9-BHX-782

Berkeley Springs

Harpers Ferry

Washington, D.C.

Charles Town

Lost River

W. Va.

Richmond

Williamsburg

V i r g i n i a

K e n t u c k y

Murfreesboro

Cumberland Gap

Bath

Jonesborough

New Bern

North Carolina

Gatlinburg

Wilmington

T e n n e s s e e

Camden

South Carolina

Columbia

Georgetown

Aiken

Milledgeville

Charleston

Beaufort

A l a b a m a

G e o r g i a

Savannah

Americus

Eufaula

Ft. Gaines

Atlantic

Thomasville

Ocean

St. Augustine

Suwannee

Cedar Key

Gulf of

Mexico

F l o r i d a

La Belle

Everglades City

North

Key West

From Florida ...

TIMELESS TOWNS

TIMELESS TOWNS

AND HAUNTED PLACES

From Florida to Maine

J. R. Humphreys

Photographs by the Author

ST. MARTIN'S PRESS   NEW YORK

For Carl and Bob

DESIGN BY JUDITH A. STAGNITTO

Library of Congress Cataloging-in-Publication Data

Humphreys, J. R. (John R.),
  Timeless towns.

  1. Atlantic States--Description and travel--1981-
--Guide books.   2. City and town life--Atlantic States.
3. Humphreys, J. R. (John R.), 1918-   --Journeys--
Atlantic States.   I. Title.
F106.H918   1988   917.4'0443   88-18161
ISBN 0-312-02300-6

First Edition
10 9 8 7 6 5 4 3 2 1

Think of the past;
I warn you that in a little while others will
find their past in you and your times.

—Walt Whitman

Contents

PART I
  In Search of the Past   1

INTRODUCTION   3
The Timelessness of Timeless Places   12

PART II
  Timeless Towns Revisited, New York to Florida   21

The Ghost in the Basement   23
New Jersey's Pine Barrens and Cape May   27
Middle Atlantic Roads   31
Spanish Moss, Florida Palms   39
The Road to Charleston   41
The Road to Savannah   48
The Road to Key West   52

PART III
  Journey: From Mangrove Swamps to Northern Pine   59

The Everglades   61
Florida   65
Georgia   70
South Carolina   77
North Carolina   88
Virginia and Greater Washington, D.C.   93
West Virginia   102
Cumberland Gap and North   112
Pennsylvania   115
New Jersey, Heading for Maine   122
New York   125
Connecticut   130
Rhode Island   138
Massachusetts   143
Vermont   150
New York Again   153
Vermont Again   157

New Hampshire   166
Maine
                                                       170
APPENDIX: Towns and Inns
                                                       183
INDEX
                                                       212

PART I

In Search of the Past

Introduction

One of these days I may yet come across an abandoned piece of highway, its cement broken and patched with weeds, that will take me through underbrush and woods, past fields and rows of split rail fences, to a roadbed of macadam that, in turn, will lead me to a town just getting the news that John Adams has been elected.

I'll come across this road where the net that captures the past has fallen. That's how I imagine it, this torn mesh, as insubstantial as fragrance or shadow. It lies in patches over our cities and towns and countryside, over highways, farms, courtyards; under it, the living remnants of another era.

A lot of what was here when America was little more than thirteen colonies is still around, some of it reconstructed, some preserved by choice or edict. There's more than a glimmer of the past around us.

I know. I'm a sometime sojourner in areas and places where the look and even the feel of history remain. It's a kind of time-traveling, with the help of early maps, avoiding major highways as much as possible, keeping to the crosshatched areas where, with a pen, I draw netlike designs, shaded places, circling the names of beautifully preserved towns, like islands in time, looking as I go for old inns moody with a forgotten period when carriages rolled up to their doors.

Twenty-eight years ago it occurred to me that a journey through the past could be charted from coast to coast. With the Atlantic Ocean at my back, I set out from New Jersey, and, with my wife navigating, calling out landmarks in the sunken past, consulting the logs of earlier navigators, we moved westward toward the forever golden hills of California and the perpetual pull of the Pacific. The book that came out of that trip was *The Lost Towns and Roads of America*—and they were lost roads; little traffic moved along them.

I've been a teacher for many years in a major university in Manhattan, and my wife Peggy and I live in a nearby apartment complex that consists of a cluster of slim, boxlike, twenty-one-story brick buildings with randomly enclosed balconies; six buildings in all, they rest on land that two hundred years ago was ragged countryside. Time moves swiftly on Manhattan.

The apartment complex obliterated a couple of long blocks of old buildings to make room for itself. Among the buildings torn down was a drugstore I worked in as a kid, dishing out sodas and sundaes behind a marble-topped counter. My father at the time was getting his PhD at Columbia. I wasn't born in New York. I was born in a small town in the northern part of the lower peninsula of Michigan, a town that hasn't increased or lost much in population since I remember it as a child.

Peggy is also from a small town. It stands in Iowa next to an Indian reservation. She graduated from the University of Iowa, taught a year, then came to New York; there we met.

New York is where our search begins for timeless places. The city streets and side streets I spend my time on now, most of them, have lost their history, so New York seems an appropriate place to begin journeys to timeless towns and haunted places. What I seem to be looking for always is a perfect sense of the past, a crossover into another time period, or at least the illusion of such a crossover.

Ours is a lazy search, taking it slow and easy, rolling along roads too narrow to be visible on the maps dispensed by gas stations. D. H. Lawrence, an extensive traveler in the 1920s, decided the world (even then), superficially at least, was "small and known." A kind of paper, he said, wrapping the earth and concealing history, had to be pierced before the traveler could be liberated from the present. We've found the wrapping gone in islandlike places in the South and Middle Atlantic, and in New England we've found it gone more frequently, the spaces shorter between each island. When we come across a village with a sense of timelessness about it, I circle it with blue pencil.

My blue circle goes around towns like Crosswicks, New Jersey, or any small, simple town blooming like a flower surrounded by a desert of historical anonymity.

Sometimes the towns aren't identified on every gas station map. Victory, and Granby, Vermont, were such towns, the two of them recognized, however, on the 1799 map we carried around for reference.

Victory, when we saw it, was a cluster of empty houses. Granby, on the other hand, ignored by our contemporary map, lived on, had a Congregational church with a congregation, a town hall, and a town clerk. Several notices were tacked to the town hall door, and a light bulb with switch chain dangled there to light the notices for those who came after dark.

I remember once searching for a tavern, looking for it all around a town in Maine called Oxford. Couldn't find it anywhere. Had it disappeared from those streets of lovely, narrow white houses, so old, founded in 1794? I walked and looked, but no tavern, or none I could find.

I went into a grocery store on the town square and asked the kid behind the counter if he could tell me where the old tavern stood.

"Craigie's Tavern?" He shook his head. He'd never heard of it.

But an older girl who had walked in ahead of me and who stood beside us at the counter had. "That place burned down. Don't you remember?" she said to the boy. "It was the old hotel that stood across the street."

"Oh, yeah, that old place."

Whole cities or large sections of cities have gone up in flames, and once a building is gone, it's hard to remember where it stood.

Revolutionary roads are sometimes as hard to find as if they've disappeared. They *can* disappear from contemporary maps. We've spent long pine-green afternoons looking for one or another of those old roads. After a while, knowing we're in its general vicinity, I'll stop at a rural farm or house to ask what's happened to it.

There was the afternoon—we were driving around eastern Vermont looking and looking for a famous eighteenth-century highway—that the mystery of where it went got too deep for me. Also, a stagecoach stop known as Elkins Tavern wasn't where my *Vermont* guide in the *American Guide* series had it located. I pulled into a farmyard. The farmer, or a man whose big hands were reddened and chapped by hard work, came out of the back of his house and led me to his front yard.

He pointed back up the road to a house we'd passed at least five times and said, "That's the old tavern, but people live there now. The book you got is a little out of date."

"Then this is the Bailey-Hazen Road?"

"Part of it, anyway. The old road ran all the way from Boston to Montreal, and travelers put up at Elkins Tavern, or stopped there for food. That's the place, and until just a while back people could still stop there to eat. It's the oldest house we got in Peacham."

"Where's the rest of the road?"

He waved one hand in a casting motion, and my eyes followed the way it led across fence and cornfield. "Gone. A lot of it. When that tavern was built, this countryside was thick with Indians. When they left they took the road with them, you might say, stole some of it. I grew up right in this house, and I can tell you, any old-timer can, there are foundations left of houses that stood along the road. Most of what's left of the old road is under grass and trees and brush, but it's out there."

Driving on, I took the cutoff once more past the tavern and then headed for Danville. Rain had fallen earlier in the day, and now, at day's end, rain once more hit the windshield. When I came to a fork where a small sign said a section of the Bailey-Hazen Road lay on my left, I cut that way onto a narrow gravel track and hit a piece of plausibly primitive road. Trees and their leaves seemed to spread and part in front of us. I slowed down, crept along, and came to an even smaller road that branched off into woods and underbrush, a road made of no more than wheel tracks cut into the earth.

When I knew I couldn't get the car down that faded trail any farther, I stopped and got out and walked on through rain, pushing aside wet leaves and branches. I could still see wheel tracks in the earth, but darkness was closing in and so was the underbrush. I had to stop, much as I wanted to go on. How far could I get with daylight gone? It was dark and raining and my hair was drenched, and so were my face and hands and clothing: the last lost traveler caught by darkness along a ghostly road without a standing farm or house or inn.

My wife had interests of her own on many of our excursions. The first of her father's family to arrive on these shores had landed in America in the early 1600s. A regular Pilgrim landing far from home, among the sea-dark stones of a savage continent. The first couple's son, Samuel, had owned a tavern we thought we'd try to find . . . if it hadn't burned, that is, or been torn down.

We pulled into Stonington, Connecticut, at dusk and drove along the business street to the beach at the end of town. A stiff wind was coming in off the ocean. A big wave hit shore as I was turning the car around, and its spray crossed twilight and orange clouds.

We stopped at the edge of the sea and looked ahead where the town broadened along a couple of branching streets, then drove around trying to find the tavern, driving along narrow streets, past old houses newly painted, many of the houses marked with small signs that gave us the date the house was built and the name of the first family who'd lived there.

We were looking for what we thought would be an early eighteenth-century house as we slowly drove along. Night was closing in. We wound through town several times as the leaves on the dimming trees around us spun in the wind.

In the town library the next morning, downstairs, flanked by book-shelves, we sat at a long table and read the papers the librarian brought us. Fluorescent lights and a hanging lamp lit our way back across eleven or twelve generations.

We looked through record books, read old letters, and learned at last that the tavern never had been in what is now the village of Stonington. The tavern stood on The Road, the old highway that ran between Stonington and North Stonington. And before we left the library we got the name of a man, a descendant of another old Stonington family, who could help us find the tavern—if it still existed.

We found him on his farm, a man in his seventies. He wore a plaid wool shirt and a red hunting cap. He'd crossed his barnyard and stood leaning at the open car window beside my wife.

"I'm glad," he said, "someone in your family has finally come around." And he looked relieved, too, a big man, retired now. "I know you're looking for that tavern, but while you're here you ought to go to the graveyard, which you may not know about, out there where the one who begot the rest of us, the two of us anyway"—he pointed at Peggy and himself—"is buried.

"We must be some kind of cousins," he said. "I'll tell you why I'm glad you came. There was a small fund set aside for care of the graves. Ellen Wheeler left it, but it was only about a hundred dollars. At the time it was enough, but not anymore, not these days. The interest from the money isn't enough to hire a man to go over and clear out the weeds and make repairs in the wall."

This Ellen Wheeler had been his great-great-aunt. She was among those buried in the family plot.

Wheeler said he'd be glad to take us there. He'd be happy to take us to the tavern, too, but nobody was sure anymore where the tavern stood.

He drove his car, and we followed him out of the barnyard and a little distance down the unpaved country road, then turned into a rutted lane that was like the last of the Bailey-Hazen trail, and there ahead of us was a plot of earth walled in by fieldstones, plowed earth all around it. The cemetery lay near the edge of a farmer's field, and there was a small iron gate in the graveyard wall. The gate hung ajar, broken.

We parked and walked to the wall of fieldstone that rose as high as my hips. The whole plot probably wasn't much larger than the foundation of Samuel's lost tavern. Down at the end of the front row of headstones were the graves of my wife's earliest American relatives, only the mother's grave still marked by a standing stone slab. On the stone, barely readable now, was crudely carved

GF A83

D M ye 7

1717

Just her initials carved into the flat surface of the chipped and weather-pitted marker.

At first we thought it was the old man's grave, the J carved backward as if it were a G. But his stone stood beside hers, the broken top half lying on the ground, any lettering it ever had worn away. We knew he had died in February, aged 84, and we knew from what we'd read in the library they hadn't survived a winter that stacked six feet of snow around their house.

A carpenter by trade, thirty-three years old, John had arrived in Stonington in 1667 with his wife Grace and three daughters. He'd settled in the country, not in town, because early Stonington hadn't followed the New England practice of building houses around a green and a church. John raised seven children, among them the son, Samuel, who owned and ran the missing tavern.

John took time out to soldier, serving as a sergeant in King Philip's War, and was said to be with the Indian guard who shot Philip as he was escaping, putting an end to the war with the Indians, though problems with the Indians and the French did not seem to have any end. Hostilities continued. The year John died, the French had just extended their system of wilderness forts from Montreal to New Orleans.

The graveyard was thick with weeds. There had been no one, said Wheeler, to tend the graves last year. There were grandchildren and relatives buried in the graveyard, but none of the couple's sons or daughters lay around or beside them.

We walked back to the car. We went slowly and thoughtfully. "My grandfather," said Wheeler, "told me Ellen was the most beautiful woman he'd ever seen. She was a widow. There was no one to look after her but a mulatto boy she'd raised. He was awful good to her. He lived in the back of a blacksmith shop. Folks around here thought a lot of him."

A year or so back Peggy had agreed to help complete a direct-line genealogy someone had uncovered on her family, agreeing more out of an obliging nature than from any real interest of her own. In the process, she heard about five cardboard cartons of documents and letters, all gathered by a man who had died before he could put together a genealogy. These data were from the time John had arrived in America and begun to beget them all.

Peggy had located those boxes of dead and forgotten names and brought them home with mixed feelings. She wasn't sure she had the time to do anything with them. If she sorted everything out and typed every-thing up, name by descending name, seven hundred pages or more, perhaps fifty people would care enough to want the book. The file was a staggering discovery, a staggering job, but about a week after we got back from Stonington, she took it on.

She was answerable, she found, to the past as well as the future. We all are. Figures out of the past stand around us, the "towering dead with their nightingales and psalms," as Dylan Thomas would have it. She set to work. Intrepid and tireless.

A long gray vapor stream of family figures rose from those names in the cardboard boxes, bridge builders, shoe dealers, soldiers, judges. . . . Justin, of the fifth generation, had a father-in-law who got a bullet through his hat in the fight at Concord Bridge. There was William, born on the original homestead farm in Stonington, who died there; married twice; both wives now lie with him, the second wife his first wife's younger sister. He was an officer in the War of 1812, and three of his sons were in his company. Stephen, of the same generation, born in Stonington, had a whale's jawbone for gateposts, high enough to drive through with a full load of hay. There was Asa, born 1855, who never married. He lived on the family farm in his old age. The story is told that he let the rain come through the roof of his stone house while he sat reading, holding an umbrella over his head.

We made a number of trips into the countryside in the fall of that year. In Litchfield, Connecticut, we came upon a building across from the green, a dark red brick structure with windows trimmed in white, every window barred. It was a jail built in 1812. The elm that once grew in front of the jail and served as a whipping post was gone. Something else that's vanished.

I looked around Litchfield for two of the town's early residents, Ethan Allen and Aaron Burr. They were there somewhere, lurk-ing. Patches of sky for eyes. Their thoughts in the shadows and grass stems.

No ghostly faces stared out at us from the jail windows. We walked across the green to the stores that stood on the other side, came to an alleyway, turned down it, and entered an open court paved with brick and stone. Two halves of a broken millstone lay in front of a fashionable dress shop.

I said, "If we were living in Litchfield in Colonial times, where would we go for coffee?"

"Oh, we wouldn't go out for coffee. We'd go out for tea. We'd have a carriage, of course, and we'd call for our carriage and have it drive us to the inn."

I had a picture of her beside me on the carriage seat, blue-eyed, blond hair piled up on her head, everything but her head flounced and draped in cloth, yellow kid gloves emerging from the sleeves of her coat, mother-of-pearl buttons, the tips of her silk shoes under a coat that brushed the floor of the rocking carriage.

"I'd go out," she said, "wearing my new hat with the great green feather." And I saw our carriage pulling away from the driveway of one of the big white houses, wheel rims gleaming.

People disappear. Become ghosts or whatever.

Like my Great-Grandfather Taylor. A studio portrait of him and my great-grandmother hangs on the wall near my desk. He's seated, she stands behind him, slightly to the side. He stares at me, a black-coated, black-vested man in a dark shirt that is buttoned, without a tie. His hands, resting on his legs, are twice as thick and heavy as my own. His head is big and square, his cheekbones high and round. A mustache conceals his upper lip. His lower lip thrusts forward as if in defiance. His eyes are shrewd. He gazes at the photographer but seems to gaze at me with an honest man's skepticism.

I don't even remember him. I wish I could.

I imagine him traveling west as a child on the canals his kind, the Irish, built. Then farming for his father, an occupation he followed all his long life, that and horse trading. Building his own cabin in the northern wilderness of Michigan as a homesteader after the Civil War. Wolves howled around that cabin.

He was one of the children of the "wild Irish," so called by those who had immigrated and settled before them; and he was wild in his way, a hard drinker, a Saturday-night brawler, a jig dancer, but with it all a hard-working man devoted to his wife and family. He was, as well, a musician, a tuba player. On Sundays in the town park he led the village band.

I'm not a naturalist, or an anthropologist, or even a historian. I'm a vague mystic looking for the best of several possible worlds, more interested in the now than in the past—but my instincts are with the

American Indians. They saw the worlds of past and present, of good and evil, as one substance and whole, one great burst of creative fire.

In the world of the past, I see the people who have been here before me, who are a part of me, and with the help of what they've left behind that I can see and touch, this moment in the seamless present is made more real by the past's added dimension.

In this room where I sit, I have books that go back to the beginning of the printed word. I have an old Westclox Ben Hur that was on my Grandmother Beam's dresser for all my childhood years, and a tiny glass mug, stained red, on which is painted, not etched: *Petoskey,* decorated with a branch of leaves and the date, 1901; on the far side of the mug is my mother's given name, Blanche. It was one of her childhood souvenirs. My desk, made by an eighteenth-century craftsman, I picked up on a slow day at an auction for sixty dollars. The top is warped. Nothing I have in this room is of great value, except to me. The pieces of the past I have around me give me a sense of the present and the past and the future, all bound up in one moment of awareness.

One day, following a cutoff road in New Hampshire, we came to a settlement called Percy. It turned up around a bend in the road and consisted of a few houses dominated by an enormous barn. I stopped the car. It was dusk. The sunlight had faded everywhere, but children were still out, playing some game that had them crouching, then running. A tag game. No one else about, not anyone, only the children who paid no attention to us. No lights on in the houses.

I have only seen a barn that size with so many small windows of various sizes in my dreams, a barn big enough to be a world in itself, with endless stables and granaries, narrow and intricate stairways leading from level to level, the only illumination coming from shafts of sunlight breaking through cracks and small windows. I could imagine a haymow four stories high, tunneled and mysterious. I could see baffling passageways that led from room to room—and everywhere people moving dimly about, carrying out errands and tasks that, I knew, never ended. All the people unhurried and silent, their faces in shadow. What's stranger than this vision to me is that I felt at home in that imaginary barn world, that I felt so at home sitting in the car on that dusky road. All very strange still, the sensation I have remembering my feelings as I saw that town and its barn appear so suddenly at the bend of an old road.

But that's what it's all about, this search along lost roads. It's a search at best for a glimpse of something ineffable.

The Timelessness
of Timeless Places

≫ When Washington was inaugurated in New York City at Federal Hall on April 30, 1789, Broadway's buildings, a short block to the west, weren't much more than piles of ruins left by departing British soldiers. One of those buildings, Trinity Church, was just getting rebuilt when Washington was sworn into office. The swearing in has been commemorated. At the top of a flight of steps on the site of old Federal Hall is a statue of the first President of the United States, Father of his Country. Washington's right hand rests on an invisible Bible.

The statue, erected in 1886 at the crowded corner of Wall and Nassau streets, faces toward the New York Stock Exchange. The building behind Washington is now a museum. Inside its doors is a rotunda, under its dome a marble floor circled by pillars. The last time I saw it, about a year ago, a sign announced daily folk music. In one of its several rooms, schoolchildren sat on the white marble floor listening to their teacher as she detailed days and times before even the recollection of a great-grandfather.

When I left, I walked toward Broadway. Trinity Church, its stones blackened by the dust of the years, was directly in front of me. In the tower of the church a clock with golden hands and golden Roman numerals told me the time. It was late, getting later.

Perhaps, as some believe, Colonial America ended when John Adams and Thomas Jefferson died. Throughout the country they had done so much to put together, fireworks were banging, bells were ringing, and speeches were being made. The United States of America was celebrating the Declaration of Independence that Jefferson had written and Adams had made possible with his stubborn single-mindedness; and when those two heroes of the Revolution departed, they took with them, some say, through the bursting streamers of rockets and the sound of clanging bells, the last of an era. Two years earlier, however, when Lafayette, an old man, made his tour of America, standing in town after town in the last glow of the Revolution, he still saw men in three-cornered hats who wore buckles on their shoes, silver-knobbed walking sticks in their hands; he could see the Colonial America he remembered around him. That's why Colonial America went on and on, vanishing slowly, ending with the Civil War as slaves were set free. Some carry it further and insist Colonial America ended only when people stopped reading by candlelight.

It is simple enough to stretch the American Colonial period past the Declaration of Independence. There was no radical change. Unlike most revolutions, in this one no aristocracy had been overthrown, no churches had to be demolished, no traditions uprooted. A people who were already independent simply put their independence into a formal declaration.

"If Washington Irving was right," wrote Henry Adams in *The United States in 1800*, "Rip Van Winkle, who woke from his long slumber about the year 1800, saw little that was new to him, except the head of President Washington where that of King George had once hung . . ."

America was, he observed, a country with "the same bad roads and difficult rivers, connecting the same small towns . . ." except that the roads that went into the wilderness ran on a few miles farther now. Fifty or a hundred miles inland more than half the houses were still log cabins, which might or might not enjoy the luxury of window glass. It took at least the war between the North and South and the abolition of slavery to put the quietus on what was left of Colonial America, and a little of it is still around today.

Colonial America is hard to find in New York City. John Adams had a country house on the corner of Varick and Charlton streets in Greenwich Village. That's gone. Fraunces Tavern, where Washington delivered a farewell to his officers, is still standing. Federal Hall, where the Stamp Act Congress met in 1767 and the Continental Congress in 1785, is gone.

City government offices were moved in 1813 from Wall Street to the present City Hall Park. Early coaches and passengers left from the bottom of the island. The road to Kingsbridge went up Fourth Avenue and near Madison Square cut east to Third Avenue. At 92nd Street, it meandered north and west across land that's now Central Park. At 110th Street it went north along St. Nicholas Avenue through Harlem, met Broadway, and continued to the 1693 bridge across the Harlem River ship canal to Kingsbridge. Kingsbridge has kept its name but it's swallowed up these days by the Bronx.

Spuyten Duyvil is at the confluence of the Harlem River and the Hudson. There's a ghost in that stretch of water, one Anthony Van Corlaer, who drowned in 1664. A trumpeter on a mission for Governor Stuyvesant, he was to swim that river and with his trumpet let the Dutchmen to the north know the British were attacking Manhattan. "I will do it," he swore, "en spuyt den Duyvl." The devil got him, dragged him under. According to Washington Irving, his trumpet could still be heard on stormy nights.

Change has been inevitable. New York City's population in 1789 was 30,000, Philadelphia's, 40,000, Boston's, 16,000. New York City after Washington's inauguration was, briefly, the capital of the country. That changed, too. But a sense of Colonial America still exists in New York at isolated places like Alexander Hamilton's home in Harlem, or in the Museum of the City of New York.

The first floor of the museum, the last time I was there, had a display showing the progress the city has made since the days the island belonged to its Indians. Around the corner at the end of a dim corridor with illuminated patches of the past, I came to the replica of a section of the Dutch fort that stood, around the middle of the seventeenth century, on the lower end of Manhattan.

When I climbed some steps in the fort to a second floor deck, I came up under the sky of a world I didn't know was there. I was in a world within my world. I stood in the heart of a great city's bud, in a seventeenth-century imaginary place. I was back at the beginning of New York. The air of my familiar world had altered, the climate and the light as well. I was caught somewhere in a countrylike town setting where nothing in sight was moving, neither on the streets below me, nor on the rivers to the east and west.

I turned and looked uptown. I saw no Empire State Building, no Central Park. I saw only a fence that marked the northern edge of the city, and a broad dirt road—was it Broadway?—that ran to the fence and a gate. Up where I might have seen our apartment building, I saw only plowed fields and wilderness.

I looked across the Hudson River: wilderness over there, too. Somewhere back across that wilderness would be the Old Mine Road. There wasn't a sign of it, however, nor of anything else across that flat, unblink-ing river, just Indian land.

Communipaw should have been somewhere in sight, and it gave me a restive feeling not to see it. According to Washington Irving in *Knicker-bocker's History of New York*, Communipaw was "the egg from whence was hatched the mighty city of New York." The Dutch, he claimed, settled there first and moved later to Manhattan.

In Irving's own time he swore that Communipaw was still a Dutch town virtually cut off from the nineteenth century—a Dutch Brigadoon that thought Holland was some place out on Long Island. "Like wise men and sound philosophers," said Irving, "they never look beyond their pipes, nor trouble their heads about any affairs out of their immediate neighborhood; so that they live in profound and enviable ignorance of all the troubles, anxieties, and revolutions of this distracted planet." There was, he claimed, one tavern in town and they met there every Saturday to smoke their pipes and toast Admiral Van Tromp who they were convinced still swept the British channel with a broom tied to the masthead of his ship.

Imagine finding then, not Brigadoon, or even Liberty Tree, but a town of Dutchmen, indestructibly Dutch, as the Amish are indestructibly Amish. Imagine old stuck-in-the-mud, kneebuckles-of-silver Com-munipaw hidden away in the urban wilds of Jersey City. Go out the rear door of a pizza parlor, follow the alley to the left, squeeze between a garage and a hedge . . . and there you are.

Change is inevitable, and nothing has transformed the appearance of America as much as the gasoline engine. Henry Ford is said to be responsible for most of the change, Ford and his mass-production meth-ods.

It was J. Frank Duryea and his brother who made the first successful American automobile with a gasoline engine. That was before the turn of the century. Duryea road-tested his car in New England in 1893; two years later he drove across the finish line ahead of the pack in America's first automobile race.

Duryea lived to be ninety-seven. In 1959, when he leaned over to take a closer look at one of his first cars, he was heard to say, "It's like a dream."

Everything changes, nothing remains the same. As Washington rolled along from day to day through his life, the scenery sliding away behind him, he must have had the tendency we all do to believe what's behind is more or less a setting that lingers on, something that we, at will, can turn back to and recapture like some lost but eternal Saturday afternoon. But nothing resists time. When we return to the scenes of our past, they're often so changed it's a letdown, a saddening trip.

We hadn't traveled the eastern coast of the United States from Maine to Georgia since 1967, and we began to wonder how much of what we'd seen had changed, how much would seem just as timeless as it had twenty years ago. To find out, we set off on a preliminary trip along the old road that ran from New York to Philadelphia, heading for Crosswicks, New Jersey. It was a road that had been familiar to Washington. He'd known it well.

From his encampment in Morristown, New Jersey, Washington could observe movement along that Philadelphia–New York highway. It was one of the colonists' early roads, cleared and roughly graded from Philadelphia to New Hope on the banks of the Delaware River. Across the Delaware at Coryell's Ferry, now known as Lambertville, it ran to Elizabethtown (Elizabeth these days), New Jersey.

Wheeled traffic had only begun to move down the road in 1764, and a sad road it was after any kind of rain, a sad sight for all the mired merchants and farmers; but a road it was and remained, something to be referred to in time as a main traffic artery.

Because it's a Revolutionary road, we knew it still had blocks and pieces of early America. We'd read in a state guide that a number of fine old houses stand along the route, now becoming overgrown with commercial buildings.

Old York Road had been served by the Swift-Sure Stage Line, and traveling the road out of New York and Newark, we decided, might be like taking my lost road that gradually led to an earlier era.

It was a February trip and at first, along Route 22, all we rolled by were factories and general blight. But those passed. Now and then, where the old road has straightened, we saw houses set at a slant to the new road; on the right a faded brick house, almost pinkish in color. Along about North Branch the road picked up a countryside charm. Here was a general store. There on the far side of the road a big red barn. When we came to Bridgewater, we turned south on Route 22.

At Larison's Corner, a road called Dutch Lane meets Old York Road and ends. It once continued across the way, but now that section is abandoned. It was a dirt road when it was closed, and trees have grown up in the roadbed, but the roadbed is clear enough to see, and so are the embankments on each side. Snow lay on the ground of the abandoned road, between the young trees in the highway that now leads nowhere, the trees leafless, bare.

Up the road, at the junction with the highway we'd been following, an inn once served the road trade. It was in this inn that Gun, long gone, cadged drinks by butting cheese off the bar.

Gun was a simple-minded fellow with a thick skull who had learned to use his head to win bets. He was something of an entertainer, and he had an act he performed for the price of a drink. A wheel of cheese would be set on the bar and Gun would back off, get a good running start, and butt the cheese to the floor. Then collecting drinks all around from the men who gathered there, usually cattlemen, he was set for the rest of the night or afternoon.

The tavern had a posted sign for these same gentlemen that said, "Cattle drovers must remove their boots before getting into bed." A rough, fun-loving, hard-drinking bunch, predecessors of the Western cowboy.

One time a couple of men in the bar got hold of a grindstone the size of a wheel of cheese and wrapped it in cheesecloth. They rounded up Gun, brought him into the bar, and showed him his target. Bets were laid. With a cheering section urging him on, Gun backed off, lowered his shoulders, and, charging the millstone, struck it a wallop, toppled the stone, and staggered. "Oh my," he said, collecting his first drink from the cattlemen, "that there, I swear to God, be the hardest damn cheese my head ever hit on."

The tavern is no more. It's gone. Fell in on itself in time, and in its place is a gas station. There isn't even a memorial to Gun, the all-time cheese-butting champion of Old York Road.

A few miles beyond Larison's Corners, at Ringoes, the Amwell Academy, built in 1811, has changed since Gun's day. It's been a liquor store since its educational luster faded, and it's now a roadside tavern, Saunders' Inn. We had lunch in the tavern's pub, thick mushroom soup and salad. Four or so people sat at the tables around us; the supports for a number of tables were old metal sewing machine bases. The stone wall of the old academy made one of the pub's walls.

Both Lambertville, New Jersey, and New Hope, New Jersey, have been discovered, first by writers and artists and then by tourists, but a solid sense of timelessness exists among their buildings and along their streets; unlike the less-well-known timeless towns seldom visited by tourists, Lambertville and New Hope have inns with meals and overnight accommodations, historic inns at that.

Along river's edge out of Lambertville toward Trenton: On the side of the road across from the river are houses, but not many. There's the canal. Then the river. Old houses and buildings. Stucco houses. Tree branches filigree the canal and river. The snow lies in free-form patterns against the dark ground.

We find a place to cross the canal and drive along the river, the canal on our left. In Titusville we pass an 1850 house. And then as we come to Trenton, the houses reach an age I would judge to be around the 1930s. Wooden porches. Now and then a Victorian house, one with a mansard roof. At Washington Crossing State Park, we come back to the main route again.

The grace of the Delaware River appealed to the eye of at least one member of a European royal family. He was the brother of an emperor and a former king in his own right, Joseph Bonaparte. He bought, without becoming a naturalized citizen, 1,800 acres of land on the New Jersey side of the river just below Trenton. But it was not the natural beauty of America alone that attracted Bonaparte to Bordentown. Rather, he fled to America after the Battle of Waterloo, leaving his wife behind.

He had some trouble at first getting assimilated at Bordentown, foreigner that he was, former king of Spain, and older brother of Napoleon. Neighboring states took to calling New Jersey "Spain." Because of him, the townspeople were called Spaniards. It made no difference that Joseph was a Frenchman of Italian descent.

Joseph spent eighteen years at Bordentown, where he was known respectfully as Count de Survilliers, or as Mr. Bonaparte to villagers who didn't go in for title talk.

The house, a large and handsome place by American standards, was up only a few years when fire wiped out its midsection, leaving its brick wings standing. His neighbors saved the furnishings. He tried to thank them publicly for not stealing everything. He wrote: "This event has proved to me how much the residents of Bordentown appreciate the interest I have always felt for them, and it shows that men in general are good, when not perverted in youth by a bad education." The locals were offended. Common honesty did not need thanks.

The count rebuilt. He liked these Americans. He built bigger and better. He put in parks, turned a stream into a lake, and upped his living standard to the level of a king's. If anyone from town knocked on his door to see how a king lived, he was welcomed in to look the palace over.

Nobody around Bordentown took the king talk seriously. To them he was a neighbor, "the good Mr. Bonaparte." When he died in Florence in 1844 at the age of seventy-six, they went about town in a state of mourning.

Change has come to Bordentown. If Joseph could return, he'd find his mansion no longer stands. But his gardener's lodge does, and a remnant of his park.

I think of Henry James's search, shortly after the turn of the century, for familiar houses and places in the neighborhood of his youth: finding his home gone, a church across the street built as though for eternity— one he had watched built—gone as well; journeying to the north and south of the United States, he saw the changing land, so many landmarks, manmade, that bound him to the past going. . . . He thought that what stood where the old had been was thinner, a little sickly by comparison, and he took that as a sinister portent.

Passing through areas I'd crosshatched or into towns I'd circled in blue pencil was for me, however, like moving into another age. Unburdened by the memory of those who had lived there and gone, and of what might have changed, the towns and areas were mysterious and remote to me; far from being sinister, they lived in an aura of immortality.

We were on our way to Crosswicks, New Jersey, because I'd taken a picture of the town across its millpond some twenty years ago, and I wanted to see if the town still matched the photograph.

Crosswicks, settled in 1677, is part of a historic district, and once a town reaches that status, little change is allowable. We remembered it as a Colonial village, as handsome and well preserved as any New England showplace.

Problem was, Crosswicks isn't on a numbered road, and though we found the highway that would take us near the place, we couldn't find the right turnoff. We reminded ourselves that the true backroads traveler moves along small roads that have no numerical identity.

"We have to sense direction," Peggy said. "What do you sense?"

"You mean, follow my hunch?"

"Go," she said, "by the shadow of those trees, go by that house shadow."

I made a turn to the left at the next small road. It led, after a while, into a dead end. The limbs of a great tree arched over our car.

"Not the road," I said.

"No," she said, "it doesn't look quite the way I remembered Crosswicks."

We followed another road, a paved road this time, until we came to a couple of men standing beside a pickup truck.

"How," I asked, "does anyone find Crosswicks?"

One man shrugged, but the other man knew exactly where it was. "Two miles," he said, "straight down this road."

Crosswicks still looks like a Colonial village, devoid of tourists, and it has any number of backyard barns. The sight of backyard barns pulls me back to the days of my childhood when barns were joyful places.

We drive back and forth through town several times looking for the pond in our picture. Can't find it anywhere. We pull over beside Crosswicks' local tavern. I go inside. It's too early for dinner. The place is dark, motif early American. The manager at the bar, a young man working at a list of figures, tells me about an old icehouse by a pond.

Following his directions we dip down a road in the middle of town and come to a barn of a building that's closed up. It's the old icehouse, but there's no pond.

I'm beginning to feel that the town I saw and photographed twenty years ago has reinvented itself. Crosswicks is a beautiful place, but it isn't the place I remembered.

Then Peggy, looking at our map, as puzzled as I am, says, "It's Imlaystown."

"What is?"

"The town in the photograph."

"It's not Crosswicks?" I can't believe our problem is as simple as a case of mistaken identity. And I still don't as we set off for Imlaystown.

We enter Imlaystown, another hidden town on a cutoff road, along a curve that passes between old white houses. And, by god, we come to the pond and the mill we've been looking for. Saunders' Mill it is. There's a plaque on it that says, RICHARD SAUNDERS OWNED THIS MILL AND IRON-WORKS. SON-IN-LAW, MORDECAI LINCOLN, WAS GREAT, GREAT GRANDFATHER OF ABRAHAM LINCOLN. The town is as attractive as I remembered. Two-story houses, long porches, shutters on windows. More than that, it's a town that doesn't seem to have changed since I took its picture more than twenty years ago. Except, the pond is dry now, and there's an inn in town I don't remember, the Happy Apple Inn.

We drive back to the inn and park and I go inside.

"How long has the inn been here?" I ask the bartender.

"Thirteen years. But the house itself was built in 1902."

And then I ask him about the pond.

When I get back to the car, I say, "It's cozy in there. First there's a bar you pass, then a dining room with windows facing the pond . . . only the pond's been drained. They've drained it for repair work. When the water flows back into the pond, the photograph will be as current as it was a generation ago."

We picked up hope at Imlaystown that a relatively timeless country-side still lies in bits and patches under the restraining, intangible net of time . . . and decided we ought to check this out and picked the East to do it: that land so many Europeans fled to, oldest and most thickly settled area in the United States.

PART II

Timeless Towns Revisited: New York to Florida

The Ghost in
the Basement

*T*wenty-eight years ago, hours after we were married, we packed ourselves into a Volkswagen camper and drove to Atlantic Highlands, New Jersey, to start off on an adventure along less-traveled roads. It led us through countryside left behind by strip cities that were rising on each side of our East-West turnpikes. That forty-five-day trip covered 7,485 miles.

Now almost three decades later it was early spring, and we were ready to set off once more on a trip through crosshatched areas on our maps, a South-North trip that would take four months and cover 11,702 miles.

Even so, in spite of all that traveling, the area we covered was so great that the timeless and nearly timeless places this account reports are only a sampling of what's out there in the eastern American countryside. This book is not, was not meant to be, a guide. As I've said elsewhere, there can't be guides to unself-consciously timeless towns. If there were, they wouldn't keep their innocence for long.

Our car, a sedan this time, was loaded. We rolled out of New York through the Holland Tunnel—on our way to Atlantic Highlands, New Jersey. From there we turned inland. On the New Jersey shore near

Navesink, we were back in time to when we'd started for California. There were changes, of course, but not many. A house had been built across the road from the place I'd rented during World War II. The old house sat at the top of the long slant of a hill, its front porch facing our car as we drove past. I waved. It was a haunted house, and I wondered if the ghost, a noisy one, still lived in the basement.

I'd rented that beautiful old eighteenth-century frame home with its wide waxed floorboards with finder's triumph. It had French doors that faced a sideyard flagstone patio and a sunken garden. There was a fireplace in the dining room, one in the living room, and still another in the upstairs master bedroom.

The house had been standing since the Revolution and belonged to a couple who were uprooted by the war. I'd rented the place furnished and was moving in with the help of a friend while I waited for my wife, my first wife, who was visiting her mother, to rejoin me.

The ghost made its presence known at once. I was getting dinner ready for Archie and myself when the ghost started opening the basement door.

There was a pantry between the kitchen and the dining room. As I passed through it, I noticed that the door to the basement was open. I closed it. I'd seen the basement, a cold, damp, windowless place, cold with a radiant chill that reached my bones, nervous-making. I shut the door that evening and carried two plates into the dining room where Archie sat. On my next trip, the door was again open. Open maybe five or six inches. I shut it and shook it to be sure it was closed.

I said, "Archie, did you open the door in the pantry that goes to the basement?"

"When?"

"Just now, while I was in the kitchen."

He shook his head.

I went back and looked at the door. It was open again. Mysterious forces were at work.

I lay in bed that night hearing rapping on the glass of the big upstairs bedroom. It's the wind in the branches, I told myself. I heard marbles being dropped in the attic over my bed. Squirrels, I thought.

My wife and her mother arrived and moved in, and her mother began to hear things she'd tell us about at breakfast. "Someone walks up and down the hallway outside my bedroom."

"It's the boards of an old house," I said. "Old boards do that."

We had given her, as our guest, the master bedroom and were sleeping in a small room down the hall.

One morning, at breakfast, she said, looking right at me, "It's you out there in the hall, isn't it?"

"It's not. June will tell you it's not me."

"Someone," she said, "is out there. Last night they rolled something down the stairs."

"Like a walnut?" I asked.

"No. Bigger than that."

"How much bigger?"

"Bigger."

About that time there was a popular British song coming over the airwaves about a queen named Anne Boleyn who, at the midnight hour, walked the bloody tower with her head tucked underneath her arm. My mother-in-law knew what was on my mind when I said, "Is this thing rolling down the steps about the size of a cantaloupe?"

She got a look of horror. "Yes," she said. "About that size."

Not long after, my mother-in-law went home, and we moved back into our room. We did some listening each night but heard no one walking about or rolling his head down the stairs.

Then one night the damnedest racket woke us. It seemed to shake the house. My wife was terrified, and I was doing my best not to be when I got out of bed.

"It's something downstairs," I said. I thought of the cold, windowless basement.

This was a steady hammering sound we were hearing, like someone pounding on the cellar door, an urgent, endless, desperate pounding. It went on and on without letup.

At the fireplace, I picked up the poker and went downstairs. I paused at the entrance to the dining room and turned on the light. Nobody there. The sound was coming from the pantry. I made it to the pantry and pushed open the swinging door. Nobody there either. The door to the basement was closed. The sound, hellish and wild, out of control, was coming from the kitchen.

I opened the kitchen door. The house had come with one of those old refrigerators that had a motor mounted on top in a metal casing. One of the bolts that held the motor in place had come loose, and the motor was banging against its housing. I still think the ghost in the cellar did it.

We lived in Navesink and Long Branch and Deal while I was stationed at Fort Monmouth. That was a long time ago, time enough for a lot of change, for some new highways and a racetrack; even so, everything was familiar, even the Navesink house with its ghost.

Those summer towns along the Jersey shore did not seem very different to me, though there has been a problem with garbage floating in the sea along the beaches. A sign of our times. Some of the old restaurants are gone, some new ones have appeared, but it's all pretty much as I remember it.

At Sea Bright the highway runs along a seawall, the ocean on one side, old summer mansions on the other; the mansions continue along the road all the way to Long Branch and beyond. This is summer mansion country.

Later on, after we left the Navesink house behind, we lived in Long Branch with our daughter, not yet a year old, in one of those old mansions that face the sea. From our windows we could watch the rolling waves that sometimes destroyed the oceanfront for miles along the shore and boardwalk.

Long Branch was a fashionable place for summer bathing long before I saw it. Its history as a resort goes back to 1788, when people from Philadelphia came to the Jersey shore to bathe. They stayed in a boardinghouse, and strict bathing laws were observed. Men and women could not wade into the surf together. When a white flag was flying, it was ladies' hour.

New Jersey's Pine Barrens and Cape May

*S*outh of the Jersey shore's summer resorts lie the Pine Barrens, an ancient, bypassed world. I saw them first when I was getting my specialty training as a Signal Corps long-linesman, laying telephone poles between Fort Monmouth and Fort Dix. When our trucks came to the western edge of the barrens above Dix, we rolled along over dirt roads through what I thought at first was a young forest. The driver I sat beside knew better. "Those are dwarf pines," he said. "They'll never get any bigger. There are places here with full-grown trees that'll make a giant out of you. I mean you can stand in trees that come to your shoulders. It's something in the soil that stunts them."

"Bad water?"

"No, sir. Best water in the world is here. Pure as rainwater."

On our noon break we drove to a shack in the woods that sold soda pop. The man who served us was tall and thin and silent. He lived in the back of the store, his yard a clutter of rusting junk. He was a Piney, and his ancestors probably had lived in the barrens generation after generation since the Revolution. There were no other houses in sight, and I learned this is typical of the Pineys. They like seclusion. Maybe the trait was passed down by progenitors who fled to the barrens to hide, among them Revolutionary War deserters, Tories, Hessian soldiers, escaped slaves, and convicts.

What I like about the Pine Barrens is the same thing the Pineys liked: the remoteness from the summer resort life to the east and from the hustling traffic to the west that rolls between Philadelphia, New York, and points north.

We entered the Pine Barrens a little below Asbury Park; from there they stretch almost all the way to Cape May, a maze of dirt roads that date back, some of them, to the seventeenth century. We did not try many of the side roads where each year hunters and hikers lose themselves and run the risk of coming face to face with the Jersey Devil.

The Jersey Devil is not the kind of spirit that inhabits houses and raps on walls and opens doors. He's a legendary monster. Bat-winged and some say goat-faced, he's been blamed for devouring pigs and, when he can, little children. Some of the Pineys actually hang out lanterns to ward him off. He lives, it's said, deep in the cranberry bogs, and he roams this wilderness at will. There are claims he's been seen beside the road in passing headlights, bat wings folded, eyes cherry red, tongue hanging from his hairy mouth.

In this area, as big as or bigger than any of our national parks, approximately eighty miles long by thirty miles wide, there is an underground lake that's seventy-five feet deep, one hundred square miles of it. The purest of water lies there. Ship captains of old sailing vessels barreled it out of the Pine Barrens' sandy-bottomed, brandy-colored streams. It's cedar water, flavored and colored by cedar roots and iron. There are canoes to rent for those who may want to paddle these waterways.

The sand roads in the Barrens were laid down by wagon traffic before the Revolution. Later, some of the roads served as stage routes when there were more towns. Beside the roads were jug taverns. Pirates—privateers, that is—liked the seclusion of these woods. They pulled their ships in along this part of the Jersey coast and unloaded their contraband. They're gone, and with them the seventeenth-century woodcutters, the eighteenth-century robbers, and the early iron towns.

We'd been cutting through the Pine Barrens for quite a while, following Route 539 south. When we came to Cotsworth, we pulled in at W. J. Busby's General Store and Eatery. At a counter inside the door we sat down to have a coffee.

The store has been standing at Cotsworth's crossroads for 125 years, pine wilderness all around it. Cotsworth is the Pineys' principal town, and a small town it is, not even a dot on our map. The sky had been overcast all day, and a kerosene heater was keeping the store warm. The counter where we sat was called, Peggy noticed, the magazine room, called this because of the magazines that roosted there, donated by a forest ranger. Not many stores like Busby's are left anymore.

Much iron was shipped from the Pine Barrens for half a century after the Revolution, ending with the discovery of anthracite and iron ore in western Pennsylvania. Batsto, a little farther down the road and off to one side, is a town that produced this ore, and it survives as a tourist attraction.

We stopped at Batsto briefly before moving on to Cape May. Batsto, meaning the place Indians came to bathe, was first named by the Scandinavians and the Dutch. Later, it became an industrial center.

In the spring of the year Batsto was a fairly deserted place. There were few other visitors. Hollow-eyed, deprived of all but its past, it sits silently now, abandoned to the sandy forest. This is the site of the Batsto Furnace, built in 1766; cannon and cannonballs were cast here for the Revolutionary Army, and cast again for the armies of the War of 1812. Joseph Wharton, a financier, bought it all—something like 100,000 acres—in 1876 for $14,000. He lumbered the land and raised or harvested cranberries and sugarbeets and livestock. When he died in 1909, nobody stepped up to buy the land around his isolated community. They lacked his vision and ambition, or perhaps had learned lessons from his failures. No one wanted it until 1954 when the State of New Jersey bought it and took it over. It's being preserved for its historic importance.

We walked the road that goes west past Batsto Mansion, a huge house that looks haunted but isn't, from all I've been able to learn. Across the bridge over the Batsto River we came to the former homes of the workers, fifteen in all. These were haunted-looking places too, their wood tanned a deep brown by the weather and streaked with gray and gold; a sandy street ran between their front doors; forsythia was in bloom in their yards. It was a picture out of great-grandfather land.

There were benches beside the doors. I walked up to one of the houses that had a sign on a two-by-twelve board. *Weaving and Spinning Exhibit*, it read. Inside, behind a wired-over door, sat a woman in a long skirt at a spinning wheel. Glassy-eyed and silent, she was permanently seated at a wheel that never moved—motionlessly on exhibit, night and day, whether observed or unobserved.

I sat down for a while on one of the benches beside the door. There were a couple of pine trees out front; under the trees pine needles colored the ground a rusty red. Moss was growing in the shingles of the house across the way. From somewhere, faintly, I could hear children playing.

The first residents of Cape May, back in the seventeenth century, were whalers. Whaling was a way to make a living in the seventeenth century in southern New Jersey. It was a winter enterprise. The Cape May whalers lived and hung out around Town Bank on Delaware Bay, a short distance from Cape May. The whalers stood on shore and kept an eye out for any leviathans passing between the bay and the ocean. Whaling was a high-risk, high-profit business. These men didn't hunt whales on the high seas, or go searching the world for them; they shoved small boats off from shore and, if they harpooned a whale, they had to tire him, then drag him back to shore and beach him.

A Thomas Leaming of Town Bank wrote that he went "a-whaling" in 1693–94 and got eight whales. He worked at whaling for another six winters, then married and gave it up. It was a business for young men or for men with sense enough to know when they were pushing their luck.

Eventually the whales steered away from New Jersey, and the whalers rowed farther and farther to sea for whale oil, farther and farther, then gave up.

Cape May is one of the towns that claim to be the oldest seashore resort in the country. It began to cater to tourists when one of the locals sought vacationers in 1801 by advertising in a Philadelphia newspaper. His hotel accommodations consisted of one large barn of a room where sheets divided the spaces allotted on one side to men and on the other to women. The resort grew and, in time, as hotels with verandas sprang up, was visited by politicians and industrialists of renown. Numbered among these mighty were Presidents Lincoln, Grant, Pierce, Buchanan, and Harrison, as well as John Wanamaker of department-store fame, and the publisher Horace Greeley.

In Cape May, our old guidebook says, visitors searched the beach for pure quartz—the Cape May diamond—its edges rounded by water attrition. Maybe there are genuine gems buried hereabouts. Captain Kidd frequented southern New Jersey. He pulled in and anchored to take on fresh water, scooped it out of Lily Pond at Cape May. This was toward the close of the eighteenth century. Not long after, during the War of 1812, the British also came to Cape May for water supplies.

Among Cape May's early tourists was Henry Clay. Women, it's said, chased him up and down the beach trying to cut locks of hair from his head.

In the 1980s, Cape May has none of the gaudiness and clamor of Atlantic City or Asbury Park. There are no gambling casinos or board-walks lined with concessions, no ferris wheels or crack-the-whips. It's a village with old hotels and houses by the sea, Victorian houses with Victorian gingerbread.

I had photographed one of those majestic white hotels on a trip twenty years ago, and we looked the place up again. It was unchanged, the hotel closed, awaiting its summer season. Peering through the windows, I didn't think too much was different inside. We'd have stayed there, locked up as it was, if we could.

Middle Atlantic Roads

~P

hiladelphia has no tourist season and, considering the scarcity of downtown motels, it doesn't seem to want one. Again and again, trip after trip, we have driven around that city looking for its Old Town near the waterfront, bewildered by its streets and looping highways, measuring our time so we'll make it across the river before the motels in New Jersey fill up and the NO VACANCY signs creep out.

Twenty years ago, Philadelphia was rebuilding, salvaging its Old Town. Now when we found it, Old Town looked as we remembered it. The area around the marketplace has been snatched from the present into its past. The trees, as always, were larger; there were more remodeled and attractive brick houses along side streets, another indication of life beyond death.

We took our usual stroll down the narrow cobblestone street where Benjamin Franklin lived, walking past the line of posts where horses had once been hitched. The upstairs windows of the houses we were passing had small reflecting glasses, about the size of side-view mirrors on a car, for the householders to view the people passing on the street. Or, to watch for Jimmy McCoy?

A one-legged news vendor by the name of Jimmy McCoy hobbled the streets of Philadelphia during the Revolution peddling a paper called the *Evening Post*. He carried a trumpet, and he'd blow the trumpet and howl, "Here's your bloody news!"

His trumpet and his now ghostly cry are still heard from time to time just before dawn along the streets of Old Town. "Here's your bloody news! Here's your fine bloody news!" Only the sleepless, I think, have heard it, those who are dreaming but awake.

Traveling from timeless place to timeless place is like slipping in and out of the past, like slipping from wakefulness to dreaming and back again, believing all the time you are awake.

Tourism, as often as not, saves—or attempts to. There's a steadily growing, even enormous, interest in our past. It got its start with the restoration of Williamsburg, Virginia. In the last twenty-five years the movement to fix earlier eras in time has spread to all the coastal cities and has moved west. Decaying city centers, so-called areas of "degradation," have taken on a revived form of life, a rebirth. Grime has disappeared. Hollow windows have new window frames and curtains. Some houses have been gutted to their walls and rebuilt according to original plans.

New Castle, Delaware, was once a great seaport, then a railroad center; bypassed by superhighways, it's now a pocket of the past. We drove into New Castle and stepped back 200 years.

After the Duke of York gave William Penn the land he needed in America for his "holy experiment," it was at New Castle that Penn landed, the oldest town in the Delaware River valley. Penn arrived on October 27, 1682. Although little of that period remains, a surprising amount of the city seems extant from the time a convention of the counties of Delaware met at New Castle to form the state of Delaware (in 1776).

Parts of the Old Court House on the north side of Delaware Street, a brick building, date back to different periods. It's thought a section of the east wing stood when Penn walked into town for the first time. The Old Sheriff's House around the corner on Market Street once had a gallows and a whipping post. They were carted away in 1901, reminders of the grim side of the human spirit that a town like New Castle could at last do without.

The Old Arsenal, an 1809 building on Market Street, is now an inn. It was a little early for lunch, but the woman who takes reservations had time to chat. "People in New Castle," she said, "have owned their homes for generations, and they're very proud of where they live and of how long they've been here. I get calls for reservations from people who start out by saying, 'I'm from Strand Street,' only they say, 'I'm from the Strand!' Strand is that beautiful street of old Colonial homes close to the river. If you go over there," she said, "be sure and look at the little alley that leads to the river, Packet Alley. That's where early travelers came up from their boats on the river, came up through Packet Alley, that is, famous people, like George Washington and John Adams, people passing through New Castle. They'd start their overland journeys by stagecoach from here. Andrew Jackson, Daniel Webster, Stonewall Jackson, and Chief Black Hawk, too."

Checking one of my old photographs, a vista of Delaware Street below the square, I found change, but so little. A stump covered with vine leaves, rooted below the brick sidewalk, gone. If I hadn't had the photograph, I wouldn't have known the stump was missing; such is the advantage, or disadvantage, of memory.

I awoke a little before five on a Monday morning in Princess Anne, Maryland, my wife and I afloat in an antique bed with a headboard that reached to within an inch of the ceiling. At five thirty I got up and dressed. Only slumber lights were on in the corridors. The downstairs door was locked. I let myself out and crossed the street to the Greyhound station and sat down on a green counter stool next to the town cop and ordered ham and eggs. When I left, day was breaking. Several blocks away a couple of dogs were bouncing barks off roofs.

The river that ran past Princess Anne had once been wide and deep enough for three-masted sailing ships to anchor; but it was a dying river then, and it was a dead river now.

I walked around behind town, following the curve of dry, grassy banks, and came, in the dawn light, to a long, low brick mansion built to face the river when the town shipped produce to Baltimore. I'd never seen a similar house in the North, but I'd seen its likeness in the South. The house was two hundred feet long; it had a central section two stories high, with a pedimented gable, wings on each side of the gable. It seemed too imposing and official ever to have been anyone's home. It might have been a governor's house, although Princess Anne had never been more than a county seat. The Teackles, a powerful local family, built the house in 1801, and now the county historical society had it.

The mansion was one of the largest and handsomest brick buildings I'd seen outside Williamsburg, Virginia, and it was startling to come across it in the shadowless dawn of another day—still elegant, draperies at the windows, as if some great and wealthy family lived there, some grand duke of a fellow inside sleeping beside his wife, his wig on a wig stand, his servants about to rise and build a fire.

The Germans, the Pennsylvania Dutch, settled in and around Lancaster, Pennsylvania. Someone in my family was among them, a man named Beam. He had his name anglicized from Boehme, or maybe had it done for him by a ship's captain. So I have always looked on the Mennonite women in their white bonnets with a special interest and curiosity. My great-grandmother wore those bonnets, and dark dresses with long skirts. She spoke German and only German, a language her son, my grandfather, never spoke again after he packed away her clothes into the brass-bound trunk in the dusty attic.

After my grandfather retired and had the time, he set down his family history. He traced it back to 1718 when Jacob Beam, just a kid off the boat from Zweibrücken, Germany, landed in Pennsylvania wearing the same black clothing that some of the Pennsylvania Dutch wear today.

Jacob was virtually an orphan. Back in Germany, during a period of religious persecution by German Catholics and Protestants, his parents, as practicing Mennonites, had been seized and thrown into a dungeon. Mennonites held, among other things, that babies should not be baptized. Baptism could wait, they believed, until adulthood. Such beliefs made them heretics. The punishment of Jacob's mother and father in those days (noted my dispassionate, non-Mennonite, grandfather a few generations later) would have been slavery or execution. Their property was confiscated. A German family took Jacob in, not the first Mennonite in my grandfather's family to be cast adrift in childhood. His mother, my great-grandmother, was another of those lost children.

Anyway, Jacob, the first of the Beams in our line to come to America, landed in Philadelphia. He already had a trade, he was a boy blacksmith. He went from Philadelphia to Lancaster, Pennsylvania, not only the youngest but the first blacksmith Lancaster County ever saw. With the money he made he bought some land and built a house. Then he married Barbara Kendig. They had eleven children. The Beams had landed in force. In America, freed from persecution, life was a whole new deal.

Martin, his oldest son—he'd have been my grandfather's great-great-grandfather—took his religion a step to the side and founded, with Philip Otterbein, the United Brethren Church. Martin, at the time, was a Mennonite bishop, apparently a man of endurance and strong conviction. He and Otterbein were revivalists, moving around the countryside on horseback, preaching in German to Germans, covering three states, Pennsylvania, Maryland, and Virginia.

Several generations down the line my great-grandmother Catherine Barnhart entered the picture. She was born in Oberseebash, Alsace, and brought to America by her parents in 1829. In short order she, too, was cast adrift. Her mother's death orphaned her. When her father remarried, she was one of a large family of unwanted small children. Some of the children found good families to take them in. Others didn't, and Catherine was one of the unfortunate.

"My mother," wrote Grandfather Beam, "related stories of privation she endured while still a small child among strangers, compelled to suffer hunger, without sufficient clothing, and going barefooted in mid-winter." When she heard, he said, of a family living on the Niagara River who might take her in, she decided to escape from the people who were, quite simply and cruelly, using her as a bonded slave.

One of her duties was to hunt for the cattle at the end of the day and drive them home for milking. So one evening when she started out to find the cows, she gathered a few of her childhood treasures and without a word to the people at the farm, off she went on her own. The cows didn't get milked on time, and the farmer was more than likely too busy when he found them to set out after her, this fleeing child. Night set in, but she knew the direction of the river, and, barefooted and bareheaded, terrified all the way that wild beasts were around her, she never paused. This was unbroken forest she fled through, in darkness.

When she came to the river, she followed it. I don't know if she waded the river or how she got to the other side, but she did cross, and followed the bank for most of the night. At last she heard the barking of a dog. She stopped, hid, and waited for dawn. When she saw smoke rising from the kitchen chimney of a house across the field, she slipped out of the woods and found shelter.

Always afterward, my grandfather said, his mother referred to the couple at that farm as "those good people." She'd apparently found a home with Mennonites, because she spoke only German then, spoke only German ever after, and went to heaven speaking German.

Catherine was living with her son when my mother grew up. My great-grandmother wore, always wore, according to my mother, Mennonite clothes: dark dresses, white bonnets. One of the plain people to the end. That was before I was born. By the time I arrived, she was a family legend.

The Philadelphia and Lancaster Turnpike, completed in 1795, was a graded road with a gravel surface, one of the wonders of its time, something to celebrate, because this road gave birth to the country's road system, though it was privately built.

Before its dazzling improvement, the old road had once been an

Indian trail, parts of it at least; and parts of the road, the "great" or "provincial" road, still exist in cast-off pieces. The provincial road that lay at the bottom of a long valley was a principal highway in the Colonial period, though before 1730 it was suitable to travel only on foot or by horseback.

The road is paved today. It runs through the countryside of the surviving Pennsylvania Dutch, some of them, the Mennonites and the Amish, unchanged in their dress and habits since their sects were established. Here on their timeless farms these timeless people live, born of the sixteenth-century Anabaptist movement in central Europe.

The Amish are an offshoot of the Mennonites, and they're a stricter sect, it seems to me, with their hard-line laws about dress and living; the customs they follow are reborn in their children generation after generation. Their hats are forever low-crowned and broadbrimmed. There are no buttons on their shirts or suits because buttons are "a place for the Devil to grab hold," in addition to being unnecessary adornments. Women wear ankle-length dresses, no matter what the lengths are in Paris. The children dress as the adults do.

Yet, strict as they are, they make room for play and sociability. Marriage is an occasion for an all-day celebration, and once a couple is married, the marriage is for good. There are no divorces.

Not all the towns or homes the new turnpike passes are owned by Amish or "plain" people. Here, among these peaceful farmers, the first long, light, deadly Kentucky rifles were locked, stocked, and barreled. A gunsmith took a week to make one, and when he finished, he expected to shoulder the rifle and knock a two-inch block of wood off a stump a hundred yards away. By 1750 everybody wanted these amazing rifles, and by then thousands were in the public's hands. Compared with the European rifle, these seemed magical, and they behaved with magical accuracy as the Revolution began.

One of the greatest changes in the look of the land along existing highways after the Revolution was the disappearance of the signs that hung near the doors of inns. Symbols of English influence were out of favor: the crown, the scepter, lions, and unicorns all were replaced, were burned. The inns themselves didn't change, God help the travelers, just their artwork and advertising.

Here, for instance, from *Wayside Inns on Lancaster Turnpike*, published by The Pennsylvania-German Society, is a 1795 letter one traveler wrote after his experience in the heart of Pennsylvania. The author is unidentified.

I set out from Philadelphia on horseback, and arrived at Lancaster at the end of the second day's journey. The road between Philadelphia and Lancaster has lately undergone a thorough repair and tolls are levied upon it to keep it in order, under the direction of a company. This is the first attempt to have a turnpike road in Pennsylvania, and it is by no means relished by the people at large, particularly by the wagoners who go in great numbers by this route to Philadelphia from back parts of the state. On the whole road from Philadelphia to Lancaster, there are not any two dwellings standing together, excepting at a small place called Downing's Town, which lies about midway. The taverns along this turnpike road are kept by farmers, and they are all very different. If the traveller can produce a few eggs with a little bacon, he ought to rest satisfied; it is twenty to one that a bit of fresh meat is to be had, or any salted meat except pork. Vegetables seem also to be very scarce, and when you do get any, they generally consist of turnips, or turnip tops boiled by way of greens. . . .

The traveller on his arrival is shown into a room which is common to every person in the house, and which is generally the one set apart for breakfast, dinner and supper. All the strangers that happen to be in the house sit down to these meals promiscuously, and the family of the house also forms a part of the company. It is seldom that a single bedroom can be procured, but it is not always that even this is to be had, and those who travel through the country must often submit to be crammed into rooms where there is scarcely sufficient space to walk between the beds. No dependence is to be placed upon getting a man at these taverns to rub down your horse, or even to give him his food, frequently therefore you will have to do everything of the kind for yourself if you do not travel with a servant, and indeed even where men are kept for the purpose of attending to travellers, which at some of the taverns is the case, they are so sullen and disobliging that you feel inclined to do everything with your own hands rather than be indebted to them for their assistance; they always appear doubtful whether they should do anything for you or not, nor will money make them alter their conduct. . . .

Most people travel on horseback with pistols or swords and a large blanket folded up under saddle which they use for sleeping in."

Travel was soon heavy on the turnpike. By the first quarter of the nineteenth century, from one end of the turnpike to the other, came Conestoga wagon after Conestoga wagon, bumper to bumper, as we say today. The Devil take the hindmost.

Spanish Moss,
Florida Palms

*T*he land changes, moods change.

All the way from New England to Florida, there is a slow physical as well as manmade change in the land and the people and their habits. New England is an older America, preserved in small-town settings in almost any direction you choose to travel. Around New York State, some of the stone houses of Dutch settlers are still standing. In the Pocono Mountains, out of season, we have felt the mood of dark regions and a silence gray as stone.

Spanish moss hangs from live oak south of the border of North Carolina. The accent, the languid tonguing of words, begins. A different kind of ham hangs in the Southern store, a hard, dark-meated ham. There's a difference in the food on menus in restaurants: she-crab soup, collard greens, red-eye gravy.

The European settlers of America absorbed a sea change on their way to the Colonies. Except for a few of the religious groups, they quickly lost the characteristics that had made them European. For many, the trip was taken to put Europe and its social setup behind them. They broke old chains and fled to take on new chains, wrapping themselves in links that were just as strong. Although they came to America to satisfy either a hunger Europe had created or to realize European ideals, they assumed new selves according to where they settled.

Crèvecoeur, writing of America at the time of the Revolution, said, "It is not composed, as in Europe, of great lords who possess everything, or of a herd of people who have nothing. Here are no aristocratical families, no courts, no kings, no bishops, no ecclesiastical dominion, no invisible power giving a few a very visible one; no great manufacturers employing thousands; no great refinements of luxury. The rich and the poor are not so far removed from each other as they are in Europe. Some few towns excepted, we are tillers of the earth, from Nova Scotia to West Florida. We are a people of cultivators, scattered over an immense territory, communicating with each other by means of good roads and navigable rivers, united by the silken band of mild government, all respecting the laws."

The roads weren't all that good, not everyone respected the laws, and Crèvecoeur overlooked the separation of men, in the South in particular, by the color of their skin.

I can't divide the territory covered in our journeys into the traditional East Coast segments of North and South according to each area's feelings about slavery. The South was temperamentally and politically divided on that issue. There were states that lay near an arbitrary North-South line that were not sure whose cause to rally around. Maryland, essentially a Southern state, lay between Pennsylvania and Washington, so it took up no cause at all. Also—the South grew less Southern in its traditional character as it extended westward.

Beyond tidewater lands were mountains and mountaineers without slaves and without sentiment for the Southern cause. Or, at the least, sentiments varied. The solid South, as has been observed, was not so solid.

Different interests, attitudes, and feelings toward slavery separated eastern and western Virginia, and finally the western section split away and became West Virginia, a state in its own right.

The Road
to Charleston

*S*even A.M. Before the sun is up, trucks come toward us, cars as well, their headlights on. Ahead the sky is pearly gray. I can make out the faint definition of clouds, a streak of pink among them. We're on a divided highway, making time, on our way to Charleston, South Carolina. Grass lies between the highways, the grass cut short like a fairway. The trees that aren't evergreens have lost their leaves. There are signs along the highway: SAM'S FIREWORKS, motels, fried chicken chains.

A line of white dashes, our center line on the paving, disappears against the side of the car, as if we are the living center of some sort of video game. Not much to be seen of the fields through which we're passing; the trees on each side are a screen, making our highway an endless green alley. Morning fog lies low over the ditch on our right. Now we pass a pond, mist rising from its surface.

This is Wade Hampton country beyond the trees. Hampton was a Civil War hero who rose to even greater heights in South Carolina as a governor after the war. He rode with Jeb Stuart, and when Stuart was killed, took over Jeb's cavalry. The North, though numerically superior in mounts, was no match for Hampton. Nor was the carpetbagger who occupied the governor's office, whom Hampton defeated at the polls to restore home rule.

Another South Carolina war hero has a large lake named after him, and the thruway we were riding southward soon cut across it: Lake Marion, named after General Francis Marion, the Swamp Fox. He drove the British crazy with the guerrilla tactics he had learned as an Indian fighter. He is supposed to have said that since coming to man's estate he had never intentionally done wrong to anyone alive or dead. Whether or not he had is a matter of moral perspective. He'd supervised the killing of a good many men. Pickets were not supposed to have been shot, but he shot them. Flags of truce were supposed to be honored, but he found an excuse to dishonor at least one. He was a master at leading the British into ambush, then slaughtering them all. I think what he implied was that he was a man of principle who had never done anything he regretted.

He was a moody man, on the short side, and proud. He could be pushed, but never pushed around. Everyone, British or American, who tried was sorry for it. He had an important character trait that he shared with Washington and Franklin, a trait that Arnold and Burr lacked: he was long on patience, and he got even.

The men who rode with Marion were farmers, some of them boys. They were riding and raiding countryside they knew, all of them fighting for something they could see, their land and houses. When fighting was slack, they went home, and when Marion needed them, they joined him again. They fought with homemade swords and bullets, without pay. They were a ragged, rugged, independent army, fighting under the taut, almost saintly control of Marion, the man of "black and piercing" eyes. He wore a leather cap. It had a silver crescent, and on the crescent was inscribed "Liberty or Death."

These men didn't pitch tents at night. They roughed it. They slept on the ground. Some had a blanket. Marion had one for a while, but it got burned in a campfire. So did his cap. He used the root of a tree for a pillow. He was then forty-eight, a tough old bach.

His young nephew was captured by the Tories, and when they realized who they had, one of them shouted, "He's one of the breed of that damned old rebel." They clubbed him and put a load of buckshot through his chest.

Marion grieved, and his men knew he was grieving.

The next day the triggerman was captured by Marion's men, and the stress of war and the need for revenge being what it is, one of Marion's officers put a bullet through the Tory's head. If it was meant as a favor to Marion, he could have saved himself the trouble. Marion was furious. He went into a rage, called in the captain of the guard, and shouted, "You couldn't stop him? What do you mean, you couldn't stop him? You could have killed that officer! You are to protect my prisoners, all of them, any of them."

Marion felt kindly toward his worst enemies, and they could depress him badly without his being able to hate them. When the Revolution was coming to a close and the British, beaten, were departing, Marion plainly wanted no more bloodshed, American or British. He was once urged to ambush some British filling up barrels with fresh water for their long voyage home, and he said, "My Brigade is composed of citizens, enough of whose blood has already been shed." And he continued, "If ordered to attack the enemy, I shall obey . . . but with my consent, not another life shall be lost. The enemy are on the eve of departure, so far from offering to molest, I would rather send a party to protect them." A ferocious soldier, he had never liked the sight of death. He hated cruelty and plundering, both so common in war. He just wanted the British to get out, and if they were going, that was good enough.

When the war was over and he went home to his plantation that is now under the water of a manmade lake called Lake Marion, everything lay broken, burned, scattered, lost. Little was left but the land. He patiently started all over again . . . on credit, since he'd saved no money. He'd never been paid.

The sun had risen by the time we turned off the thruway to look for a back road to Charleston. As soon as we headed down Route 15, we came to a line of two-story white wooden frame structures with brick chimneys, second-story balconies directly over the front porches. A couple of men, both black, were picking up bottles, beer cans, and assorted highway trash, putting it into large bags.

In St. George I got out of the car to take a picture of a house set back on a lawn and surrounded by half-grown trees. On one side of the front door was a bay window, to the left of the door a porch with a balcony above it. It was a weathered old clapboard place, half-Victorian, suffering a confusion of identity. No one seemed to be living in the place, this home approaching extinction. Bushes, untrimmed, grew around the front steps and across the bay window. I moved around the yard among the bushes and trees, trying to get a clear shot of the place.

Peggy was in the car studying the map. She rode with books, maps, and thermos carefully arranged around her feet. I noticed now her attention was off beyond the car, and then I saw that someone had been watching me, observing me, from the sidewalk on the corner.

He was a young man in his thirties, wearing an orange cap with a long visor. Parked across the street behind him was a shortbed pickup truck.

When you're driving a car, as we were, with out-of-state plates, picture-taking of old houses and churches arouses curiosity. When a driver actually gets out of a pickup truck, as this man had, to see what you're doing, it can sometimes mean trouble. Once a woman wanted to know what I, with New York plates on my car, was doing photographing her church, and she got to screaming at me while her husband tried to calm her down. Northerners have made a lot of trouble for Southerners over the course of the last hundred-plus years.

I told this man the same thing I told her, that I was interested in old houses and in towns and streets with the look or mood of an earlier America.

"A history buff?"

"You could say that," I said. "We're on our way to Charleston."

"The turnpike to Charleston is behind you if you've been coming down from the North."

"I know. We're shunpiking. I figure we'll see more of the kind of thing we're looking for on side roads."

He nodded. "My wife and I, when we're on vacation, we like to do that. We have a camera along, too. That's a pretty good camera you got there."

"It's a Nikon. Had it for years."

"If you want to take a picture of a really big old house, there's one over on Ninety-five you ought to see. An old couple lives in it. They won't mind you taking a picture of the place."

"Who lives here, do you know?"

He shook his head. "I don't know if anyone does."

"These old houses don't last long if they're left empty. There's a lot of beauty to that house. It's worth fixing."

"This is a very poor area," he said.

When I got back in the car, Peggy said, "What was he asking you?"

"He just wondered why a stranger in town, someone passing through, would want to take a picture of an unpainted, deserted old place."

"He drove past us once," she said, "and then turned and circled the block."

"He was mostly surprised," I said, "that anything in this town would interest a stranger enough to want to take a picture of it. He wasn't hostile, he was puzzled."

On Route 17: swampy ground, the kind that rice likes, on both sides of the road. According to Francisco de Miranda, rice and indigo made

South Carolina the richest of the colonies at the time of the Revolution. We pass shanties, small houses with long roofs that slant down to become the cover for a front porch, unpainted places, weathered wood. People seem to be living in the houses, but no one appears in any yard.

Middleton Place, fourteen miles from Charleston, is an old plantation, now reconstructed and open to the public. It's a National Historic Landmark, a parklike place with walking paths and a cluster of work buildings near the ruins of the manor house. The gardens were laid out between 1717 and 1784. Four generations of Middletons lived here before the plantation was burned by General Sherman in 1865. A wing of the main house has been rebuilt, using fallen bricks, following the original lines.

We had lunch in the restaurant, formerly a guest cottage, stepping down into a room with nine tables, a grand piano, and a fireplace. The bricks in the fireplace were scorched with use, and the room had a smoky odor. There was a bar. A dining porch ran around two sides of the building. Beautiful views. Moderate prices.

After lunch we joined a group of about twenty for the tour of the main house. As if we were part of that form of experimental theater, called apartment theater, that uses houses and apartments as its stage, we moved from room to room, each room furnished in a luxurious eighteenth-century manner, listening to our guide, the only actor, a woman monologist, a voice that took us back more than a hundred years.

In the first room hung portraits of the Middleton family, generation by generation, portraits that were hidden just before Sherman arrived. These were the faces of Southern aristocrats, politically powerful men, among them a president of the First Continental Congress and his son, whose signature is on the Declaration of Independence. Our guide was speaking. We heard, as if firsthand, of the anguish the people of the South suffered, things I'd never known growing up in the North. The eyes in the portraits stared at us. Our monologist, a gray-haired woman, spoke with a Southern voice. "In our defeat," she said, "we were hungry and confused. We did not know where to turn, who to turn to. When our homes were burned, neighbors took us in, or we just kept walking."

After we left the house, we went up old steps to an iron gate that hung open. To the right, fallen bricks lay banked against a standing brick wall, all that was left of the first main house.

Plantations are disappearing. It's difficult to save them even as curiosities. There are chains across driveways that lead into abandoned plantations along Southern rivers. Chiggers in the underbrush guard old ruins. Farm land, I've been told, is sold by the acre, plantation houses thrown in with the deal. The land is bought by people who have no need for the houses. There's not enough money, anyway, to put the houses into shape, and workmen capable of restoring Colonial houses are harder and harder to find.

The next day, entering Charleston, we penetrated ring after ring of time or commerce, beginning with shopping centers and gas stations, reaching at last the Spring Street Bridge, then following Calhoun Street down to the restaurants and boutiques that press in on the heart of Charleston, that area below Broad Street where the Ashley and Cooper rivers join the Atlantic. We hadn't seen this area in twenty-five years.

The Charleston we had returned to was a town of quiet charm and unaltered atmosphere, still a great place to walk, with its houses that stand sideways to the street, its houses with steep slate roofs, its stuccoed brick houses that crowd up against the sidewalk, its wrought-iron gateways in high walls, its secluded streets and alleys and gardens. Among its many nineteenth-century buildings is the 1801 Hibernian Hall. Founded by eight Irishmen, it had an unwritten law that alternated its presidents between Roman Catholic and Protestant year after year. Here the St. Cecilia Society Ball is held, Charleston's notable social event.

Not only has the historic area of Charleston been well preserved, something like two thousand buildings have been restored. Charleston's historic area is one of the best examples of how tourism can save a town or a neighborhood from developers. Tourists come to see a city of tradition, not a new city. And an insular society holds the traditions of Charleston together, a society that places more emphasis on family than on money. It's this society and its influence that have kept Charleston so ageless, surrounded as it is by tour buses and tourists looking inward for the secret city looking inward on its past.

We are lucky to have those Colonial buildings left in Charleston, because the British, when they were evacuating, could have burned the town. They didn't. They asked simply to be allowed to leave quietly. It was understood, of course, that if they weren't allowed to ship out in peace, the town would be burning when they left. They left in mid-December 1782, six and a half years after Charleston had come under naval guns. The British had sat in occupation for two and a half years.

Charleston, exposed to the sea, has had its oceanic disasters. In 1752 a hurricane blew in that flooded its streets. Water rose ten feet above its usual highest tide. Houses on Bay Street were battered by ships that broke from their moorings. People went up to their roofs to sit out the storm.

We stayed at Planters Inn, an 1840 building that was once a warehouse. There have been no changes to the outside of the building, and on the inside the second floor's original flooring has been preserved; even the building's moldings, of Charleston design, are intact. On this occasion, as a gesture to the Early American grandeur of Charleston, we checked into a suite. Folding doors closed off the four-poster bed in the bedroom. The living room was early nineteenth-century with high ceilings, the tall windows draped in swags and festoons. Everything was new to sight and touch: travertine marble in the bathroom, French milled soap, thick-pile towels, antique furniture, carpeting, the TV set recessed behind cabinet doors.

Sheldon Church in Prince William Parish near Beaufort, South Carolina, is unchanged since 1780 when it first became the handsome ruin it is today—the work of the British army's torches. Passing Sheldon Church on their march to Charles Town (now Charleston), the Redcoats thought burning the church would be practical. It was rebuilt after the Revolution and destroyed again during the War between the States, but I guess it's correct to say it's unchanged since Revolutionary days. Sherman, in 1864, used the church as a stable, then burned it by way of completing its return to the ruin it was in 1780. Services are still held on Easter Sunday in the church, the sky for a roof. Perhaps the grass inside the walls has been cut since the last time we were here, but I'm not sure. It looked the same to us.

And Peggy looked the same, too, as she walked across the grass under the roofless old edifice where she walked when I photographed her there twenty-five years ago.

The Road
to Savannah

On the road, the sun behind us, our car casts its shadow ahead on the paving. Cars coming toward us, perhaps from Savannah, drive into the rising sun with headlights on. The trees on each side of the road no longer look like stunted forest. They're bigger, broader evergreens than the ones we've been driving past for the last two days. This is Route 170 going west. In a while the sun is high enough to slant beams down through the trees on our left and to lay belts of light across the road. The strips of sunlight rise into the trees on our right and light an open circle of land in the forest big enough and isolated enough for two Colonial gentlemen to settle their irreconcilable differences.

In and beyond the forests of the North American continent, the men and women in the English colonies had three enemies, besides themselves, to worry about. Great areas of land the colonists claimed were also claimed by the French, the Spanish, and the Indians.

Enter James Edward Oglethorpe.

An English aristocrat, he guided Georgia's first English settlers across the Atlantic to Charles Town, and from Charles Town to the mouth of the Savannah River. There he and his followers built a town called Savannah.

He had a godlike way about him. He would go without food if any one of his followers was hungry. His eye marked every sorrow and discomfort, and he did what he could to dispel misfortune. So there he was, founding the last of the thirteen colonies, adored by his men, or by most of them. He had a shrill voice, but he was respected. He was a soldier and a statesman. He was more than a match for the Spanish, and he tamed the Indians with gifts instead of rifle fire. He forbade slavery. He enforced the prohibition of booze and, naturally, deplored the bootlegging that went on, and the smuggling. He had problems, but his patience at the beginning was rarely pressed into explosive rage.

He had carried Georgia across the ocean from England on his shoulders. He'd set it carefully down between forest, river, and ocean. He'd sighed and said to himself, "Let this be Paradise."

He spent ten years in Georgia. When it came time to leave America for good, he had earned considerable fame and immortality at the expense of two failed attempts to defeat the Spanish at St. Augustine. But he had defeated the Spanish at Frederica, a defeat big enough to throw them back into Florida. He left Georgia a brigadier general, forty-six years old—and tired.

Georgia grew and changed, adopted slavery, started drinking rum openly and legally. But Savannah still has as much the aura and ambience of a semitropical paradise as any city in the United States.

East Bay Inn in Savannah, for breakfast, at a table against a brick wall, some dried flowers on our table in a gray vase. The floor is brick, but darker than the wall. Spotlights overhead, between beams, are trained downward. Even so, the lighting is subdued, and we eat our first meal of the day, curiously, by candlelight.

We look for Savannah's Colonial burying ground, driving past a square every few blocks, each square a small park. Bull Street has five of these squares along its length. According to the original city plan of Oglethorpe and Colonel William Bull, the squares were to be part of the city's defense against the Spanish and the neighboring Indians.

We drive past an assortment of houses with tall windows, fanlights over doorways, grilled gateways. The Colonial Park Cemetery was Savannah's burial ground from 1753 until 1861, and it's like a park in itself, another of Savannah's quiet centers around which the city's traffic moves.

I was there to pay my respects to the memory of Major General Nathanael Greene, but I'd come 86 years too late. After 114 years in the Graham vault, both Greene and his son, who had been named after George Washington, were shifted to Johnson Square in Savannah, where their ashes lie under a white marble shaft on a granite base.

There's a grave, I note, of a duelist in the cemetery, not far from where General Greene lay for so long. The duelist's story is on his tombstone. James Wilde was his name. On January 16, 1815, he turned up at the appointed hour on the Carolina side of the Savannah River. There, on the fourth exchange of fire with Captain Roswell P. Johnson, he took a bullet through the heart, from "the hand of a man who a short time before would have been friendless but for him, and expired instantly in his 22nd year, dying as he had lived with unshaken courage and unblemished reputation. By his untimely death the prop of a mother's age is broken, the hope and consolation of sisters is destroyed, the pride of brothers humbled in the dust, and a whole family, happy until then, overwhelmed with affliction."

As I walked back to where Peggy was standing talking to a black woman, I heard her say, ". . . but I can't find the bird." Both women's heads were tilted upward, looking into the trees. The black woman said, "You can tell he's happy. He doesn't have a thing to worry about, not a care in the world."

We had lunch in the Boar's Head Tavern by Factor's Walk and the Savannah River, a place where iron balconies face the water and the passing ships. The cotton factors have gone now, and shops and restaurants have angled their way in among these cobbled streets. The tavern we sat in was here when we last visited Savannah. Out on the river a freighter was passing, its smokestack painted blue and white and red, passengers on the aft deck waving as if to us.

As we left the restaurant, we saw a man on the sidewalk washing a small white Christmas tree made of springy metal needles. Across the way a narrow park ran along the river, and out on the river the wind was kicking up little waves. We climbed the cobblestone roadway along Lincoln Ramp to where we had parked the car.

Magnolia Place Inn, one of Savannah's bed-and-breakfast inns, has the atmosphere of a house steeped in its Victorian past. It faces Forsyth Park, another of Savannah's green and leafy places, these twenty acres laid out in 1851.

Our room, looking out on a garden, had a gas fireplace, common now that wood-burning fireplaces have destroyed so many houses, a pencil-post bed, an armoire, and a couple of antique chairs. A chair rail extended around three sides of the room. A couple of times a black cat wandered by and looked in from the garden—having, I suppose, noticed our out-of-state plates.

The Road
to Key West

*T*he territorial limits of Florida, claimed by the Spanish around the turn of the eighteenth century, were extensive. Farther up the East Coast, the British had carved out New Jersey, Maryland, Virginia, and Carolina. Spanish Florida ranged from the Atlantic Ocean to the Pacific; that is, it ran west to the Rocky Mountains and there joined Nouveau Mexique, which was then all of the West. The area that is now the northern half of the United States was disputed with France. Florida was, by far, Spain's largest territory.

Development in Florida, however, did not begin until the British took over from the Spanish in 1763, when by treaty Cuba went to Spain, and Florida, as we know it today, went to the British. For the first time, under the British, roads were cut, and colonization was encouraged. Fifteen hundred Greeks and Minorcans formed a settlement near New Smyrna, Florida. But in 1783, Florida went back to Spain in exchange for the Bahama Islands. One more switch came in 1821, when Florida was formally transferred into the hands of the United States.

As recently as the 1880s, the state had been relatively unexplored. Then Henry M. Flagler opened St. Augustine to tourism and built a railroad line along Florida's east coast. The Ponce de Leon Hotel, which he built as the flagship of his hotel chain, still stands, but it no longer takes in guests. It's been Flagler College since 1968.

Even with time, some things do not seem to change. Here is a shipwrecked sailor's description of St. Augustine, Florida, in 1696: "At the north end of town standeth a large fortification, being a quadrangle with bastions and each bastion will contain thirteen guns. The wall of the fortification is about thirty feet high, built of sawed stone, being only sand and small shells connexed together, being not very hard till exposed to the sun."

Two hundred years later the fort was still standing. This description by J. W. Davidson appeared in *Florida Today* in 1889:

> The oldest city in the United States, is . . . noted for its picturesque beauty; its crumbling old city gates; its odd streets, ten to twenty feet wide, without sidewalks; its coquina built houses; its overhanging balconies, with a scent of days gone by; the hoary ramparts of its year-laden [*sic*] San Marco; its medieval-looking Moorish cathedral. . . . The ancient San Marco is now the Fort Marion. . . . The moat is dried up and overgrown; but there are still the drawbridges, the massive arched entrance, the gray barbican, the dark under-ways, the sullen bastions, and the crypt-like dungeons.

Nearly a hundred years later, the fort is still standing, still in good shape, strong of outline at the edge of the sea and Route 1. We passed by it on our left as we drove into town. This route into St. Augustine displays something of a midway atmosphere with tourist attractions like the Old Jail House, the Alligator Farm, Ripley's Believe It or Not exhibits, and the Fountain of Youth.

"The Fountain of Youth?" Peggy said. "Listen, that's reason enough to come here."

In Key West I was lost. I hadn't seen it in thirty years, and I didn't know where anything was anymore: new hotels, new shops, and streets, like St. Augustine's, jammed with cars and tourists. Even so, its past, like St. Augustine's, was not obliterated. In 1898 it was described in *Florida Today* as a Spanish-looking town with "buildings of all sizes, and of every conceivable style . . . joined or seamed to each other by a wealth and profusion of tropical foliage." That was still true, yet it was not a town I recognized. It was not the Key West I remembered.

We had to leave the hotel/restaurant area at the end of the road where Florida and the United States end and walk back into town before things began to seem more familiar. On Whitehead Street, looking for Ernest Hemingway's house, we came at last to his gate and looked in between pillars at the big yard of a Spanish Colonial house set on an acre of land. It is 130 years old. Hemingway owned the house from 1931 to 1961, and it was here he wrote *A Farewell to Arms, The Green Hills of Africa*, and *For Whom the Bell Tolls.*

His house is high on the list of places to visit in Key West, and people waited for the next guided tour in chairs outside the front door. The woman who now owns the place sat inside selling tickets.

Hemingway's house stands as he left it, complete with the furniture he brought from Spain, Africa, and Cuba. His books are there on the bookshelves. Clippings from his interviews lie under glass. In one of the clippings he is quoted as saying he never did anything he enjoyed that was legal.

As we approached the house, it hadn't looked promising, not at all. Too many tourists. But for the surfer searching the world for the perfect wave, the number of people crowding the sand on the beach doesn't matter when the wave comes. The wave came, the wave that brings the past into the present.

To begin with, there were the descendants of all those Hemingway cats running around outside on the porch. Once we were inside, it was the sink in the kitchen, made higher to accommodate his size; it was the 1920s furniture that belonged to Hemingway, left behind, as if he'd be back to rejoin his family as soon as he left the woman who had spirited him away. It was the sense of only temporary absence of Hemingway himself.

The wave of the past went over my head as I stood in the upstairs bedroom by the oversized bed, the tour having gone on without me. Again, later, when I climbed the wooden stairs of the small two-story cottage in the rear, I was locked into the past as I peered through the doorway at the small wooden table holding his typewriter.

We left Key West the next morning and drove back to the mainland, passing on our right a small key that I'd read about in our Writers Project guide, *Florida*, and in a book called *Florida Wars* by John T. Sprague. At one time in the last century, Indian Key had rivaled Key West in size and importance. In 1840, however, the Seminole wars put the whole island out of commission. The Indians attacked in the night, massacred everyone they could get their hands on, and plundered and burned the buildings. They leveled the island and slid it out of history.

The Indians, who had been at war with the Florida settlers since 1835, were after a man by the name of Houseman who'd had the effrontery to place a $200 bounty on each and all of their heads. This Houseman was an entrepreneur who, seeing the money to be made from ships that ran aground, had set up a ship-salvaging center on the island. By the time the attack occurred, he had built docks, warehouses, a blacksmith shop, a carpenter shop, and a hotel. There were homes on the island as well, including that of a well-known botanist and his family, the Perrines. All the structures went up in smoke, with the exception of one small building.

Chief Chekika and his band landed between two and three in the morning. The Perrines were startled from their sleep by the sound of breaking windows. Dr. Perrine sent his wife and children into the cellar of the house to hide; he stayed upstairs.

The Indians broke in, and down where Mrs. Perrine and her children were hiding, she could hear her husband talking to them. They shortly left.

The botanist went to the cellar to tell his family that it wasn't over yet, to stay put. As he left them, he dragged a heavy chest loaded with seed over the trapdoor in the floor, concealing it. He then locked all the doors and went upstairs and into the cupola through another trapdoor, bolting the trapdoor behind him.

Mrs. Perrine and the children crawled from the tidal bath into a more secluded hiding place, the turtle run, a cage of palmetto posts where the tide was already rising.

When the Indians returned, it was with the sudden and terrifying sounds of shouting and a steady hammering at the front door. The door gave way, and into the house they rushed, running from room to room, then up the stairs, where the shouting and the hammering started up again at the trapdoor to the cupola. The trapdoor gave, and the Indians found Perrine and killed him.

Mrs. Perrine and the children, huddled together, heard the sound of feet above, and the sound of chairs and dishes thrown about, trunks dragged over the floors. Then directly overhead they heard the voices of two Indians bossing the others. One began to pry at a plank above their cage. They sank as low as they could in the water as the plank came loose. The Indians looked down, peered around, saw nothing, and went away. Even after the Indians had left the house, the family huddled together and did not move.

A little after dawn the house began to fill with smoke. The burning house, timbers cracking, fell into the cellar. Their hiding place was now so filled with smoke they could no longer see one another. To protect their faces from the heat, they smeared themselves with mud and threw water against the burning boards.

The boy began to scream. His mother clamped a hand over his mouth to shut him up. "The Indians will hear you," she said.

He broke away, squeezed between a couple of palmetto posts, and was gone. The gap between the posts wasn't wide enough for Mrs. Perrine, and she began to dig with her hands until she dug the post free. Then she and her daughter were out under the wharf, crawling for shore. Burning coals fell on their backs. Once away from the docks, they saw the boy, on the shore, no Indians anywhere.

Near Houseman's wharf was a boat big enough to hold them all; Mrs. Perrine led the children to it. It was loaded with trunks and stacks of clothing, a barrel of flour, a box of tobacco, soap, molasses, brandy, prizes of war the Indians had piled there; also an oar, a paddle, and two poles. She got in with the children and shoved off, poling and paddling.

An American boat, the schooner *Medium*, took them aboard at one o'clock in the afternoon. The Housemans, also on the *Medium*, had managed to escape by driving the Indians away with clubs. Other neighbors were on the schooner, but at least thirty people on Indian Key were dead.

We took the excursion boat to Indian Key, a barge with passenger seats, powered by two ninety-horsepower motors. Half a dozen other tourists were with us. Two Park Service guides rode along, guiding the boat and feeding us details about the massacre and its aftermath.

Houseman was wiped out. He lost his fortune and had to go to work again in the salvaging business at its lowest level. Staking a claim was the dirtiest of the salvage jobs, and that was one of his tasks. It consisted of swimming with a rope line from the salvage boat to the stranded boat, then claiming it with his rope. Houseman, given that job, swam off and was crushed to death between the two boats.

After we landed, we took a brush jungle trail across the island to the far shore where the settlement's houses and sheds once stood. All that was left were foundations. Beside the site of the Perrine house was a sea grape tree. It had little to tell us.

We moved on. The day was warm, and the sun was bright coming off the water. Our feet, moving up the paths, made the only sound. We came to a clearing. Our guide knelt to grab a half brick. He showed us how the center of the brick had kept its pink color, and the rest had turned dark from the fire that had burned here over a hundred years ago. He seemed to hold a piece of that night in his hand.

Shushan, New York, a village in the keep of time.
It seemed to me I'd climbed those steps as a child.

Note: Some of the photographs in these pages were taken in 1967 on an earlier journey up and down the East Coast. Where the intervening years left the scenes unchanged, I have used them.

Harrisville, New Hampshire. The last hundred years have seen little change in this forest-hidden factory town.

New Castle, Delaware. Houses in a town on an island in time, where the flag of the Thirteen Colonies still flies.

Old roads lead to timeless towns and places in the past, some with their timelessness reconstructed or preserved by choice. Jockey Hollow, Morristown, New Jersey, where General Washington spent a miserable winter, is preserved for its historical importance.

Colonial roads still pass through covered bridges in rural
countryside. Stark, New Hampshire.

The haunted house stays with us. Almost every child grows up near one. St. George, South Carolina.

Signs of timeless roads. This ancestor, ten times, or generations, removed, died May 7, 1717, age eighty-three, Stonington, Connecticut.

Children live in a timeless land. Colonial Williamsburg, Virginia.

Flag of wood composite. Lloyd's Bookstore, Georgetown, Washington, D.C.

"I believe of all those billions of men and women that filled the unnamed lands, everyone exists this hour, here or elsewhere, invisible to us, in exact proportion to what he or she grew from in life, and out of what he or she did, felt, became, loved, sinn'd in life."—Walt Whitman

We went for a walk in a town that hasn't changed visibly, we were told, in the last fifty years—though the state around it has boomed. Everglades City, Florida.

Ochopee, Florida. A post office not much bigger than its mailbox.

The ancient San Marco, now Fort Marion, oldest standing fort in the United States. Construction, begun by the Spanish in 1672, was completed in 1756. St. Augustine, Florida.

In Cedar Key, Florida, a Model-T Ford was parked along the main street. It took me back thirty years and more to other Florida towns I remembered.

Savannah, Georgia. Forsyth Park, where the statues in the fountain spout on and on, are always there when I return.

So is James Oglethorpe,
who planned the city
and all its leafy, languid
squares.

Washington, Georgia. The
popularity of columns in
Southern architecture is
attributed to Thomas
Jefferson's classical influence.
Many of these columned
mansions survived the Civil
War; many burned.

Dawsonville, Georgia. A mill town surrounded by pecan orchards.

am Oliver, river ferry operator
a break in a back road. Near
urfreesboro, North Carolina.

Carl Johnson in his shop—one of the
vanished who unexpectedly reappeared.
Georgetown, South Carolina.

HORSES
ON
SIDEWALK
PROHIBITED

Camden,
South Carolina.

Entrance to the former Hutton Plantation. Near Georgetown, South Carolina.

Perrine died in a war that sent American soldiers wading into the swamps of southern Florida to destroy the crops of the Seminoles, all in an effort by the United States to starve the Indians into a general surrender. The soldiers found it tough going. These Indians were to be moved west, and they were obstinately refusing to go. It made no sense to the American government. This land was too thin for decent crops. What did the Indians want with the swamp they clung to with such fervor?

What the Indians knew that the American government didn't was that the soil in the hummocks, those rounded islands of earth that rise above the flatness of the land, is the richest in Florida. The Indians, with escaped slaves, the Spanish, and other outsiders who'd joined them, scattered into small parties and fled ahead of the soldiers, moving by night, covering their footprints behind them. They walked backward, jumped from log to log, crossing and recrossing their tracks.

Into and across the unfamiliar swamps went the soldiers, through undergrowth that at times was impenetrable, through grapevines and scrub oak and palmetto, cutting paths with axes, water around their legs four to six inches deep. In cypress swamps, the water was from one to three feet deep. On the soldiers went toward an enemy they could never reach.

Nobody, except the Seminoles, had gone into the Everglades until the Indian wars; few go into that maze of shallow waterways without a guide today. The thinly populated 'Glades' natural inhabitants are mostly fish, alligators, and birds. It was toward the Everglades we were now headed. I liked the idea of starting our trip north on the edge of an American forest primeval, a Southern wilderness of cypress and mangrove swamps to match the remaining wilderness of Maine's northern pines.

PART III —

Journey: From Mangrove Swamps to Northern Pine

The Everglades

O n the west coast of Florida, fifty to sixty-five years is a
long time. In 1923, for instance, the settlements were few: Naples, Marco
Island, Chokoloskee Island, Everglades City, that was it. Their population
totaled around 1,000. A railroad line north of this area had reached Fort
Myers in 1904, but didn't extend to Everglades City until 1928, the same
year the Tamiami Trail, connecting Tampa and Miami, was opened to the
public.

Where Everglades City stands today, a lot of dredging had to be
done. The land itself was raised by using fill from the riverbottom. The
town site rose higher, and the channel in the river grew wider and deeper.
Even then there wasn't enough dirt for the town site, so the dredge went
to work and dug out the lake east of town, using the fill from this
man-made lake to lift 760 acres beyond the reach of high tide and storm.

In 1924 Everglades City existed, but as a boat stop only. No automobiles or wagons arrived and departed because no road, even then, ran into
and out of the place. The river was the town's main street. Nevertheless,
they had a church, a school, a fraternal order (the Tamiami Trail Lodge
of the Masons), and, by 1925, a hotel—the Rod and Gun Club. The
Everglades were already attracting sportsmen. By 1928 Everglades City
had a road to the outside world.

The Rod and Gun Club, where we checked in, was the former home of the Shorter family. It was a touch of luxury out of the twenties, sustained over the years, unabashed about its age. In the wood-paneled lobby there was a big stone fireplace beside a pool table, dim lighting, and, in a room close by, a small bar with a few tables. Everything was clean and casual. In recent years the hotel had added a swimming pool.

There was nothing fancy in the way of decoration. The walls of the lobby displayed mounted fish. A comfortable, much-used sofa faced the desk. When we were there, no clerk regularly sat behind the desk, because business wasn't that brisk.

In front of the hotel flowed a stream; there were docking facilities. The large dining room off the lobby had windows facing the river.

Our accommodations were small, and although they had television sets, the rooms were clearly designed for the age of the radio. Which was what we'd wanted, a place where the atmosphere of times gone by was still around.

We went outside for a walk. There wasn't much to see—an old bank, empty lots, open grassy space, a short main street with a supply store for fishermen. The center of town, compared with Key West, seemed abandoned. My guess was that Everglades City hadn't changed greatly in fifty years. The few houses we saw beyond the main street didn't have the substantial look of a settled farm service center or industrial community. Everglades City obviously served those who came for the wilderness, as we had the previous Christmas.

A cold Christmas that had been, the air brisk, much colder than we'd expected that far south at the end of the year. In the morning when we set out in our canoe, we took along the winter clothes we'd had on when we left New York.

That was a long trip, cold at night and sometimes rainy by day, paddling hour after hour, past mangrove forest that grew to the edge of the waterway, mangrove roots rising like tangled legs, the trees crowded against each other. On and on until we reached our campsite, with only the birds and the leaping mullet for living company, and an occasional launch or motorboat. And, once, porpoises.

We were surrounded in our canoe by the Everglades, a region originally occupied by the Calusa Indians, who had been there for something like two thousand years. Hour by hour we passed the same scenery; only the width of the stream changed; sometimes it was as narrow as a country lane, sometimes as wide as a lake. We steered by compass. We lunched on peanut butter, cheese, and crackers. The only other times we paused, once underway, were to get our bearings or to train our glasses on the birdlife along the shore. Mile after mile we passed unbroken mangrove forest, observed as we went by ibis, ospreys, egrets, herons, and anhingas—those snake birds that swim along underwater like submarines with just their heads in sight.

That had been last winter; now we had come to Everglades City again. It was spring, not winter, and mosquitoes were out by the millions. I didn't feel like renting a canoe for a day, but I did stand on the ramp behind the ranger station looking at the bay with a tinge of nostalgia.

We had our dinner that evening on the screened porch beside the dining room. Pelicans, singly and in formation, were flying up and down the river, looking for dinner themselves. As we ate, the sky darkened, and over our heads in the dining room orange ceiling globes began to glow like moons over a planet too far from the sun to catch more than a dying light.

In the morning, checking out, I talked to a man wearing tinted sunglasses who lived in town and who'd dropped by the hotel, a man in his early sixties whose hair was still black. He'd lived in Everglades City since the end of World War II, brought here by the Everglades City girl he'd married while he was in the service.

"My father was a commercial fisherman and that's what I meant to be until I got into the army. My wife and I met," he said, "in northern Georgia. I was serving with Special Service, otherwise known as the 307 Rangers. We were the Green Berets of our time."

He had the solid sort of jaw that would have gone well with a ranger's beret. "In all the time I've been here," he said, "there's been little change. Where I grew up, and down here after the war, there was a real frontier atmosphere, and some of that, but not all, is gone. I don't think we're going to see a lot of change. We're essentially a town in a national forest. There are things that are different, of course, but not things an outsider would notice. We used to leave our doors unlocked, but not anymore. And we'd leave fishing tackle in our boats. Had to give that up."

"Lots that's different over along the Keys," I said.

"Oh, yeah. When I was a kid, those keys weren't connected by a highway. At Marathon in 1947, you had to drive through shallow water to cross to another key."

The manager of the hotel had come over and was listening, and I asked him if he thought the Indians had changed. We had passed their small villages along the Tamiami Highway on our way to Everglades City. They charge admission for tourists to look at their houses, and they sell souvenirs in shops up front.

"Oh, they don't live in those villages," he said. "But they do live in thatched houses like the ones beside the road. Over near Marco Island there's a settlement of about five hundred Indians, and they're preserving their culture carefully. They don't mix easily with the rest of us. A friend of mine worked at a gas station near the settlement and saw the chief frequently, but it was five years before the chief would say hello or talk to him."

"Do they have TV sets?"

"Some of the villages even have dish antennas that bring in a variety of programs, but the chief my friend knew only let his people watch one channel."

The man with tinted glasses said, "You folks should go to the north-west part of Florida where I grew up, if you like timeless places. Every time I go home it's just the way I remember it."

Florida

W̶e started north, through unpopulated landscape.

Along Route 29, highway signs warned us of panther crossings. ONLY 30 LEFT, said one sign. PLEASE DRIVE CAREFULLY, said the rest. This was isolated country, no houses, no towns. At Sunniland, a tiny place, a sign outside a small restaurant said in hand-painted black lettering, TERRIBLE FOOD. THE SERVICE IS WORSE. I figured the owner must have put it up himself and decided a Southerner's word is his bond.

At La Belle the streets and big yards were darkened by live oaks and other trees. It was a city in caves of leaves and tree limbs. There were orange, grapefruit, and tangerine trees growing in yards, always a curious sight to this Northerner.

As we sat at a counter in a diner having coffee, huge trailer trucks loaded with oranges went by on the street outside. When we got back on the road, taking the same turn the trucks did, oranges lay scattered along the ground.

Beyond La Belle, orchards; fewer palmettos and cabbage palms in the fields; more and more pines; and distant cattle.

All night outside the motel where we stayed, orange trucks rolled by every ten or fifteen seconds, big semis, carrying oranges along the edge of my sleep for stores and supermarkets all over the country. Oranges coursing through the night, endlessly.

We left Route 27 at Leesburg and took Route 44 west, the hood of the car wet from the drenching rain we'd come through, tornado rain; the sky ahead was clear. A white heron came flying across the road ahead of us, about twelve feet above the paving.

Twenty miles north of Leesburg, where we turned, near Ocala, was Ma Barker's home base. Ma was a gangster with two sons, both into crime with her, and they were principals in the Bremer kidnapping in Milwaukee when I was a senior in high school. I remembered reading about the day the law caught up with them.

On January 16, 1935, the FBI surrounded Ma Barker in a cottage on Lake Weir, Florida. Ma cut loose on the G-men with a submachine gun, and the battle was underway. It went on for hours, big stuff for those days in the relative quiet of the early part of this century. Finally, there was silence from inside the cottage. Ma Barker and her son Fred were dead.

The terrain reminded me of the thirties, when I was in Grand Rapids, Michigan, another sandy place. It made me think of cottages on streets near wooded lots, of milk bottles on porches, of Saturday movie matinees, and of roads that led to towns where the Depression had put people out of work. I was not to be so strongly reminded of that era again until we reached northern Maine.

We made our way north and west to the shores of the Gulf of Mexico, and there our road spanned ocean to an island that's a national wildlife refuge. It's a key, with a town that carries the same name.

Cedar Key, Florida, looked to me like Key West thirty years ago, without the tropical foliage. Its main street runs along the Gulf front, stretched out between two piers; white frame buildings face one another with breaks in between; up the sides of the buildings run railed stairways with wooden steps. An old Model-T Ford was parked along the street, as if to give the town a finishing touch. The streets themselves were empty of people walking and of traffic.

The place is not exactly undiscovered. New motels have gone up at the edges of town, and there are restaurants on the pier, shops on the main street. The Second Street hotel, however, didn't seem to have been altered since it was built.

While I was moving around taking pictures, Peggy walked down Second Street and came to the Crafts Cooperative Shop. She went in and bought a hand-crocheted cotton sweater. The woman clerk asked, "Have you been here before? I just ask because we have so many people now who come back, and some of them are buying houses in town."

"There don't seem to be many tourists."

"Right now, no. But things pick up. At craft fairs, when we have those, the street outside this shop will get so crowded I can't look out and see across the street. We have three of them a year."

"Those look like new motels you have in town."

"We're changing."

"Doesn't that bother you?"

"Well, it bothers an awful lot of people. But I've lived here my whole life, I'm seventy-nine, and I know that we have to grow or we're going to die. I think growing is better."

"Is anyone controlling the way the town grows?"

"Plans are all reviewed. Our historical society sees to that. They review plans and so forth. For myself, I wish some of the new buildings had been designed different than they were, but it's better to have people employed than it is to see them out of work. I live in a hundred-year-old house a few blocks from here, and there's another old house next to me. There are still unchanged areas in town."

"My husband," Peggy said, "says your town reminds him of Key West thirty years ago."

"I've never been to Key West, so I can't say. But I've heard that from other people."

On one side of town there are new white frame hotels, and a houseboat, called the *Santa Fe,* was moored beside one of them. A blond woman was on the foredeck with a long-handled scrub brush, working away on the railings, sweeping the brush back and forth without benefit of suds or water. She was getting rid of spiders, she said. Her husband was below deck checking out the motor. They'd have left Cedar Key before this, but the tide was holding things up. They were eager to get going. The houseboat was a big part of their lives.

"My husband's a car dealer and every few weeks we have to go back home so he can tend to business, but the job allows him enough time to devote to the boat. We bought the boat in Louisville and, making about a hundred twenty-five miles a day, we've gotten this far. We've been moving along the coast very cautiously, very conservatively."

Through the windows of the cabin, I could see a wicker picnic basket on the floor.

"Where you headed?"

"The Tamiami Canal next, then on to Fort Lauderdale."

Late in the afternoon we took a walk around town, following the shoreline, and we came to a place where, on a small sandbar, a boat was stranded. We stood in the chilly, dusky light staring at the boat, our hands in our pockets. A man in a warm-up suit with a white stripe down the sleeves and pants came by. He was walking alone. He stopped and said, "Is that your boat?"

We told him no, it wasn't, and introduced ourselves. The boat, he said, had run aground that day, another had run aground yesterday, and a boat had sunk last week. It sounded as if the salvage business might be as good here as it once was on Indian Key.

We wondered if he was a tourist. It turned out he lived nearby, at least part of the year, and we asked him if Cedar Key was usually this cold. "No," he said, "this is unusual." He was retired and had lived on the island with his wife for the past four years, spending six months on the key and the other six in Kentucky, where they had another house.

He said they'd come to Cedar Key originally because his wife had read about it in a magazine. "The first time we were here, we stayed at the hotel in town, the Island. That inn, you know, goes back to the middle of the last century. It's not run down, but it hasn't changed much either. There's still a coal stove in the lobby. We checked in, my wife and I, on one of the hottest nights of the year. After dinner we went out on the second-story porch with a bottle of scotch and watched couples going in and out of the bar next door. A local would go in with one girl and come out with another. I sat there miserable with the heat and I thought, What are we doing in this godforsaken place? Our room had an iron bed, there was no air-conditioning, and there was one tiny lightbulb dangling from the ceiling. But we kept coming back, and finally we bought a house." He laughed. "Now we think Cedar Key is the most wonderful place in the country."

Suwannee, about twenty-four miles off the main road north of Cedar Key, through forest all the way, was the place where the man I'd talked to in Everglades City had grown up, the place that he said hadn't changed. It's too far off the beaten track, he said, and the area is too poor. The people who live there, mostly in trailers, are commercial fishermen, always have been. He loved the place and said, "You be sure and see it."

The trailers, nondescript things, put us off at first. That was the only kind of housing we could see. They seemed so temporary, so artificially alike back among the trees, resting haphazardly on the sandy soil, no one around any of them. But from what we'd heard about the place, this was the way it had looked for a couple of generations at least. The fishermen, we guessed, were out in their boats.

The road through the cluster of trailers in this shaded place ran beside a stream that rolled along to the Gulf. We passed no stores, no shopping center. We were hungry, and there were no restaurants in sight.

Then a woman walking along the road told us about Carol's Place. "You have to look sharp. The restaurant hasn't got any sign, but it's close to the bridge and there's a small parking lot beside it."

It didn't need any sign because everyone in Suwannee knew where it was, and Suwannee was the end of the line. We pulled into the parking lot and walked to Carol's across sand and fallen leaves. The settlement, I realized now, had a wonderfully relaxed and peaceful atmosphere. The people here live close to nature, on the sea and in town. They fit their trailers into a natural setting, as natural as the sea they ride across in their boats. Since that day, rural trailers have looked less to me like a curse on the landscape than like latter-day log cabins among the trees. A hundred years or more ago a similar town would have been constructed from whatever was at hand.

Inside Carol's small restaurant were half a dozen tables. Good-time laughter came from the kitchen. Out of that kitchen, hot from the oven, came cornbread. Our waitress was Carol herself, her coffee the hottest I've ever held in my hand. There was animated talk at a nearby table where five people sat.

A woman entered the front door, went into the kitchen, and came out holding two boxes of strawberries. Just before she reached the door, someone at the big table yelled, "Hey, one of those strawberries is mine," and the woman at the door, in a half turn, shot a strawberry through the air, a perfect arc. The woman at the table who'd called out caught it with one hand. And Carol, near the kitchen, quipped, "Anybody for softball?"

We moved northward, on our way to Wakulla Springs, the sky clear, passing houses with tiled roofs and stucco walls that came in with Florida's real estate boom.

Wakulla Springs—and the entire northwest region of Florida, for that matter—has a reputation for the curative powers of its water. One town is even named Panacea. According to our WPA guidebook to Florida, there's an Indian legend that in the waters at Wakulla Springs on certain moonlit nights, figures of long-haired men and women, all about four inches high, can be seen cavorting in the very clear depths. At a certain hour, goes the legend, an Indian warrior appears, paddling a stone canoe, frightening the little people away.

In the parking lot in front of the Wakulla Springs Lodge were seven antique cars, as shiny as if they'd just been minted. One had a license plate from Maine. A foreshadowing, these cars, of the thirties atmosphere inside the hotel's doors—and of the trip ahead of us through antique countryside.

Before we left the lodge the next day, I felt I had to ask the manager if anyone had seen the little figures frisking about at the bottom of the spring. He gave me a careful look. No one had seen them, he said, not in the twenty-six years he'd been there.

Georgia

*T*homasville, Georgia, is a few miles north of the Florida border. We drove into and out of town on Dawson Street, past a long row of early Southern houses with pillars and second-story porches. The houses were getting care. Ladders rested against their sides. These were freshly painted places—except for the Seixas house, built in 1835, which was up for sale. Beautiful old homes, all of them. The Lapman-Patterson house, a state historic site, had been painted yellow. Azaleas grew in its sideyard. A woman out front was clipping flowers.

An early Spanish road, once an Indian trail, passed through Bainbridge. The town has a square with a mustached Confederate soldier, his rifle in front of him, both hands on its barrel. In a pool behind a low wrought-iron fence floated fallen leaves from a live oak. Goldfish swam around under the leaves and two cannons, slanted downward, dripped water into that pool. There's a bandstand in the square with a brick floor and ceiling fans, and around it were azaleas in lavender and white bloom.

We studied a couple of memorials, one a steamboat bell from the *John W. Callahan, Jr.*, mounted on a three-foot brick pedestal. A similar pedestal holds a glass-enclosed Bible open to the Psalms, a memorial to Miss Mary Davis, a local teacher who died December 7, 1946.

Our car, soon after we left the Everglades, had picked up a shimmy that was getting worse. I also had a bum leg that wasn't getting better. I'd twisted my knee on a piece of broken sidewalk back in New York; I was walking, but I was limping. In Colquitt, at an automobile supply store, I limped in and asked a clerk where the best place was to get tires balanced or aligned. It turned out to be just down the block at the Chevron station.

Tully, owner of the station, said we needed a new set of tires. He was a Southerner, born and brought up in Colquitt. In spite of the glasses he wore, I thought he looked like Chuck Yeager—more like a test pilot, that is, than a mechanic. He moved quickly, squatting at each tire to show us how the tread was worn and how the right front tire was coming apart at the seams. He spoke quickly. His attention was everywhere at once. While he was talking, he knew what his men were doing in the garage and at the pumps, and from time to time he addressed side remarks to them.

"I'll charge you," he said, "the same price I'd charge anybody in town for four Michelins." I knew I needed the tires, and when he gave me the price, I knew it was more than fair. It was a bargain.

We had forty-five minutes to wait, so Peggy and I walked around the square. Its stores, unlike the courthouse, were early twentieth-century. The old courthouse, said our WPA guidebook, had entertained checkers players and horseshoe pitchers on its lawns. No more checkers players, and no one slung horseshoes on the lawns anymore. The new courthouse, built in the last few years, is a contemporary brick building with arched entrances. We crossed to it, looking maybe for the last score of the last horseshoe game. No loungers or loafers sat on any of the benches. Inside the building, walking down the hall, we passed an open door where a woman who looked as if she might remember the old courthouse sat at a desk facing a typewriter.

She said the new courthouse got built because there was a fire, and new office space was needed. "The old courthouse would never have been torn down. It was too beautiful." She had come to town forty-six years ago, she said, and the buildings around the square hadn't changed in all that time. "The horseshoe players and the checkers players, they were before me."

Back at the gas station, talking to Tully, I found he shared what is said to be a Southern man's consuming interest in hunting and fishing. He took off with a rifle or a fishing rod, he said, every chance he got, and so did all the men who were working for him. He took me into the station and showed me a green plastic picnic chest filled with what looked like sunfish and bluegills that must have been caught that morning.

We asked Tully about towns we might want to explore, and he recommended Fort Gaines up ahead. Eufaula, on the Alabama border, he said, should not be missed. Tully was someone else who liked what we were doing. He and his wife had taken trips together, sometimes on a motorcycle, sometimes in a car, often just the two of them, other times with friends.

Tully was a veteran of World War II. Along with the annoyance of aging, he had come to dread, he said, the afflictions that come with it. Cancer had taken his wife from him just eight months ago; one of his close friends had suffered a stroke and facial paralysis; another friend and fellow motorcycle rider recently had a triple heart bypass.

Tully stared off for a moment. A thoughtful moment on a busy day. "Sometimes," he said, "driving with my wife, she'd go to sleep. She'd drift off easy, and I'd drive along with her sleeping in the seat beside me until I got tired myself. Then as soon as I pulled over to sleep, she'd wake up. She'd do it every time." And he spoke not with rancor or even with lingering amusement, but simply of a matter one dealt with on long trips. It had happened, that was all, and he was recalling something about a woman he missed without showing the pain of missing her.

Fort Gaines was old, all right, as Tully had said. Founded in the early 1800s, it had first been a log fort. Today it was a town of Greek Revival homes. We came upon a hotel called Dill House that, like the town, seemed ageless behind the wrought-iron fence that bordered its sidewalk.

Dill House had a couple of rocking chairs on its front porch; a balcony ran along the upper floor. The front of the building had been painted in the recent past, but not the sides of the house. There were several impressive live oaks in the yard. The place seemed mysterious, the house deserted. Because we'd heard that Dill House rented rooms, we walked to the porch and let it be known in the dim interior that we were at the door. No one came. Inside, on a table against the wall, was a guestbook.

I'm fascinated by these old, often furnished but deserted hotels. I have the feeling that doors inside their rooms lead not to closets but to secret rooms with trapdoors to lost years, ours and our ancestors'. I grew up with that feeling about old houses. I felt it strongly now. Attics, of course, are loaded with memorabilia of bygone days and suggest such openings to the past. This hotel certainly brought the past closer, but its front door was locked, and there was, I thought, something significant about its locked grip. It seemed to be inhabited now by ghosts protecting their privacy.

⸺   ⸺

Eufaula is across the Chattahoochee on the Alabama side of the river, a bluff city founded in 1857. As we came into town, we saw on both sides of the street Greek Revival and Victorian houses, and azaleas in bloom. Once there was a brisk river trade here, with plantations all around the town's outskirts.

The South went crazy over those dignified round pillars they spaced in front of and around their white homes. The love of Greek pillars swept what was then, and almost still is, a nation within a nation, and they're as significant as any flag.

Outside Americus we passed close to the airfield where Lindbergh made his first solo flight in a plane he bought for $500. The road leads on to Andersonville, one of the South's military prisons during the Civil War.

Andersonville made me think of my Great-Grandfather Taylor, who looks out at me from the photograph in my study. "He finished his war," I tell Peggy, "the Civil War, that is, in a camp like Andersonville. It was farther west. He was hardly a fighting Irishman then. The only battle he ever got into was a skirmish in which a mule was killed. Then he settled down to prison parades, playing in the prison band, and suffering starvation and dysentery."

"A prison like Andersonville?"

"Maybe not as bad. How could it have been?"

Andersonville had been a human slaughterhouse that did not use gas to kill its inmates. They died of neglect, of starvation, and disease—by the thousands.

In the Andersonville yard, where prisoners were fenced in, they made shelters out of anything at hand. A stream flowed through the yard, and this was all they had to drink from after they'd washed in it and used it for a latrine until, miraculously, a spring appeared in the yard, bubbling up through the earth.

I'd known someone besides my great-grandfather who survived a prisoner-of-war camp, a friend of mine from Michigan who now lives in Georgetown, South Carolina. Carl came back from the Second World War so thin I barely knew him. We were on our way now toward Carl's.

We reached Macon in time to make it out to the Ocmulgee National Monument before closing. It's a park with a long Indian history, most of it buried or lost, and what's buried, the pots, the artifacts, are riddles. Long-gone days lie below the land we were walking and under the mounds we were climbing, sunk as deeply into time as 9000 B.C. The area's earliest Indians were hunters, replaced by a farming culture called the Mississippians around 900 A.D. The farming Indians built the mounds. Nobody's figured out what happened to those Indians or where they went. They were replaced, it's known, by the Lamars, and the Lamars were the Indians that De Soto ran across in 1540. Between 1690 and 1715 the plateau was occupied by Creek Indians, then the Creeks were defeated by white settlers in the Yamasee War (1715–16), and that was that; the village at Ocmulgee was wiped out. The Creeks, driven to Florida, joined the Seminoles. Ocmulgee is vacant, sacred Indian land now, under the control of the National Park Service.

We made our way to one of the ceremonial mounds, crossing a footbridge to a small hill and entering the hill through a low tunnel that emerged into a dusky round room with a single smoke hole in the roof. The earthen benches around the walls were once privileged seats in a holy chamber.

It's a haunted place. We sat there, earth under, around, and over us, and it was as cool as the basement of that house I'd lived in in New Jersey during World War II.

Georgia has a lot of haunted places. Thirty miles to the north, on one of Milledgeville's old streets, there was, I had read in our WPA guide, a haunted house, haunted by a ghost who had followed a migrating family from Wales all the way to Georgia. It was the Williamson-Jones-Ferguson house on the corners of South Liberty and Washington streets. The ghost was described in a book called *White Columns in Georgia* by Medora Field Perkerson as "a little old lady in brown." Mrs. Ferguson had sighted her twice at dusk between the boxwoods. How many more times she'd been seen or heard, and where and by whom, I didn't know.

When we got to Milledgeville, we drove around until we found the right corner and parked to take a closer look at the house and at the sign in front. The sign said: HOMESTEAD. c. 1818. Not at all what we expected.

Two fir trees flanked the walk to the porch, both covered with vines. The bricks of the walk were sprouting grass. Four windows faced the street, two upstairs, two down. Chimneys on each side of the house. The house, as the book said, had beautiful proportions. Someone had set a pot of Easter lilies outside the front door. The corner was right, and the house fit the book's description. Everything matched but the sign. I wondered if the owners no longer wanted it identified as a house with a haunt.

I went up on the porch and knocked. No one answered. This was another of those houses, it seemed, like the inn in Fort Gaines, a house that did not respond to the human knock.

It was eleven thirty in the morning, Easter Sunday. Perhaps everyone was in church except the ghost, and the ghost, through one of the upstairs windows, watched me walk away.

Milledgeville, designed and built as the site of an early state capital, has streets, some at least, that are 100 to 120 feet wide. It is a splendid city, but it wasn't destined to be the permanent state capital. As Nelle Womack Hines, historian, wrote, "Milledgeville was born a capitol in the fading light of an Indian war dance. It died as a capital city in the fading light of a burning bridge as Sherman passed."

Four columns of Sherman's army converged on Milledgeville. He had moved southeast from Atlanta with 62,000 men plus Wheeler's cavalry against 3,000 Confederate troops. His policy was to burn only warehouses and buildings that might be of aid to the Southern cause. At Milledgeville the penitentiary burned, the prisoners setting it afire themselves. The rest of the town escaped destruction, and that included some forty houses built before 1840, as well as the house with the Welsh ghost.

Thank you, General Sherman.

Elloa Mitchell, an eyewitness to Sherman's famous march, was the daughter of a family that lived in Sandersville, along a road Sherman's troops took after leaving Milledgeville. Sherman's men, Wheeler's cavalry to be exact, were in hot pursuit of the Confederate soldiers. She wrote:

> We were at breakfast, father lying on a couch, mother, brother and I at the table and the baby in the nurse's arms. We heard firing of rifles and yelling of men, then came a clattering of horses' hoofs and a rain of bullets on the roof. Wheeler's men went dashing by, firing as they went. . . . The road was a mass of blue men. The surrounding fields were full of them. In a few minutes our house was filled with the surging mass. In a little while there was not a piece of china, silver or even the table cloth left; and food disappeared in a second. Fences were torn down, hogs shot, cows butchered, women were crying, children screaming, pandemonium reigned. Then the jail, the court house, people's barns and a large factory that made buckets and saddle trees were all ablaze. . . .

Many small Georgia towns have heritage tours. At Eatonton, where Joel Chandler Harris was born in 1848, we followed the tour that begins with downtown brick-front stores. Around the courthouse are blue wooden benches saying, WELCOME TO EATONTON. A Confederate soldier's statue is in the square. We passed lots of frame houses, some of them with at least eighteen rooms, some Greek Revival, some Victorian, some a combination. This is another timeless town. I learned that much when we visited the Uncle Remus Museum on the outskirts. A white-haired woman guide said she had lived in Eatonton all her life and had seen little change in all that time.

Eatonton also had its haunting presence, the ghost of Panola Hall. This ghost's name was Sylvia. She was young and attractive, and she didn't flit about among the hedges in the yard. She lived in the house, walked its halls and rooms, and took the stairway between floors, as would anyone in the living world. Nobody knew her history. She was frequently seen, once on the stairway by a visitor who thought she was flesh and blood and smiled and bowed as Sylvia passed. She was wearing a hoop-skirt and had a rose in her hair, he said; he was disappointed to learn she was an insubstantial presence. She was observed another time by the librarian across the street who saw Sylvia through the window of the house, standing behind a chair where the master of the house sat with a newspaper; she was reading, it would seem, over his shoulder.

In Greensboro, I went into a store to pay for gas; near the counter were boxes and boxes of tins of snuff.

I was still curious about the house with the ghost in Milledgeville. When we got to Augusta, we looked for the state tourist office, but no one there knew the story behind the house now known as the Homestead. A woman I spoke to said she knew someone who did, said she'd get word to me.

Before we parted, I asked her if she thought customs in the South have changed in recent years, at least where women are concerned; she didn't think so. "For example," she said, "Southern women still want to play the old feminine roles. Women still expect the door to be opened for them. And women aren't promoted to positions of authority. I worked in a bank for sixteen years, and there was only one woman executive in the entire bank system."

A few weeks later, back in New York, I had word from her. An elderly lady, she wrote, lived in Milledgeville's haunted house, and there is a ghost. I'll come to the rest of that story later.

South Carolina

*I*n Aiken, a city of many boulevards, we strolled around and came to Hopeland Gardens. The gardens' undulating brick walls, higher than our heads, extended to our left as far as we could see. When we found an entrance, we saw that inside the walls the sun was slanting through trees and falling among flowering shrubs and over raked sand paths. There were markers along the paths. Nobody was on them. We had, it seemed, an enormous garden to ourselves.

"A Garden of Eden," said Peggy

Signs were to be our guide, little oblong signs that stood about waist-high and told us what tree we stood in front of or what plant, with each one's name; but, strangely, as we went along, the signs began to tell us what to do with our hands and our noses; the tour became a feeling and sniffing walk through the garden. "Lift your hands," said one sign. "Feel the leaves, feel their softness. . . . Smell them. Smell the odor they leave on your fingers. . . ." I felt like a child again, in some kind of wonder-garden.

And then we saw we were not alone in this Eden. Another couple was walking in the distance, holding hands. She came about to his shoulder. He wore a blue T-shirt, and the sun for a moment flashed off a gold chain he wore around his neck. Her long red hair was gathered at the back of her head and fell along her back in a single strand.

They paused long enough for him to run his hand over one of the signs, then they on went toward a large fountain where they stood like living statues and did not move as we passed behind them. They seemed to be sensing the garden, picking up its odors, feeling the sun on their faces, feeling the slight breeze that was blowing. I became more aware of the fragrance around me. We walked on, following the trail. The garden seemed endless.

It wasn't until we finished our walk that I realized our guided-tour signs carried more than lettered information and instructions. There were also messages in a code of raised dots: braille.

Sherman's men burned almost the entire city of Columbia, South Carolina, so there is little left of its architecture prior to 1865. Sherman's men got out of control. Columbia, for one thing, was a "surrendered" city, as Milledgeville was, and Savannah later; therefore, according to the customs of war, it should have been spared. Then, too, Sherman had assured the Mother Superior of the Ursuline Convent, a family friend, that she and her nuns could safely remain in their convent. He reassured her twice, the second time when, after hearing rumors that a fiery night was in store for everyone, she wrote Sherman a worried letter reminding him of his promise of protection. Again, he told her to stay where she was.

She did. But that night Columbia was put to the torch, and the convent burned as brightly as any place in town. The nuns fled. Father O'Connell, an elderly priest, followed by the Mother Superior, led the procession of nuns through firelit streets. The account I read, from *South Carolina Women in the Confederacy*, said: "Father O'Connell led the procession, a crucifix held high above his head. . . . Even the drunken soldiers seemed silenced for a little while. . . . The roaring of the fire, the scorching flames on either side as we marched down Blanding Street, did not create the least disorder."

O'Connell came to where Blanding meets Assembly Street and, choosing between the safety of a cemetery and a standing church, led the nuns into the church.

The next morning, the Mother Superior and General Sherman met face to face when he came to apologize. She met him halfway down the walk to the church. Surrounded by her nuns and some of her pupils, with "graceful, dignified bearing," she received the supreme commander of the Union Armies in the West.

"As he approached the Mother Superior, he removed the cigar he was smoking; in his embarrassment, he restored it, nervously chewing . . . then took it out again and held the cigar slightly behind his back."

"General," she said, "this is how you kept your promise to me, a cloistered nun?"

The fire, he said, had got completely out of his control. Besides that, his soldiers got into the liquor they found in the houses. It was the men of Columbia who had left that liquor behind, he insisted.

When he could see his explanations were getting him nowhere, he offered her and her nuns any house left standing in town as a gift.

"General Sherman," she answered, "I do not think the houses left are yours to give, but when I do make arrangements for my community and pupils, I will thank you to move us and provide food for the large number it will be hard to feed."

Around noon of that day, ambulances arrived to move the nuns to the Methodist Female College.

"We had," the account read, "one pot to cook the meager rations in, and a broken tongs, washed and scoured, to stir the mess we called a meal—rice, or hominy, and a piece of meat, when so fortunate as to get a scrap given us, to flavor the cereal. . . . Wooden paddles, on the order of 'chopsticks,' took the place of spoons and forks." Two nuns "too delicate for such hardships, finally entered 'into that peace which passeth all understanding.' "

On the morning of the army's resumption of its march to the sea, word came to the Mother Superior that the soldiers were planning to burn the house that belonged to the Prestons, a family that had protected the nuns for years. "This," she said, "cannot be permitted."

General Sherman got word at once, by messenger, that the nuns, having been offered any standing house, wanted the Preston home. Sherman complied, and "after many years, the nuns paid their debt of gratitude to the Prestons . . . by saving their elegant home from the torch of Sherman's soldiers."

We stayed at Claussen's Inn that night in Columbia, 120 years after Sherman picked up and moved on. The hotel, a brick building that was a former bakery, is a blend of the best of the past and the present. The hotel is handsome and quiet. The lobby is long, narrow, and high, rising past the balcony railing and the second level of rooms. There are antique reproductions in all the rooms, and we reminded ourselves that antiques were once new, or contemporary with their times.

We had a luxurious two-story suite, the kitchen, living room, and bath on the ground floor connected to the bedroom and another bath on the second floor by a wrought-iron spiral staircase. I kept going up and down the stairs; the things I needed were never on the floor where I thought they'd be.

We remembered Camden, South Carolina, from an earlier trip. Twenty years have gone by, but Camden hasn't changed. I thought at first the sign requesting horses to stay off the sidewalks was gone, but it wasn't. A woman at an inn told us where to find it. The imperative still stands.

What we saw as we drove Camden's streets was an abundance of beautiful old Greek Revival and Victorian houses, most of them on Lyttleton Street and Broad Street.

Camden was one of the state's oldest inland cities, first settled in 1733–34, incorporated in 1791. By 1760 it had sawmills and gristmills, indigo works, a tobacco warehouse, and a distillery. During the Revolution, the British captured the town, and the streets ran red with the blood of executed American prisoners. There were many Revolutionary battles fought here, fourteen in all. In one, General DeKalb was killed, and General Gates was soundly defeated by Lord Rawdon. Another battle had a distinguished observer in the prisoners' stockade, a future president who was then thirteen years old—Andrew Jackson, his eye to one of the chinks in the log wall.

Blood continued to flow between the Revolution and the Civil War. Many duels were fought in Camden; for a while it was the place to go to get lessons in pacing off and firing.

Today most of the town's violence takes the sporting form of racing. The town holds a steeplechase at the end of March, and at that time the biggest party in the state is thrown, a social event for those with racing blood. We'd missed that, but not by much. The love of horses and racing, we noted, has not passed with time from the Southern scene.

What I'm glad we didn't miss was lunch at a little off-the-main-road, back-of-town restaurant we were directed to. It reassured us that Southern cooking is alive and well.

We weren't sure, when we pulled up beside the place, that it was a restaurant. The Rainbow Shop, that's all the sign said. No window showing a posted menu. Inside was an open kitchen and two small rooms with chairs around several tables. One table was free. We took it and sat among the black and white patrons.

A couple of gentle ladies sat at the table next to us, and the thin one turned to us and said—she seemed to know we'd never eaten there before—"Order the child's plate. Unless, of course, you're ravenous. Portions are large here."

"Is the food as good as we've heard?" Peggy asked.

"I think you'll find it so. What she cooks is greaseless, and delicious."

We looked over the menu and ordered fried chicken, collard greens, cornpone, cornbread, hush puppies, black-eyed peas . . . every traditional Southern dish we could see.

I hadn't been happy with most of the Southern food we'd had. Hush puppies, for instance, had tasted like doughnut balls, as if the

South were modifying its food to suit Northern tastes. Cornbread crumbled in my fingers and was flavorless; in the same way, supermarkets have taken the bold corn flavor out of Mexican tortillas and given us something bland in its place. Everything is leveling out. But not at the Rainbow Shop.

Our cook and owner, we learned, had come to Camden from the North, from New York City, where she had cooked for a Jewish couple. When our food came, it was full of flavor. I tried to buy more of the cornbread to take along when we left, but they wouldn't let me pay for the huge piece they gave us.

As we got back in the car, I said to Peggy, "I could see living in Camden and eating here every day."

I'd asked one of the women at the next table whether there'd been quite an influx of Northerners into the South, and she, with the longest face, thought about it and nodded. We were headed toward the home of a Northern friend of mine from high school. He and his brother had married a couple of girls, sisters, as chance drew their lot, from Georgetown, South Carolina. Bob, the oldest, had married Bernice while he was still in the army, and Carl had married Snookie after he got out. The last time I'd seen them was twenty years ago. Bob would not be there this trip.

We drove Route 52 toward Georgetown, a two-lane highway with few towns. Tobacco warehouses began to appear on each side of the road: tall, narrow buildings without windows. On our left a flock of egrets were following a plow that was churning up tidbits.

Georgetown is on the Ocean Highway, sixty miles north of Charleston. Its history includes Spanish galleons, British occupation, and a visit by Sherman during the Civil War.

We pulled in beside the office of a motel, and I signed us in, then drove back to our unit. It was situated beside a stretch of water like a stream that separated the motel grounds from the more solid ground of the marsh. I sat looking at a log on the far bank. I said to Peggy, "See that alligator over there?"

Peggy said, "Oh sure, and see the other one just beside it?"

Inside the motel we unpacked. I got our binoculars, and went out again. A chain-link fence ran between the motel and the stream, but where there might have been a gate, there was none, just an opening wide enough for a truck to drive through. One recently had, leaving its tire tracks in the grass.

Looking across the stream, I focused the binoculars on two alligators. They weren't logs. One was about fifteen feet long, and the other about twelve. Their eyes were closed. They were sleeping, sleeping the deep sleep of water monsters.

Peggy came out and we traded the glasses back and forth. "Those," she said, "are the real thing!"

We had paddled through the Everglades expecting to see an alligator and had seen none; here, practically in the backyard of a motel, were two huge fellows, big enough and old enough to run for mayor.

We got something to eat, returned to the motel around dusk, and I called Carl.

"This is Dick Humphreys," I said.

He thought that over, and said, "Who?"

"Is this the Carl Johnson who went to Comstock Park High School?"

"Yes."

"Then you and I were classmates."

"Is this Hump?"

I said, "Listen, I want to see you."

"Hump!" he said. "Where are you?"

"I'm in town." I told him where, and he said, "I'll be right over."

We hadn't seen each other since the sixties. At the motel room door, we took about a three-second appraisal of one another. He was taller than I remembered by about the three inches he stood over six feet. His face was fuller. He'd put on some weight about the waist. His hair, though thinner, was as dark as ever. He stood characteristically square-shouldered, his chin tucked in. My hair had gone white since he'd seen me last, and that surprised him.

Bob and Carl had settled in this Southern town with their Southern wives and gone to work for the International Paper Company. On the side, they practiced a skill they'd imported from Grand Rapids, Michigan: upholstering. They had their own shop where they restuffed and re-covered chairs and davenports in the evening and on weekends. Since last I'd been here, Bob had lost a hard, long bout with cancer. Now Carl, retired from the paper company, carried on the upholstering business alone.

Carl's shop was just across the street from our motel. When we told him about the alligators we'd seen, he said that one once wandered across the motel parking lot and came around behind his shop, but he didn't know it was there until the police came.

"I went out back to see what was going on, and I saw this police-woman staring at an alligator about seven feet long. It had its chin up the trunk of a tree and wouldn't move. It wasn't going to move. So the other cop, a man, picked it up and put it in the trunk of their patrol car, and they drove over to the marsh and turned it loose."

"Alligators are protected?"

"Oh, yeah. And they're breeding all the time; more and more of them, getting bigger and bigger. They're like pets over where you're staying. Tourists feed them stuff, scraps of chicken, half-eaten hamburgers, bananas . . ."

"They look," said Peggy, "as if anything would be acceptable."

One summer, no work to be found, Carl and I had hitchhiked to northern Michigan. We got rides to Charlevoix, where I had a grandfather and grandmother my mother didn't like, who hadn't seen me in years. These were my father's parents. My mother's family had lived in a town about twenty miles away. My mother had met my father when she was in Charlevoix one summer working at one of the summer hotels.

My father died shortly after I was born, a long time before Carl and I walked into my grandfather's drugstore and I told the old man who I was, what I was to him. His eyes brimmed and he held me by both shoulders.

He took us to his house at the top of the hill on the street that ran through town. I met my grandmother, a woman who sat erect and spoke softly. "Lace-curtain Irish," I'd heard my mother call her. She carried a quiet authority.

I was meeting family I'd never known, a family that had come to America in the seventeenth century, settled in Newbury, Massachusetts, and worked its way west over the succeeding generations. They were only distantly related to the Braintree Adamses, if at all. They were one of my direct connections to the crazy mystery of creation, so I've always been sorry about the way things worked out.

Carl and I slept there that night, in a house my father, interred in a vault in the cemetery across the road, had slept in when he was growing up. It gave me the creepy feeling I was my father's ghost come home.

The next morning Carl and I went to work in the drugstore. It was a few days before my father's family, the Adamses, realized my mother had married again and was using a name other than Adams for me. "Hump," Carl would say, speaking to me. "Hey, Hump."

My grandfather said, "Why does he call you that?"

One thing led to another, and we both lost our jobs. Carl and I hit the road. I never saw any of them again, but my fascination with the historical Adamses did not end.

Bernice, a short brunette, has large dark eyes. She met us the next day. After Bob died, Bernice had married a retired army colonel who shortly left her widowed again. "There have been quite a few changes since I saw you last," she said to us at lunch.

We were sitting in a restaurant in the midst of hanging plants and expansive windows, lots of light coming in. The restaurant was connected to a dress shop where Bernice had a job as bookkeeper.

She'd always worked, always had some job around town. She had been the hostess at Oliver's Lodge in Murrell's Inlet twenty-five years ago, the year I located Bob and Carl again. We'd lost touch with one another after the war, and then this curious event occurred.

As I was paying our check at Oliver's Lodge, once a private home, then a fisherman's lodge, now a restaurant, the woman at the cash register said to me, "Are you the Humphreys who went to school in Comstock Park?" She had taken our name as we waited on the porch for a table.

We were standing almost dead center inside the lodge, waiters and busboys moving around us, every table filled. Peggy crowded in behind me. We stared at her. How had she heard of Comstock Park? It's so small it's almost unknown in Michigan. "Yes," I said; and she said, "My husband lived there. You must remember him, Bob Johnson." She turned to a busboy, stopped him, "This is his brother Carl's son." Having heard about me, through the brothers, it was as if she'd been waiting for years for me to turn up, knowing one day I would.

About forty-five minutes later, because it took that long to drive from the lodge to Georgetown, guided by a child with earnest eyes who sat on Peggy's lap telling us with a Southern drawl where to turn, we arrived in Bob's garage and got out.

Bob, the child's father, opened the kitchen door and stood looking at us. He wasn't exactly the same Bob I'd known. Since I'd seen him last, he'd busted his nose cracking up in a small plane. But it was Bob, no doubt about it.

We didn't say much. Inside, he picked up the kitchen phone, dialed Carl, and said, "It's him." Then hung up. That was Bob, abrupt and straight to the point. No frills.

I felt I'd gone down one of those roads where the underbrush comes up on all sides, narrowing the road to a vanishing point, had gone on beyond the vanishing point between the present and the past, and there stood Bob, and a little later Carl as well, almost as if no time at all had gone by.

Now, at a table near us, six women were reading the menu, waiting to have their orders taken. They were different ages. Two of the women were black. That was one of the changes in the South. A couple of tables away I could hear Yankee voices like our own.

"Houses are going up on Sandy Island," Bernice said.

"The island Bob took me to? Where the Gullahs were?" I hated to hear that. The island, as I remembered it, was a primitive paradise. ·Descendants of the Gullah Negroes, Bob had said, live on Sandy Island; we were in Gullah country. The Gullahs, he said, are Colonial sons and daughters with musical intonations in their speech unlike any other accents in the country. He wanted me to see them. A boat was the only way to get to Sandy Island.

We took his cousin's speedboat along the Inland Waterway under hanging Spanish moss, the water dark with tannic spill, the edge of the boat sun-hot to my palm.

Sandy Island looked uninhabited, wooded, remote; but there was a small dock. We tied up and went ashore under big trees, under trailing moss. We followed a boardwalk down a span meant to stand above the sea at high tide, the tide then out.

The village was a scattering of houses around what seemed to be a field or park shaded by trees from the sun. It was a village of sand streets, tawny lanes. Nobody around. The houses were small frame places; some had fences. Paths ran off everywhere; then, near a chicken pen, we saw children moving, not furtively, but at the edge of the wake of intrusion we made in the dusky air. We passed garden patches and a yard where kids were playing baseball, using a rubber ball and a flat board for a bat; about six of them, ages ranging from six to twelve.

We came to a tiny white-haired woman who had come out of her house to stand at her gate. I had my camera hanging around my neck. When Bob said hello to her, she looked at me and said, "You can tromp me and beat me but don't you take my picture."

She was wearing a white sailor hat, whiter than the whites of her eyes or her hair. Her hand on the gatepost was withered and hard. She stood straight as she spoke, her head stiff and high. We were strangers to her, but she wasn't about to tell us to clear out. She was curious, that's all.

Going back to the dock, we met some Sandy Islanders arriving from the mainland, a man and a couple of women. One of the women was coming up the bank from the dock balancing what looked like a sack of flour on her head. Bob knew the man, a Mr. Prince Washington. They were coming home from their jobs.

We stood a while talking, and when Bob said I was interested in the history of the island, Washington said, "My great-grandfather bought up a lot of Sandy Island. There was white people living here then."

"Where'd he get the money?" Bob asked.

"He saved it up from his job. He was a slave driver."

Bob looked astonished, and I must have, too. Thinking of Simon Legree, I suppose, I asked, "Were there black slave drivers as well as white?"

"Yes, and there was white slaves as well as black, you know," said Washington, giving us a lesson in history.

After our lunch with Bernice, I walked over to Carl's shop. Just inside the door was a room loaded with furniture, some of it there for repairs, a lot of it piled up for storage. In the next room, just as filled with sofas and chairs and upholstery materials, sat Carl behind a sewing machine, near him an antique loveseat on a couple of sawhorses. He still doesn't need glasses to work.

"Come on, I'll take you for a tour of the town," Carl said. He walked me through the old part of town. Georgetown has more historic houses than at first seemed apparent. "It's hard," Carl said, "to know how old some of the houses are. Too many documents, because of the Civil War, got lost or destroyed."

We stopped in front of the Tarbox House, a building that rises straight up from a hill beside the street. "Whoever lives there," I said, "has a lot of stairs to climb."

"I know her," Carl said. "She's an old woman, but she manages."

My knee felt sore again just looking at the house.

"A place like that," he said, "goes back to 1737. That warehouse across the street was also built in Colonial times."

We walked down a street of brick-front stores from early in this century, all of them freshly painted. In front of the Chamber of Commerce building, a tour wagon was parked, and under a nearby tree stood a horse and tour buggy, empty and waiting.

We went inside to see if there was any easy way to visit Sandy Island, but there wasn't.

"You could still get there," Carl said, "if you wanted to take the trouble. A ferry goes over to Sandy Island, that's where the houses are going up, but there's no road from the ferry landing to the settlement, and it's a big island. Anyway, the settlement is still the same. It hasn't changed."

Peggy and I moved to a beach cottage that Bernice owned. The view from the screened porch at the rear took in a length of yard that led to marsh and bay water, about seventy-five yards of sand and grass bounded on each side by trees not more than a foot or two thick. Islands of marsh grass lay in the bay. Over to the left, visible through the trees, was a long thin dock.

Birds came at all hours of the day, birds full of birdsong and bird cries. They came in pairs; small tan doves, boat-tailed grackles, cardinals, orioles, finches, rufous-sided towhees. The grackles came in flocks, black birds with iridescent wings, so big I thought from a distance they were crows. They raised their heads as they drank from the fountain in the yard, stared straight up and thought about what they'd done. No song-birds, these fellows. Squawkers all. They fought one another; made shrill, piercing cries like squeaky machine-gun fire, so loud they could be heard for half a mile around.

Late in the afternoon a female cardinal sat in the tree at the near corner of the porch and sang into the evening air for ten minutes, a virtuoso performance.

North Carolina

On a rainy Saturday that seemed more like a Sunday, so few cars were on the streets, we followed a driving tour through the historic area of Wilmington. The tour took us past the Bellamy Mansion, built in 1859. It has three stories and imposing pillars that must be twenty-five feet high. Union forces used the house as a headquarters during the Civil War. Shutters, closed on the second floor, were open on the main floor, giving the house a lived-in though sleeping appearance, as if an orderly might have been left behind in case the general returned.

Wilmington's historic district is a conglomeration of various periods, bits and pieces of time scattered here and there. Flotsam and jetsam, says Peggy. Older buildings stand in the midst of modern buildings, much the way Rome and Athens live with their antiquity.

We park and walk along a herringbone brick sidewalk over rain-matted leaves past a red brick Victorian house with a curtain blowing from an open window. Iron steps rise to a porch with a rocking chair and potted plants.

A socially prominent woman, a Confederate spy by the name of Rose Greenhow, lived in this town. She drowned near Fort Fisher in 1864 while running the Federal blockade and is buried about a mile northeast of Wilmington.

Cades Cove, Tennessee. Here time took a stand, stood still.

Gatlinburg,
Tennessee. The
Wonderland Hotel.
Old-time peace at a
modest price.

Cades Cove, Tennessee.

Williamsburg, Virginia. Where the illusion of Colonial America has been made visible and available. Inspiring; an example of preservation at its best.

Annapolis, Maryland.

Romney, West
Virginia. The oldest
house in town,
probably built before
1760 by Lord Fairfax.

Harpers Ferry, West
Virginia. The lingering
ghost of a building,
all that's left.

We could see Devil Anse through the trees before we got to him, an erect figure like a bearded ghost, surrounded by leaves. There he stood, patriarch of his clan, dominating the Hatfield family cemetery as he'd dominated the Hatfields in his lifetime. Near Matewan, West Virginia.

Spring Grove, Pennsylvania. Sometimes the log cabin grew an extension and sometimes, as in this case, it was the other way around.

Horse-and-buggy days are not yet gone for the Amish. Lancaster County, Pennsylvania.

A Pennsylvania Dutch barn.

Near Carlisle, Pennsylvania.

Bethlehem, Pennsylvania.
Beneath flat gravestones
Moravians await their day
of resurrection . . .

. . . and each Easter morning, as the sun rises, a Moravian trombone choir
serenades them.

You can even find a horse and buggy in the heart of Philadelphia. Market Square.

Philadelphia, Pennsylvania. Bladen's Court. Elfreth's Alley.
Benjamin Franklin knew the alley well.

Cape May, New
Jersey. A Victorian
village by the sea.

Batsto, New Jersey.
Worker's cottages in a
time-lost village in the
New Jersey Pine Barrens.
From somewhere, faintly,
I could hear children
playing.

New Castle, Delaware.

The Dyckman House, 1748, the only Dutch Colonial farmhouse left in Manhattan. Apartment buildings rise around it. New York, New York.

The Tewksbury wine festival at Lebanon, New Jersey, where we spent a
bucolic afternoon: grassy fields, tents, wine stands, and the mind drifting in
timeless contentment.

Tewksbury Wine Cellars, Lebanon, New Jersey.

We go into St. James Episcopal Church to see the painting of Christ rescued from plundering pirates; salvaged, that is, from one of three pirate ships that around 1748 attacked the Colonial town of Brunswick, North Carolina, fourteen miles below Wilmington. The pirates were driven off, and one of their ships was sunk. The portrait of Christ was in the captain's cabin. It was declared to be of the Spanish school and given to the Parish of St. James in Wilmington. There it's hung, ever since, on a wall of that old church.

In this painting Jesus wears a crown of thorns and a red robe. There is a rope around His neck. His hands are bound, and He holds what seems to be a bamboo stick.

On the lawn of the church, through a window near the painting, we could see a couple of grackles. The same grackles we saw in South Carolina drinking from the backyard fountain? Are they following us north? Across the street a child about two years old is standing in front of a house; he seems to be waving to us.

Pirates have not been forgotten in this countryside. Far from it. Motor lodges are named after them. Buccaneer Lodge, for instance, is on a road sign we pass. Blackbeard is remembered. He lived for more than a year in Bath, North Carolina.

On Route 101, heading north for New Bern, we come to the Intercoastal Waterway just as a bridge swings open to let a tugboat push several barges through. The tug is blue and white and seems to have three decks. A man with his hands on the ship's wheel stands in the wheelhouse on the top deck. The barges and tugboat are followed by gulls that whirl around above the water stirred by the tug. A couple dip to the surface and rise again.

The next day in New Bern, North Carolina, we come to a sign that says: POLITICAL DUEL, JOHN STANLY KILLED RICHARD DOBBS SPAIGHT, FORMER GOVERNOR OF NORTH CAROLINA, IN A DUEL NEAR THIS SPOT SEPTEMBER 5, 1802.

New Bern looks as if overnight some fairy with a sparkling wand visited and transformed the houses. A good deal of restoration work has been done and is still going on. It's extensive, block after block. It was hard to find a street that didn't seem to be lined with historic homes.

We go over a bridge, the masts of tall sailing ships on our right, into Bath's city limits. It's the oldest incorporated town (1705) in North Carolina. In 1708 Bath had only twelve houses and a population of fifty. The first thing we notice are the fields, empty lots, and big lawns around the houses. This was the meeting place of the state's general assembly in

1744 and 1752, but Bath went into a decline after the county seat was moved to Washington, North Carolina, in 1785. The town soon fell under the shaggy net of timelessness.

Blackbeard lived on a point of land across the water from Bath. His ships were hidden when he brought them in from plundering excursions. The governor of North Carolina lived on a nearby point of land. Not all of those who cut themselves a piece of the swag sailed with the crew and swung a cutlass; the governor and Edward Teach, or Blackbeard, are said to have had a working relationship, i.e., a mutually profitable understanding.

Teach lived up to every boy's nightmare of a terrifying pirate. He looked terrifying, just to begin with. Blackbeard he was called and black was his beard, extending from under his eyes to his chin, hair down his body to his waist. Preparing for battle or a hostile boarding, he livened up his appearance by twisting his beard into little tails tied with ribbons, looping the ends of the ribbons behind his ears. Over one shoulder he wore a sling with holsters for three pistols. He was, in action, as evil as he looked. Treachery and murder and rape came as naturally to him as the barrels of rum he drank with his crew. He roared and yelled and murdered with equal ease.

The governor of Virginia got sick of it. He was losing too many ships, cargo and all, to Blackbeard, and his complaints to the governor of North Carolina had no effect. He decided to take matters into his own hands and hired a naval officer named Robert Maynard to lead an expedition of fifty-two men in two sloops against Teach. They outmanned the pirate but lacked the cannons the pirate had aboard his ship. On November 17, 1718, Maynard set sail with the greatest secrecy, hoping to surprise Teach.

Teach, however, learned he was coming. Treachery abounded. In the morning hours the battle began, and Blackbeard, maneuvering, grounded his ship. Maynard, seeing this, ordered his men below deck and then, shot flying around him, headed for the pirate's grounded sloop. Teach didn't wait to be boarded, though he should have wondered what Maynard was up to with only two or three men in sight. Bellowing to his men to follow, he and his pirates swung onto Maynard's sloop, and as Maynard's men swarmed up from below, hand-to-hand fighting began.

Maynard and Teach brought the battle down to a personal level as they blasted away at one another with pistols. The naval man was the better shot, and one of his bullets hit Teach. Wounded but still on his feet, Teach fought on. They closed in on one another with swords. Teach, with one of his swipes, broke Maynard's blade. Maynard went back to his pistols, fired again, and hit Teach, but like the man from hell the pirate claimed he was, Teach kept up his cussing, swinging his cutlass.

When at last Blackbeard lay on Maynard's deck, the battle over,

Blackbeard's men pleading for mercy, a carnage count was taken: Blackbeard was dead, along with nine of his men, and nine wounded had been taken prisoner; twelve of Maynard's men were dead, twenty-two wounded. It had taken five pistol shots and twenty sword wounds to his body to put an end to the pirate.

Blackbeard's head was cut off, and it swung from Maynard's bowsprit as they sailed for Bath to tend to the wounds of Maynard's men. At Bath more of the pirate's men were arrested and carried off to be tried in Virginia.

Blackbeard's head is said to have dangled for many years at a spot called Blackbeard's Point at the mouth of the Hampton River. Tradition has it his skull was eventually made into a drinking cup.

Edenton, an old Confederate seaport, has a turn-of-the-century main street, beautiful Court Street, a boulevard. We walk along the waterfront. Wisteria is in bloom on an iron fence. The Confederate soldier across from the municipal building has raised his rifle, as if he shifts position as we move from town to town. Now he's pointing it off to one side at something he alone sees.

A breeze of romance at Murfreesboro arises from the past, from as far back at the 1850s. A family in town had arranged a marriage for their daughter with an old general; she wasn't happy about it. She was in love with a young man a few blocks away, and though she was forbidden to see him before the marriage, the night before the wedding she managed to signal to him with a candle from the window of her upstairs room. Before the dawn of the wedding day they were gone, leaving her family and the aged groom with raised fists of frustration.

She was disowned by her family. The couple moved to Tennessee, where they founded another town named Murfreesboro. He became a doctor, and they had many children.

The upstairs of the house she fled is open to the public, and the rooms seem to have preserved the period of the elopement. In the upper hall is a harpsichord that conceals a phonograph. In one room there's a high four-poster bed with steps beside it.

North of Murfreesboro a sign at the head of a road posted a ferry schedule. We turned to see where the road led and drove over a couple of miles of paved road and four miles of gravel. There we found the ferry, a metal raft at the edge of a narrow stream. The boat had a flat deck and a small engine house. A cable guided it from shore to shore in this narrow part of the Meherrin River.

We parked and walked around. Trees supporting great cloud banks of leaves shaded grass and water. Across the river were several frame buildings. We stood and studied them, and as we turned, we saw that behind us, from a small house, the ferry operator was studying us. He wore a green cap with a visor. A tall black man with a round face, he weighed well over two hundred pounds. He stood waiting to see if we intended to cross the river . . . or what, if anything, we wanted besides the picnic sandwiches we sat down to eat at the table near the ferry.

We grew more curious about the buildings across the water, so I walked to the ferry house and spoke through the screen door. Could we make a trip, I asked, across the river and back? The ferryman came out, and we followed him to the ferry.

He had as pleasant a job in as tranquil a setting, I thought, as anyone could want. His name was Sam Oliver; he lived in Murfreesboro and had been running the new ferry for two and a half years. Earlier, when a wooden ferry made the run, he'd churned it back and forth for five years. It took us only a couple of minutes to cross the river.

The mysterious buildings on the far side housed fish and fishermen. They'd piled the fish they'd pulled from the river into boxes; catfish, eels, white perch, and herring. The herring, a saltwater fish, had come up the river to spawn; now it was headed for local restaurants and markets. There weren't as many fish to pack, however, as the men were used to. There had been ten inches of rain in the last two weeks, fishing was poor, and a lot of their nets were lost.

When we ferried back, we faced the far bank, feeling the spell of the current under us. In the time we'd spent at the crossing, not a car had come by from either direction. All the way back to the highway we had the gravel road to ourselves.

Virginia and
Greater Washington, D.C.

W e were in Virginia going to Surry by way of the Colonial Trail; on the road beside us, a long white fence. The fence gave out before we got to the road that led to the ferry. On the ferry to Jamestown we saw in the distance, as if they were a patch of the past, a couple of galleons at anchor.

Colonial Williamsburg, Virginia, is where the re-creation of the American past began that's still going on all over the country, a re-creation bringing us closer to something that lingers in our blood and minds but is almost lost. Williamsburg is a timeless town preserved. Never mind the people in contemporary clothing wandering its broad streets and crowding into its buildings. It's the grand illusion of Colonial America made visible and available.

We stroll down Duke of Gloucester Street, not a car to be seen; no horse and carriage for that matter, though horses and carriages are here. People are wandering up and down the street. It's like Sunday afternoon in a town where automobiles are unknown, although, paradoxically, the street is paved, bending the illusion of timelessness through a refracting lens.

The leaves in Williamsburg were past budding, magnolia trees had bloomed. We were still following the edge of spring northward. We passed a vegetable garden behind a white picket fence, and then behind a similar fence passed the greenery of a formal garden.

At last we reached the jail where Blackbeard's men were kept until tried and hung, a Colonial jail with twelve-by-fifteen-foot rooms, its walls and floors made of planks. The cell doors were thick wood, swung on iron hinges.

In front of the jail beside the gate to the street stood a woman in Colonial dress, one of the restored city's Colonial Dames. We asked if she knew whether Blackbeard had a wife. It wasn't a question she'd heard before so she thought about it.

"He had a house in Bath," Peggy said, "so we wondered if he was married and, if so, what happened to his wife."

"If he did have a wife," the woman said, "I don't think he'd have taken her with him to Bath. He only lived there for a year and a half."

I said, "I think I read somewhere he had several wives, and it's possible because bigamy wouldn't have bothered him."

"No, not him. He was a law unto himself to the end. Too bad he didn't live to hang like the others."

"Well, he did. In a way."

"His head, you mean?"

"That hung on high for a long time."

"Oh, yes. Here, for a while."

"What happened to his skull? There's a story it was made into a drinking cup."

She thought about that, picturing perhaps, as I did, a grim chalice.

"I never heard that story. But if anyone drank from his skull, they must have had a strong stomach."

Now we were in Richmond, driving past the capitol designed by Thomas Jefferson, the first classical building to rise in the United States; then down Monument Street, which turns into Franklin, moving between fine old mansions.

Richmond's old Jefferson Hotel, now the Jefferson Sheraton, is a good example of how a building sliding into oblivion can be snatched back. The hotel had become a run-down rooming house when a man named George Ross borrowed $34 million, and the Jefferson, instead of disappearing, took on new life.

I'd gone into the manager's office to ask about the renovation, but he was out. The sales manager, too. As a sign of how well tourism is doing along the East Coast from Florida to Maine, it wasn't always easy to find people of authority in state and local tourist bureaus, or hotels, to answer questions. They were often too busy working with tour groups or television crews or clusters of journalists to take the time. I had the impression the tourist business, in city centers at least, is boiling over.

A man in the manager's office, there to make reservations for a large dinner party, said, "May I say something about the hotel? I'd like you to know the people of Richmond are delighted with what's happened to this place." His name was James Melvin, a fifty-year-old native of Richmond, dark-haired and trim. When he was a boy, he said, the hotel was the winter social center of the city. "People came here from their homes in the countryside to winter for three months. Whole families." At that time the lobby of the hotel, he said, was downstairs, which was—and still is—the most impressive entrance because of massive, honey-yellow pillars on all sides. Guests walk in toward a broad staircase that rises to a second level, where people these days register—up where a statue of Jefferson faces the new lobby entrance. Near the statue is a pool with an alligator floating above it, a creature of the air.

"When I was a boy, that upper level had real alligators in the pool. They tried to bring the live alligators back when the hotel was remodeled, but the authorities didn't see how the alligators could be made to stay in the pool. So today there's only one alligator and he's stuffed and not going anywhere. But I just want you to know how proud we are of the hotel. It's turned out to be not only a favor to the people interested in its history, but also a profitable enterprise. This hotel is booked solid most of the year."

In the capitol we stood looking up at the statue of George Washington where he stands under the dome. A gray-haired hostess came over and in a quiet voice began to explain that the part of the building we and George Washington were standing in was first completed in 1793. Jefferson had designed the building while he was a foreign service minister in Paris.

Peggy pointed to the open doors of the room behind her and asked if that was where Aaron Burr had been tried. Yes, that was the room. We all walked in, desks behind railings on each side of us. "And where," I asked, "was the balcony that collapsed, killing sixty-three people?"

"It wasn't just a balcony," our guide explained. "The whole floor caved in. Too many people crowded the room. Downtown," she said, "they thought the capitol was on fire at first. It was plaster dust. Plaster dust just filled the air like smoke."

As we were leaving, I asked her if she knew any towns around

Richmond that hadn't changed much in the last fifty to seventy-five years. "What hasn't changed? Everything has changed."

A few miles above Richmond, we put Ashland behind us and moved north on Route 667, following a narrow blacktop road between flowering dogwood trees, fences, and farms, beautiful undulating hills around us. It was a slow, deliberate, approach to the area around Washington, D.C.

Mist hung in the air as we drove through Fredericksburg, past old brick houses, and it hadn't yet burned off the fields beyond town. Thousands of soldiers lay in National Cemetery earth on each side of our road. Between tall monuments stood a soldier in stone. He was shading his eyes, peering into the mist, as if waiting for someone as ghostly as himself to appear.

We came into Alexandria on Fayette and moved over to King Street, the street that divides the city north and south. Christ Church, where Washington used to worship, was undergoing restoration. Restoration is needed periodically. Similar work was done on the church in the early 1890s. At that time the church was 120 years old.

Inside the church the enclosed and numbered pews are white, their symmetry broken only by the aisles and the natural wood grain of the pews' upper edges. There are red velvet seat cushions in each pew. Facing the congregation is a wineglass pulpit. The overall impression is one of light and purity, of age well tended.

I heard a bell somewhere tolling about once every four seconds. Leaves beyond the church windows were blowing in a breeze, moving in the wind, moving in memory of memory.

A note: Washington, D.C., would qualify as a Southern city on the basis of the pillars in front of so many of its houses; some wooden, some cement, some fluted, some plain. Jefferson, because of his interest in Greek architecture, influenced that Southern love of graceful white pillars.

Jefferson, that cool cat and aristocrat from the countryside of Richmond, had staked out in his mind an America of unified states that lay like a flagstone patio all the way to the Pacific.

He spread his fingers at the sides of maps while his wife lay dying in another room. There was no god he could ask for mercy.

I see him as someone with a deep faith in his fellow man, someone who held the individuality, or singularity, of each man sacred. He put a premium on a man's right to self-discovery. When he was defending himself for being an anti-Federalist to Francis Hopkinson, he said in a letter, "I am not a Federalist, because I never submitted the whole system 'of my opinions to the creed of any party of men whatever, in religion, in philosophy, in politics, or in anything else where I was capable of thinking for myself. Such an addiction is the last degradation of a free and moral agent. If I could not go to heaven but in a party, I wouldn't go there at all."

In Annapolis, Maryland, we parked near the Severn River and walked streets laid down so long ago that Englishmen weren't yet ready to walk them dressed in English elegance. That was still to come with the beginning of the eighteenth century. Puritans were the first settlers. Elegance came along when the early wooden houses went down, and brick mansions began to appear in their place; inside the houses were intricately carved woodwork and cut glass chandeliers that glittered in their own candlelight.

Annapolis became a social as well as a business center. There was much partying, dancing, gambling, theatergoing, right up to the Revolution. Some of those days are left, are still there, the feel of them, the look of them, in the streets around State Circle where the state house (1772) stands. Annapolis has many timeless houses. George Washington's nephews attended St. John's College, chartered in 1784. The Dorsey House at 211 Prince George Street is believed to date all the way back to 1685.

Prince George Street was the same as when we saw it last. Except for the trees, time seemed not to have touched it in a couple of decades. At one corner, dogwood had blossomed, white petals with a center of golden green. The street corner carried the street's name. Rust had run down from the chain that held the street sign. I'd have thought the streets would have had more traffic, but I couldn't hear the sound of a car anywhere, only the cry of birds.

On Route 50, heading for Middleburg, Virginia, we come to Aldie and stop to ask the owner of a bed-and-breakfast if he knows where Ox Hill is. A Civil War battle took place there, and a wounded officer left a record of it; the details of his account are painful.

The author was a young lawyer. He'd been given, to his everlasting surprise, the command of a company of veteran troops. "I am by no means," he wrote in a letter, "qualified to assume immediately the command of a company in actual service." But assume it he did, and he gave it his best as they faced the great Northern army.

He had, as he admitted, much to learn about the realities of a soldier's life.

We had no tents after August 6th, but slept on the ground, in the woods or open fields, without regard to the weather. Once I slept on the wet ground in wet clothes, with my socks so wet that I wrung water out of them next morning before starting to march. The weather was generally hot and dry, but with some showers and hard rains. Sometimes the dust was very oppressive. We generally made forced marches. We were often without cooking utensils to prepare our rations. . . . I started from Gordonsville with a slight attack of flux, which, under ordinary circumstances would have kept me on my back for awhile, and which, I very much feared would force me to the rear. I seemed, however, to march it off, and none of the labors or exposures of the campaign seemed to have any other than a good effect on my health and strength, which I found improving all the while.

Marching and fighting continually as we did without time to wash our clothes or our persons, and sleeping on the ground all huddled together, the whole army became lousy more or less with body lice. . . . It is a calamity which the soldier bears without shame, and with that wonderful patience and calm philosophy which is characteristic of him, and which is infinitely more poetic than the dirt and toil and suffering which calls it out.

A couple of months later he had need of all that patience when he was stung by a good deal more than lice bites. So far all the North's minié balls had missed him. In the aftermath of battles he had pried the slugs loose from tree trunks with his knife and examined them curiously. Most of the trees had been struck not once, but many times. It seemed marvelous to him how many of his men escaped being killed.

The hottest fire to which my company was exposed, I think, was at the battle of Ox Hill or Germantown when only three of the little squad that was left of us to go into battle escaped unwounded. In the twilight, towards the close of the battle, I had thrown myself on the ground sitting with my body raised so as to rest on my elbow, and my legs stretched on the ground, across the fire, instead of towards the rear as they should have been. I had just been talking to Capt. Morris who was sitting by me in a similar attitude, and had turned my face from him to observe and speak to my men, when I felt an awful pain in my leg, and said, in my ordinary voice, Captain Morris, my leg is broken. A musket ball had passed through my right leg, a little nearer the foot than the knee, from side to side, about the middle of the leg, and as the surgeons afterwards informed me breaking both bones. Very soon afterwards I felt another severe blow upon the same leg, and said to Captain Morris in the same tone, I am wounded again in the same leg. . . . After some conversation with Capt. Morris, commenced perhaps before I received the second wound but finished afterwards, I determined to try to crawl to the rear in search of some of the infirmary corps to bear me off the field as I was utterly disabled, and feared that an artery might have been severed which would require prompt surgical aid. I managed to drag myself about ten steps when I stopped from exhaustion, finding myself in an open place caused by a little road, and a little more elevated than the fence at which we had been fighting. . . . While lying there I had sand thrown on my cheek twice by musket balls which struck the ground by my head. And the shells from a Yankee battery which was enfilading our line, and which I now had leisure to listen to attentively seemed to pass in fearfully close proximity to my body. I wondered afterwards at the degree of calmness and resignation to my fate which I felt in this very alarming situation. . . .

It had rained hard during the night, and I was chilled and thoroughly wet when I was found a little after dark by one of my men. As none of the infirmary corps seemed to be near I was borne off by four men on my blanket stretched between two fence rails, I believe that I had no groan or outcry till they commenced moving me. . . .

On that night, Sept. 1st, I was carried about a quarter of a mile to a house where I was laid upon a narrow porch already so crowded with wounded men that there was only room for me at the entry, where my wounded leg was struck occasionally during the night to my great torture by the feet of persons passing in and out. On the next morning I was carried on stretchers about three quarters of a mile, and deposited on the ground in an old field where some wounded men had been brought together. Here I lay without receiving any surgical aid till about ten o'clock on the morning of the 3rd, when to my great relief I found that several surgeons were in attendance and ready to proceed with the amputation of my leg. I was placed under the influence of chloroform, and my leg soon taken off by Dr. Shaeffner surgeon of the 33rd NC, and the stump dressed. I waked up just as the dressing was completed without retaining the slightest consciousness of any part of the operation. . . .

Soon after my leg was taken off I was laid in a bed of rough and heavy army road wagon without springs, to be hauled to Middleburg in Loudon Co., Va., distant about 24 miles. The road was rough, it seemed to me very rough. We traveled all the rest of the day and till some time in the night about a mile beyond the village of Aldie, and still 4 miles from Middleburg. . . . The first day's ride in the wagon, it seems to me, had caused me to undergo more pain than I had suffered in all my life before I was wounded, every little jolt of the wagon causing a pang which felt as if my stump was thrust into liquid fire, and was as fierce as that awful pang which first announced that my leg was broken. . . .

I suffered comparatively little severe pain after reaching Middleburg, but I was very much exhausted. . . . The days were like months. But my wounds did well, and after I began to sleep I improved rapidly.

In Aldie the owner of the bed-and-breakfast tried to help us solve the mystery of the place where the officer had been lying when he was wounded and where he'd had his leg amputated. We decided the battle was probably at Manassas, and Ox Hill might have been the name of a local hill near Jermantown. Jermantown, he told us, was the correct spelling for Germantown.

Beyond Aldie, Route 50 is a well-preserved road through the past, though the traffic was heavy. We passed an old fieldstone fence and a lot of frame houses that went back to the early part of this century, and farther.

Middleburg showed us its German, or Jerman, influence in its stone houses, old houses on all sides of us. In Upperville, on the other side of

Middleburg, we drove by a red brick church that had green moss clinging to its bricks. Then we were in mountainous country, shifting gears.

Paris, a small place, nevertheless has an inn in a house built in 1829. Its black shutters lie against white stucco. There are working fireplaces in the front dining room, the taproom, and the library. The rooms, furnished with antiques, have country views from their windows.

The road into Winchester goes through rolling countryside, past farms with herds of cows. Where there aren't cattle cropping the grass, machines and men are at work. Fresh leaves are coming out on the trees. We pass forests beside the road that glow with a greenish-yellow subaqueous light, an earthly monochrome world.

West Virginia

*H*arpers Ferry is in a hollow of mountains at the confluence of two rivers. After breakfast at Hilltop House we take a hillside drop
down into Harpers Ferry. There John Brown made his stand, behind the
brick walls of a firehouse, against the federal army. On the way we roll
by someone's home built with a combination of walls I have never seen
before. The front half is stone, the sides are weathered brick. Doors of
the town's shops are beginning to open. Rain is falling. The streets are
damp and deserted. Our road drops us into the past around the turn of
the century and earlier.

George Washington took an interest in Harpers Ferry. The potential
to produce water power seemed great, and it was at his urging that a
national armory was set up there in the 1790s. Washington had not
foreseen the problems flooding could create.

John Brown's raid was in October 1859. From that time on, not
because of Brown but because of the Civil War, the town went into an
economic decline. The arsenal was burned in 1861 to keep it from falling
into Confederate hands, but what really wrecked the future of the town
were devastating floods by the waters that at first held such promise.

North of Harpers Ferry old Route 340 is now Route 180. The old route, with a new number, is a scenic and almost forgotten stretch of road.

The names of towns keep changing, too. Shepherdstown was once called Mecklenberg and dropped its German moniker in 1798 when the town was enlarged. It's known as West Virginia's oldest settlement and dates back to around 1730 when migrating Pennsylvania Dutchmen and their families put together a community. They didn't bother to pick up title to the land. They just settled in and named the place after their hometown in Germany, then chartered it in 1762. At that time they had ninety-six log houses, each twenty feet long by seventeen feet wide with brick or stone chimneys, an early community development.

Today, all the mills along a stream called Town Run in Shepherdstown have disappeared except for one. That mill has been there for one hundred years. It was built in the 1880s and stands on the site of an earlier mill built by Thomas Shepherd between 1734 and 1762. The mill has a working forty-foot waterwheel, a span big enough to bring the mill worldwide admiration.

There's a Lutheran graveyard with stone slabs inscribed in German. In the Shepherd graveyard, a private resting place, is the unmarked grave of the man after whom the town is now named.

Shepherdstown also has, or had, a haunted cottage. It was a story-and-a-half log house covered by siding and, by reputation, still occupied once a year by a murdered shoemaker. Our only clue to its location was an old folder that said it was on the campus of Shepherd State Teacher's College.

We drove around the campus looking, but none of the students we spoke to had ever heard of it. A man I took at first to be a college teacher or administrator said he thought the log house had probably been torn down. "These academic institutions are not very good about preserving old houses on their campuses."

He was from Wisconsin, a pipe-smoking man, tall, slender, gray-haired. He had just come back from a trip to Maine where he thought the people were quite cold compared with Southerners. Southerners, he said, are much more cordial and polite. "Awfully good people here in this town. There are many younger people along with retirees like myself."

When I asked about the mill, he said, "If you go down to the mill owner and ask him if you can see the mill, depending on the mood you catch him in, he might very well take you inside. Otherwise it's only open on special occasions."

"Have all the early log cabins been torn down? I expected to see more around town."

"No, they're here, most of them in the black section of town. Not that the houses were abandoned and blacks moved in. The blacks here are not like blacks who have recently moved north and settled there. The blacks in Shepherdstown have been here as long as the white inhabitants. But you won't see the logs in their houses. They've been covered over with siding."

We stood on the sidewalk near the car. I took him over and introduced him to Peggy. "The town is so beautiful," she said, ". . . and so undiscovered. One way we rate how discovered a town is is by how many antique shops it has, and so far we've seen only one."

"No, there aren't many, and I don't know who the dealers sell to. I think they must sell to one another."

But the town had a bed-and-breakfast where we stayed, and when we checked out, I asked the woman if many of her guests were disappointed when they found their rooms had no telephone or television set, a characteristic of B&B places all over the backroads map. "Not at all," she said. "People who come here are looking for something that isn't in the motels along the highway. We have a TV set in the common room for those who want to watch anything special. What we do is take people out of their ordinary lives, give them a hearty breakfast, and send them on their way."

The courthouse where John Brown was tried in Charles Town, West Virginia, is a tall brick building with a clock tower. The room he was tried in would have had trouble crowding a hundred people into it. Its windows are at least eight feet tall. The air, as we stood looking around, was cool. Toward the front of the room is a railing, behind it a long table.

It was here that Brown and his men heard their sentences, and a few blocks away the sentences were carried out.

They tied Brown's arms, sat him on his coffin in a wagon, and drove him out to a stubble field beyond town to the scaffold. From the scaffold he looked out over 1,500 soldiers commanded by General Stonewall Jackson and said he had no idea the governor considered his execution so important.

Charles Town, over the years, has grown out and around that field. If the scaffold were still standing, it would be in the sideyard of an aristocratic Victorian mansion, behind a black iron fence. The house is a brick structure, three stories tall. The yard, an extensive stretch of lawn, is carefully kept. There are trees and bushes. We peered at the area through the rain washing down the windows of our car. It would be hard to imagine a place a gallows once stood more moody and beautiful than this site has become with time.

What I'm beginning to suspect is: the houses we see along this road, approximately sixteen by twenty feet, are log cabins covered with siding, in temporary hiding, biding their time, and one day they will all reappear.

In Darkesville on Route 11, between Martinsburg and Inwood, four log buildings once stood on the town square, all of them taverns. Boyd's Tavern, at the moment, is in the process of coming out of hiding. The house, built in 1789, was turned into a tavern by the Boyd brothers in 1846. It's a two-story place. The narrow side facing north still had clapboard over its logs the day we saw it and stopped.

While I was standing across the road looking at the place, a woman came out of the house behind me. "Go on over," she said. "They like to take people through the rooms and show them what they're doing."

Her home, as it turned out, was also log, covered over. "Are these log houses warm in the winter?"

"Mine is. It's very good."

We stared across the way and then she said, "That house over there is a much better-looking place with the logs out and showing. We're renting our place or I'd sure have the siding off."

I limped across the road to see if I could get invited inside, but nobody was home, as if, once again, something was shutting me out.

We leave Martinsburg, West Virginia, following Route 9. The road seems to go back to the thirties, as if the people in the houses we're passing listen to radio instead of TV. Two houses skim by with hanging pots of flowers on their porches. A woman sits watching cars, as if cars are a relatively new phenomenon in her life.

In Berkeley Springs I decide that if the warm baths were good enough for George Washington, they ought to help my sore knee; and I'd bought myself, for the first time in my life, a soak in a tub with health-bestowing waters.

The tubs are in cubicles between walls of glazed tan bricks. Lifting my knee with care, I climbed into a white tub and sank into water registering 102 degrees. I lay there with the water just below my chin.

The soak lasted fifteen minutes, about the time it took for perspiration to run down over my ears and eyes. Then I got on the massage table across the room, and a heat lamp with an aluminum reflector was placed above the warm, damp towel they'd wrapped around my knee. The knee was already feeling better.

In the next stall the only sound was the whir of a ceiling fan. Berkeley Springs has passed in and out of fashion a number of times. After the Civil War, a lot of its regular customers, Southerners, refused to return to a spa that had shifted from being in a Southern to a Northern state. When the masseur came around again, I asked him where most of his customers came from.

"They come from all over, from as far away as Washington and Baltimore. I have regular customers who come on weekends."

"Do any of them have a torn ligament?"

"Oh, sure. Those can take up to six months to heal."

"This is my first try. And I came feeling skeptical."

"The Roman baths. The Roman baths, along with the massage, really do good."

This strip of West Virginia we're traveling, between Maryland and Virginia, is in the West Virginia panhandle. Half Southern, half Northern, it's remote enough in time for log buildings to turn up beside the road and for wood-burning stoves to send smoke up the chimneys of some of the houses we pass. Kindling to fire up those stoves lies piled in sideyards.

Beside our road a thirty-foot-wide stream runs over rocks, flowing off behind us. Peggy says, looking up from the map on her lap, "It's the Potomac."

We cross briefly into Maryland and come to Oldtown, situated on a former branch of the Indian highway known as the Great Warriors' Path. It was used by the Indians of the Five Nations. During the French and Indian Wars a stockade was built here. Braddock's troops, after his defeat at Fort Duquesne, used it as shelter.

Michael Cresap, an Indian fighter, Peggy reads aloud, cleared the forest in this area and built a log house that's still standing. A brick addition was added in 1781. Oldtown, the town he created around him, never prospered and so retains its picturesque setting.

Cresap, during the Revolution, moved his men in a hurry to the aid of Boston, covering 550 miles in 22 days, and as a consequence died from the exertion before he could return home. The old Indian fighter is buried in New York City beside Trinity Church, a man who gave it his all and then some.

Heading for Springfield, West Virginia, we find a river in front of us, with a tollgate at the entrance to a narrow wooden bridge. Near the tollbooth a stop sign, black against orange, rises with a clank. A tin can welded to the end of a fly swatter comes out through the tollbooth's window. A woman's hand holds it. "Fifty cents," she says. We pay and pass.

The bridge is about fifty yards long, too narrow for two-way traffic. Wooden planks rumble under us; below them is the Potomac again, we think. The trip is worth every penny.

In Springfield, in the rain, we drive past the log house beside the road I fixed in time on a photographic print twenty years ago. It is still standing, still unoccupied, a little bent and showing its age. Vines and weeds have grown around it, the tree's grown larger.

Route 29 winds its way through rural West Virginia past pickup-truck society, in stretches wooded on both sides of the road. Mountaintops tower around us.

All the cabins were taken when we got to Lost River State Park, so we stayed that night near Lost River at a place called The Guest House, with virtually no signs to guide us there through the wilderness. Looking for it, thrashing around on dirt roads, lost, we blundered into a Baptist religious retreat. A woman Baptist pointed over the trees and said that just beyond the ridge we could find accommodations. And we did.

The Guest House, isolated in a wilderness, gets its guests through advertising and word of mouth; it's a genuine hideaway. Wood paneling, quilts, and wallpaper. Rustic luxury at moderate prices.

I gave my leg another water treatment that evening in their Jacuzzi. Amazingly, there were no mosquitoes. A frog serenaded us. At dusk, as we soaked in the Jacuzzi, our host brought us each a cold glass of white wine. We could hear shouts of merriment coming from the Baptists beyond the ridge. They sounded like kids in a crowded swimming pool.

At breakfast the next morning we were served by a woman wearing a Mennonite cap. Her name was Esther. Her husband was a minister in the Mennonite church, "a volunteer minister," she said. "There's a group of us who support the church. My husband is also the principal of the elementary school in Mathias. Before coming here we lived in Wisconsin. My husband was from there. I was from Virginia. My name wasn't a Mennonite name. I married into the Mennonites."

She talked about her garden. She had, she said, a wonderful garden. "My tomatoes come ripe all through the summer and into the fall until the first frost."

Around noon we stopped at Upper Tract at a combination gas station and grocery store to get the makings for a picnic lunch. Beside one

of the doors going into the store was a sign: REPORT TURKEY AND BEAR KILLS
HERE.

Log cabins are no longer an unusual sight along these back roads.
We're heading west over old Route 60, a two-lane road slipping its way
through mountainous countryside. There's a two-story log house on our
right, its logs chinked with white, an old stone chimney at one end, a
small porch in front.

Mountain rain has come again, patting on the hood and the roof of
the car, darkening the road ahead. CHEW MAIL POUCH TOBACCO, says the
side of a weatherbeaten barn. That's a sign I've been seeing beside the
road for as long as I can remember.

We pass an adequately named burial ground called Trail's End.
We're in coal-mining country. A little beyond Clintonville we come to a
shop selling coal jewelry.

Turning on Route 19 toward Beckley, we cross the world's largest
arch bridge, below us an immense abyss. An abyss in the wilderness so
vast the face of the earth sinks under us as if we are leaving it behind.

I have a picture of Devil Anse Hatfield, a tall thin man in baggy
trousers and jacket, standing with a pistol in his right hand, the barrel
of a rifle resting on the ground in his left. His pants and jacket don't look
as if they'd been pressed since the day he bought them. He's a mountain
man, wilderness-based, not far from the Kentucky border and the Tug
River, a horseback ride from Logan, Matewan, and Williamson, the only
towns of any size in his southwest corner of West Virginia.

In another picture the rifle is there, steadied by his left hand, and
his right hand rests on the back of a chair. He's in shirtsleeves now, his
suspenders showing, a narrow-shouldered, narrow-chested man. He
stands on a board porch, or a board floor. The picture in the book is
fuzzy. Debris seems to be scattered around the chair and his feet. Perhaps
it's fallen leaves. His pants, turned up at the bottoms, bag at the knees.

His back, as always, is protected by a wall. A black cloud seems to
hang about his head because the wall at his back is discolored. The
wide-brimmed hat he's wearing has a high crown, creased at the top. He
looks wiry and willful, though frail, not at all like a devil or a terror of
the hills. Still, he doesn't have a face anyone would want to cross. This
is a man who has his principles, who believes in what he believes unshak-
ably; and he has the ammunition to enforce or defend his principles if
anyone should drive him to it.

And the McCoys did. Shortly after the end of the Civil War, the
Hatfields and the McCoys were picking each other off at a steady clip on

the mountain trails and wagon roads near Logan, West Virginia. Their private war went on among mountains so steep and wild Logan's law officials were helpless to stop it.

At the center of it all on the West Virginia side of the Tug, guarded by sentinels along a network of mountain trails, was Devil Anse. He had been a captain in the Confederate army and was a sure-shot marksman. They were all marksmen, those mountaineers, and proud hospitable hosts to strangers who weren't McCoys or men with badges. Anse had twelve children; his brother Randolph had thirteen. Behind those two were numerous rifle-toting relatives and in-laws.

For target practice, which the mountaineers never neglected, they stood on the banks of a river and shot the necks off bottles as they floated downstream. Sometimes, just for the hell of it, they shot at trains chuffing through the mountains.

In those days the Tug River was so far west that a character like Frank James roamed the countryside around it looking for banks to rob; Anse Hatfield, distrusting all strangers, once had James in his rifle sights. He had this stranger on horseback, in black string tie and black slouch hat, all lined up, but some instinct or streak of decency made him lower his rifle.

Anse didn't know it, but James that day was trying to outdistance the posse that was after him and the rest of the James gang; the gang had already robbed a bank and split up. James sat tight, watching the mountaineer come down the slope. James spoke first. He said he'd been thinking of crossing the river but had changed his mind. "That's best," said Anse, and James rode off. Off, off beyond Devil Anse's rifle sights, beyond the posse too, losing himself in that cavalcade of pleated mountain ridges.

Anse, when old, a man who had outlived his feud, was asked by a reporter to demonstrate his marksmanship. Anse obliged. Without taking aim he pointed his rifle at a tin can a hundred feet away and shot it full of holes.

Asked if he was a religious man, he replied, "Not a church member at least." Then he thought a while and added, "If you want, I guess you could say I'm a member of the devil's church."

He died with his boots off, in bed, in 1921, brought down by pneumonia. A family memorial to Anse, a life-size presence of the man, was carved from a block of marble in Carrara, Italy. Shipped from there to the United States, it was drawn by cart and mule to the Hatfield hillside cemetery where it stands today.

Along Route 85 we pass through company coal towns where the miners live who succeeded the mountain people. Their houses all stand alike, grimly the same, garden patches among small frame or brick buildings, as if all were built at one time, overnight. Clean towns, with lawns. People taking pride in what they have.

We swung left off 119 onto a two-lane road toward Matewan, a town that has seen some gunplay involving the Hatfields. Its main street buildings, most of them on one side of the street, are reached by a high sidewalk. The buildings are brick. A railroad runs behind the stores, as if at one time the store fronts were reversed and faced the railroad tracks . . . making it hard to visualize the gunfight Cap Hatfield, Anse's son, got into on Election Day 1896. But the railroad underpass he ducked under is still there.

Cap had gone to Matewan, taking along a fourteen-year-old nephew, another Hatfield marksman. Though John Rutherford of the McCoy clan was in town and all of them were carrying weapons, the day proceeded peacefully.

Drinking proceeded, too, and everyone was well liquored up when Rutherford got out his six-shooter and opened fire on Cap Hatfield. Cap, carrying a shotgun, blew him away. By the time Cap got a pistol out of his hip pocket, people all over the place were firing. Cap emptied his pistol, then he and his nephew headed for the underpass at the end of town. Cap reloaded, took further aim, and another Rutherford went down. When the firing all over town stopped, two of the McCoy clan were dead, another man was dying, and Cap Hatfield and his nephew were heading for the hills at the edge of town.

It was remarkable that among so many sure shots, so many shots were fired without effect in these skirmishes. Anse, once asked about this, said that human beings were a cunning lot, turning their bodies sideways and showing the gunman no more than about four inches of "life space"; even then "he keeps dodging and frisking about so when the bullets come along they can't find him."

I could think of nothing better to do than go into a bar and ask about Anse Hatfield's grave. The bar was the Town Tavern near the railroad tracks. Three men sat at the bar, two older men and a man in his late thirties. The two older men rivaled one another telling me about the Hatfields and the McCoys, and the younger man sat listening as if most of what he heard was new to him. Nobody, however, could tell me where I'd find the Hatfield family graveyard.

Then I ran into someone who could help us, a minister I met in back of the main street stores, up by the old railroad station. John Taylor. He wore a white T-shirt and glasses, and looked like a local businessman. He was interested, he said, in the area's history himself, wanted to see the old railroad station rebuilt and made into a museum. He was in communication, he said, with the railroad line about the reconstruction and was waiting for some action.

We followed him to his home so he could make a call to a McCoy he knew who, he said, would know where the graveyard was.

His parsonage was on the side of a steep hill. He showed us his backyard, and said it had been cleared by a previous minister. "They bulldozed it to level it, and as they started dumping the dirt over to one side, they found these strange stones, rocks, that turned out to be headstones. This was an old Civil War burial ground for unknown soldiers, dead soldiers nobody knew what to do with, so they dumped them here. Put up little stones. Nobody will ever know who they were. That's a family plot over there, another one there, a tiny one, just one grave, and in the woods beyond is another cemetery of relatively recent graves. There's a fence around it, somebody put a fence around it."

We went inside, and just before he called to get us the directions we needed, he showed us the local telephone book. It was crowded with McCoys and Hatfields.

Mountain people, I knew, were a superstitious lot. They believed in the influence of the moon on their crops and planted accordingly. Potato eyes went into the ground during the dark of the moon, corn, peas, and beans while the moon was bright. Hogs, furthermore, had to be slaughtered during the full moon, otherwise the meat was tough. Mountain people studied the moon to determine the weather. A new moon with its horns turned upward like a bowl in the sky was holding back water. A dry spell was to come. Horns turned downward meant rain was on its way: the moon was spilling water.

Hill people today have the help of the TV weatherman. They don't cut trees to make a home. They live in trailers or in small frame houses supported by cement-block foundations. The older the house, the more likely it is to be covered by tar paper. On the road we were taking, Route 44, some of the houses had to be reached by short single-lane bridges.

The Hatfield cemetery rose partway up the side of a ridge of land beside our mountain road. The driveway to the graves looked too steep to try to drive with anything short of a four-by-four. We parked. My sore leg took the slope while Peggy went ahead. I made my way slowly, rocks and pebbles rolling off behind my feet.

We could see old Devil through the leaves long before we got to him, an erect figure, all white, like a bearded ghost surrounded by trees. He wore no hat. Coming closer I could see he lacked the rifle I thought I might see in his hand. There he stood, deepset eyes, hooked nose, the fenced-in patriarch of a mighty clan, surrounded by the graves of at least fifty kinsmen, most of them Hatfields. His army in deathly isolation.

Cumberland Gap
and North

O ut of Jonesborough, Tennessee, we rode close to the old wilderness trail on our way to the Cumberland Gap, now a National Park, passing a few old barns that had gone gray with time; we traveled between green fields along 11E to Morristown, passing a small post office, its flag flying, passing weathered wooden telephone poles.

We stayed for the night in Morristown where 11E and 25E met. Had breakfast in the Red Ball Diner, a guy there playing the poker machine, feeding it nickels, playing from the time we sat down at the counter until we got up. Then up along 25E, a scenic road (part of the Daniel Boone Trace and the Warriors' Trail), mountainous all the way to Tazewell, not many houses. The road climbs and drops and dips and turns, goes over the Clinch Mountains, and follows, for a while, the Clinch River. A wilderness feeling comes over us, the sun shining on tops of forest trees, cool air blowing in at the windows. Twenty-three miles to Tazewell, fourteen to Cumberland Gap. A four-lane road. At Tazewell a sign says CUMBERLAND GAP, and an arrow points us ahead. The road gets busier, more signs along the way; we rise slowly, slip into a piece of Virginia, and then almost at once we're there.

Cumberland Gap is an old, once-busy town. Today it's bereft of its houses. About all that's left of the original settlement is a small two-story log house, stone fireplace, and the town's old mill.

America's first Southern route into the West began here in 1775 when Daniel Boone and thirty axmen leveled trees and brush for over two hundred miles (much of it buffalo trace, clear of impediments) into what is now the State of Kentucky. It took Boone and his men about three weeks, averaging ten miles a day. The settlers who later took his trail seldom covered the ground any faster.

Never a great road, no four-lane highway of its day, it was little more than a foot- and horsepath, but thousands went over it. From 1775 to 1796 more than 200,000 travelers went west by the Cumberland Gap passage.

Later travelers taking the road through and past the gap made no better time than Boone and his men, ten miles a day from sunup to campfire. Wolves howled through the night and, in the winter, freezing wind numbed ears and hands. Carts were jammed with household wares and furniture for the new place; for some, the place was Boonesville, Kentucky. Livestock trailed behind.

Indians were troublesome, treating those on Boone's trail as invaders, murdering any of the intruders they could. It was a risk of life to take the gap west: flint arrowheads, musket balls, and hatchets took a steady toll in the early years. The wise crossed the gap in groups. In 1796 a wagon road was finally completed, but by that time the period of the gap's major importance had pretty much passed. Still, it served, and until 1850 was one of our most important highways to anywhere.

When Boone pulled stakes and moved west, he was a disenchanted man. He owned not a single acre of land, was loaded with debts, had lost a son to Indians, and was homeless. The land he had held as a reward for his roadbuilding and pioneering was stripped from him through the courts in legal maneuvers he did not understand. Civilization and claim jumpers drove him to Missouri and into a wilderness he could cope with.

By 1808 Boone's Trace through the gap was no longer the primary highway west. The National Road to the north was putting it out of business.

Only a short stretch of the original trail still exists. It runs out of the town of Cumberland Gap, starting from behind the mill, runs through forest, curving gently higher and higher under shade, through forest silence, looking a little too narrow and parklike to be the old road once traveled by bands and throngs.

We walked the trail for a way without wanting to go to the end, because it runs nowhere now, ending at a highway, or so I'd heard. We took it far enough for the woods to close in around us. I listened for birds and heard not a peep. The path, for it's really a path, was so smooth I moved, I imagined, as soundlessly as Boone himself.

Our return to New York was northward across Virginia along the Blue Ridge Parkway. If timeless towns exist as islands in time, we weren't merely island-hopping now, we were island-vaulting, covering distance rapidly by highway and thruway.

Spring is the best time to drive the Blue Ridge Parkway. The azaleas are in bloom, the shadblow and rhododendron and mountain laurel. Spring, for that matter, is the best time to visit the South. But the views any time of the year along the parkway are spectacular; there's no interruption to the viewing as the road winds on and on, almost all the way to the Middle Atlantic states.

The first sense of the North—north of the Mason-Dixon line, that is—comes just south of that line in Frederick, Maryland. Nineteenth-century brick houses built side by side stand behind short lawns, thrifty architectural arrangements to be repeated in town after town after we reach Pennsylvania.

Pennsylvania

*T*his sign on the side of a gray-green cantilevered barn:

PREPARE TO MEET THY GOD
HAVE YE RECEIVED THE HOLY GHOST SINCE YE BELIEVED.
STILL WATER AND STILL
RELIGION FREEZE THE QUICKEST.

Just before Carlisle, Pennsylvania, we picked up Old York Road, now Route 74, a good road for old houses and barns. We passed a windowless Amish carriage, black against the black pavement, an orange warning triangle on the back, a father and son in black inside.

At Carlisle we crossed the Pennsylvania road that in 1751 ran from Philadelphia west to the Allegheny Mountains. It was the most important of the colonies' highways to the Great Lakes country, a prehistoric trail the colonists adopted. Before the trail was widened, pioneers heading into the wilderness loaded their pack horses at Carlisle. At Carlisle the wagon road from the east ended. That road, today, links with Route 30 to the south.

We were in Carlisle driving down a street with brick houses on both sides, windows in the doors; on our left, a brick house with columns; the columns look red, but it's only reflected light from the bricks. There are many old buildings, most of them around the center of town, red brick with stoops and white frame windows.

Carlisle was a supply center during the French and Indian Wars, and it was Washington's supply center during the Whiskey Rebellion. Carlisle had its own Declaration of Independence, a separate one, signed in one of its ancient churches.

There's a local story about Regina, a child captured by the Indians, who was reunited in Carlisle with her parents when she was a woman. She didn't recognize them until her mother sang a lullaby she remembered as a baby in her mother's arms.

Penn's Tavern is north of Harrisburg at Fisher's Ferry, Pennsylvania, a pre-Revolutionary stone inn that sits below road level on Route 147, its back to the Susquehanna River.

At the time the two-story tavern was built, the country around would have been solid forest, all of it virgin timber. There was once a ferry crossing nearby. Down the road a bit a great stone chimney rises out of field weeds. The hearth, at least seven feet wide, is the relic of a fire. There are always ruins around us, always have been. Penn's Tavern, however, has faced the hazards of time and come through.

The present owner serves drinks and meals, but doesn't rent rooms. The building, he told us, has probably been a tavern since its beginning early in the eighteenth century. It could have been built as early as 1690.

He was a tall man wearing a blue visored cap, a T-shirt, and shorts, his working clothes. He was remodeling. The plaster was off the walls all the way down to the stone.

It was a long time since we'd seen the tavern. Since then the bar had been moved. The staircase near the door was gone. But the newspaper clipping about the woman who had died in the arms of William Penn's grandson was still on the wall. In the room's shadowy light it was difficult to read.

John Penn, the story goes, met a girl his family considered beneath his social status, and John couldn't be convinced he should be satisfied with a flirtation or a discreet affair. He married the girl in secrecy and presented her as a fait accompli.

The family split them up for "their own good," and packed John off to Switzerland, but he wasn't there for long. He returned and the couple were reunited. This isn't a story of how love triumphed, but that seemed the case for a while. The stern and powerful Penns pursued the pair of lovers, or their influence did, until John's bride disappeared. He searched everywhere and would not give up until he was convinced he would never see her again.

. In time, he was appointed lieutenant general of Pennsylvania. Stopping one night at Fisher's Ferry, he heard persistent coughing through the wall. Pity and sleeplessness got him to the next room. There he was reunited with his lost wife, but only briefly. She died, it's said, in his arms, and is buried on a hillside near the tavern.

A man sat silently beside us at the bar. The owner spoke to him from time to time, and the man responded with a couple of words, then continued sitting in silence.

"Have you ever," I asked the owner, "heard ghostly coughing upstairs?"

He looked startled, then shook his head. The man at the counter said, "I heard the old owner once did."

On Route 772 moving toward Philadelphia, we pass at the Intercourse exchange another horse and buggy, the buggy as black as a hole in space, carrying a spectral Amishman in black hat and suit and beard.

Philadelphia proves that it isn't only in designated historic areas that buildings are being preserved. At the turnoff south on I-95, glancing across the highway at the line of houses that face the river, Peggy points out all the well-preserved, old-style houses, some of red brick, windows trimmed with white, dormers jutting from the roofs.

Philadelphia had grown so much in size and splendor by the time of the Revolution that it had become America's finest and largest city. Only London housed more people who spoke the English language. Philadelphia's streets, travelers took note, were clean and well lit at night. Security guards were posted at every corner. It was one of the most pleasant and well-ordered cities in the world.

Said Mrs. Anthony Trollope of a visit to Philadelphia in the late 1820s: "The great and most striking contrast between this city, Philadelphia, and those of Europe, is perceived after sunset; scarcely a sound is heard; hardly a voice or a wheel breaks the stillness. . . . No shops are open, but those of the apothecary, and here and there a cook's shop. . . . This stillness is so great that I almost felt it awful."

On Easter morning in Bethlehem, Pennsylvania, we stood in predawn silence among eighteenth-century buildings, watching the door into the Moravian Church. The trombone choir had gone silent. It seemed half an hour before the door opened and the choir came out, carrying their trombones, wearing overcoats and hats. We'd left the church early to get a picture of the musicians coming down the steps. A crowd gathered around us for the march to the cemetery, and a chilly wind followed us up the hill. Trombones pressed to cold lips led us on. The light of street lamps lay on our faces, eyes in shadows. The sounds of people walking and talking and the music of the trombones made our progression seem like an unearthly festival.

When we reached the graveyard, the musicians reformed. They faced the graves, and we lined up on each side of the graveyard. Limbs of trees hovered above us. The choir didn't begin to play at once because the sun had yet to rise. We waited.

The gravestones lay flat on the ground, varying in size. The sun was on its way, and the grass around the stones began to pick up morning color.

A man in his fifties with a camera slung over the front of his topcoat stood beside me. He had a German accent. He too, he said, was a visitor in town for the Easter service. He was a Moravian who had come all the way from Germany.

He spoke with pride, with delight, about the flat headstones and their simple inscriptions. "It is so that no headstone stands higher than another. And the men and the women," he explained, "have their own areas in the graveyard. The married women and the widows lie side by side, apart from the married men and widowers. That is so those who had most in common while they were alive are together as they wait for the day all will rise again."

And then he said, standing with one hand outstretched and sweeping it slowly from left to right, in both indication and blessing, "This is God's field. It is God's acre."

The custom had started in Germany, in Saxony, in 1732. In that year, as the sun rose on Easter morning, some of the Moravians in Herrnhut gathered in their graveyard and sang hymns. Three years later, the first Moravians landed in America, fleeing, as the Amish had, religious persecution. They landed in Georgia, tried to settle there, then moved north in 1741 and settled in Bethlehem.

Music became so closely woven into their lives that Moravian musicians followed their workers to the fields at harvest time; they gathered to play for the dying as well, the dying choosing the hymns that were played.

In the early years, to announce a death, four trombonists, soprano, alto, tenor, and bass, climbed to the steeple of the church. They played three dirges. From the dirges chosen, townspeople could tell the age and sex—as well as the worldly status—of the dead man or woman.

Moravians went beyond hymn-singing. Benjamin Franklin said of a stop he made in Bethlehem, "We listened to very fine music in the Church close by. Flutes, oboes, French horns and trumpets . . ." Today those who admire Moravian music come to their Bach festival held each May. But tourists are not usually drawn to the sunrise service at Easter. It's not a performance, not a spectacle for outsiders, although outsiders are welcomed.

Where we stood, looking across the grass and flat stones, we could see houses that have been standing since Colonial days, facing the graveyard, witnessing, Easter after Easter.

The sun appeared in its own good time that morning—as trombones played and the congregation sang. The sun came slowly up behind the trees. The flat gravestones were luminous in the early light. As their gray glow brightened, the stones were like so many doors in the earth that led to an underworld where the dead wait, their hands pressed against the underside of life. It was a moment that went back beyond Moravian graveyards to a desert wilderness and the moaning of a ram's horn. The sky brightened. The sun rose.

When we got back to our apartment in New York, there was a letter from the tourist representative in Georgia who said she'd learned what she could about the house with the ghost in Milledgeville. Here it was: House built in 1818 by a Peter Williams. House passed down to a Sue Williams, who lived there all her life and on her death in 1906 became the resident ghost. Ghostly Sue Williams was the great-great aunt of Katherine Scott, present occupant. Miss Scott, a ninety-two-year-old woman who lives there with a housekeeper-companion, had recently rented a room to a student who heard the ghost stirring about. According to Miss Scott, a retired schoolteacher, the ghost is widely enough known so that trick-or-treating children avoid the house on Hallowe'en. If I wanted to call Miss Scott, she'd be glad to give me more ghostly details.

I called her at once. Miss Scott said she'd been home the day I came around, that I was knocking at the wrong door. Her entrance is at the rear of the house. The house, she said, has a ghost all right. She called her ghost Miss Sue and said she was a tall, mean woman in life, but in death this ghost had never shown herself.

"The roomer we had here was in his room upstairs when he heard someone on the steps out in the hall. It was someone coming up the stairs. He heard the person go into the bathroom and shut the door. And he wondered and wondered who it could be because nobody else was on his floor. Nobody, he thought, is supposed to be up here but me. He even went and looked in all the rooms to be sure. He never heard the bathroom door open again, or anyone come out. He waited, then he opened the door himself, and there was nobody inside.

"And so he, the next morning, came down and described his visitation. I told him about Miss Sue, and I said, 'I guess we'll never see you again.' But he wasn't scared. He stayed right on.

"On a later occasion he heard someone in the bathroom again, even heard the toilet flush, and when he went in, water was still boiling in the bowl. But there was no one there.

"He told us about it, and we all decided this was the smartest ghost we'd ever heard of. She'd died in 1906 before this house had indoor plumbing. Always had outdoor plumbing in her time. And yet she knew the how and wherefore to flush that toilet. And so we decided she was the smartest ghost around.

"She came one more time to visit Joe, but this time he just called out, 'All right, Miss Sue, you go on about your business. Just help yourself to the toilet.' She must have decided she couldn't scare him because she hasn't been back since. That was last year Joe was here."

Her house didn't sound like the house our guidebook said was inhabited by a ghost from Wales. That house and ghost were still unaccounted for. But it did raise the question in my head: How many ghosts inhabit this land? Real or imaginary? More, it seemed, than I'd suspected.

One thing for sure, when ghosts appeared, like Hamlet's father, and spoke, they were the projection of the imagination. Ghosts have no vocal chords. Or flesh and bones, for that matter. So how do they flush toilets? Or set loose the motors of refrigerators?

I believed in ghosts until I was eight or nine. I slept with the light on. Darkness terrified me. I must have got fed up with this fear because I remember one night turning out the light, and then, tingly with apprehension, saying aloud, "Show yourself." The room wasn't absolutely black. The light of a lamppost down the street came dimly in through the window. My grandmother, whom I was staying with at the time, was out. I got up and went through every dark room in the house. There wasn't a ghost anywhere, and I haven't expected to see one since.

It's only in my dreams that ghosts still threaten. I had a dream once of an old, empty mansion. I was alone and in a mood to explore the place. I went up a flight of stairs to the second floor and started going from room to room, all the furnishings gone everywhere I went, and I came to a room so large it must have been built for receptions and dances.

Something was in this room, but it wasn't anything I could see. It was inside a coldness. I was walking into it, moving toward the center of the room across a parquet floor, when I came to a cone of icy air. Just as I was about to step into that icy cone, I heard my mother scream,

"Richard! Richard!" And I stopped. She was screaming my name in warning. I didn't see her anywhere. My mother was dead. She'd been dead for several years, and her warning, in itself, was terrifying.

It was the same iciness I'd felt in the cellar in Navesink, New Jersey, and that I ran into in another dream, this time in a similar cellar place. In that later dream I tried to force my way into the cold place, just as I had forced myself to go from room to room in the dark house. I couldn't do it. This time what I feared was too powerful, and against my will it hurled me back.

New Jersey,
Heading for Maine

*M*oving west across New Jersey along Route 78, a little more than halfway to Pennsylvania, on our right, we came to the road to Oldwick. In a few miles we were heading into the past. As we drove through town, Oldwick gave us the impression of a Colonial-Victorian heritage.

We were on our way to a wine festival, one we'd attended before, one we wanted to revisit. We were headed for Tewksbury Cellars.

Oldwick was the start of a drive through one of the most timeless areas of New Jersey, a hidden part, not guessed at on main roads.

The first time we'd been to the fair, we heard its music, country music, coming through the trees on each side of the road, and now we heard it again. We pulled into a field that had been turned into a parking lot and walked toward a stone farmhouse. Below the farm, between the farm and its barns and the wooden platform where the musicians were seated, we saw tables loaded with bottles of wine; on the green grass, big yellow-striped tents. Horses in the near distance stood in a corral.

Tables were set for those who wanted to sample the wines, thirteen samples for four dollars. We made our way to the food tent by the pond where a big yellow dog who had waded in was swimming. I had a hamburger, Peggy ate a hot dog. We sat on a bale of straw near strolling men and women who were carrying babies or leading small children around. It was a hot day. Most of the people wore shorts. One of the women, holding a child, was dancing to the music.

Peggy, with a glass of wine in one hand, fanned her face with a brochure. "I'm still a little hungry," she said. I got up, went to the tent behind us, and got us each a slice of watermelon.

The dripping dog came out of the pond and walked slowly up to where we sat. He didn't shake any water over us, as dogs will do, so I gave him my piece of watermelon. He took it down at a gulp.

"What a lovely place," Peggy said. "I love it here."

Beyond the fair, a wooded road wound around and around and took us that first time, and this time, too, to Mountainville, a silent village of a few houses, a deli-grocery with two weathered gas pumps, one gray, one red, and a pond full of ducks, nobody on the banks to feed them.

It's an uncharted Colonial town, a surprise. One of the first houses carried a sign, Mountainville Hotel. We stopped. It hadn't been operating as a hotel the last time we came through; the idea that it might be this time around made me check its status.

I knocked at a side door.

The woman who answered said, on sight of me, "Haven't I seen you before?"

At least two years had passed since I'd stopped to ask if the hotel was open, but she remembered me. I detected a look of annoyance.

"We're still hoping," I said, "that we might come through one of these years and find you've reopened a room. This is a beautiful town."

She shook her head.

"Anyway, I saw the inn sign, and thought I'd ask."

"That sign doesn't mean anything anymore. We're an antique shop now. An antique shop, is all. If you're hungry, there's a grocery on down the road."

A tunnel of leaves led into town, and we left by another green tunnel. The road continued, curving, and we came to Cokesbury, one more uncharted Colonial-Victorian village hidden in woods, one more village without accommodations. It was big enough to have two churches, although one of them, a gargantuan brown frame building with Gothic windows seemed to be a church turned into a private residence.

We pulled over to study it. Two joggers in shorts came up behind us and went on down the road as we watched their tanned bouncing backs.

A little farther on, we came down off a high ridge into Califon, dropped back into a time out of my childhood, to backyard sheds and barns. The railroad through Califon has not picked up or dropped off passengers in many years. Although the stone station still stands, the tracks are gone, stripped away. Geraniums were growing along the station's back wall.

It used to be we had only haunted houses, but today our landscape has haunted railroad stations as well. And haunted drive-in theaters, with junked and haunted cars near them.

New York

At Port Jervis, New York, we picked up the Old Mine Road, a road built by the Dutch from the Delaware Water Gap to the Hudson River at Esopus, New York, now Kingston. It's one of the oldest cart and wagon roads in the country.

The Old Mine Road is hard to find because roads, like rivers, change with time. What we have of the Mine Road today, most of it at least, has been altered and paved. Out of Port Jervis, heading north, it follows Route 209.

Along this route, the towns of Marbletown and Hurley still carry their history. In the 1800s Hurley supplied so much milk for the making of cheese that the town was said to have cheese mines.

During the Revolution, Kingston, just up the road, then the state's capital was burned by the British; people fleeing the city had no place to go. As in the South at a later time, they took to the highways. It happens in all wars: the dispossessed jam the roads and get in the way of the serious business of the military. When the refugees got to Hurley and Marbletown, people took them in. At that time Hurley briefly replaced Kingston as New York's capital, serving the state and sheltering its homeless citizens.

Only a few houses in Kingston survived the fires the British set, but

Kingston was rebuilt. Today, its downtown has good streets to stroll, lined with more historic buildings than we expected.

Kingston's Dutch Reformed Church, organized in 1659 and built in 1729, went up in flames. It was rebuilt and rededicated in 1852. Nearby are slate sidewalks edged with brick. Across from the church is a frame house built around 1789, yellow, with green shutters and a fanlight over its front door. Some of the sidewalks, on both sides of the street, are shaded by balconies.

The old Catskill highway lay ahead, what was left of it. It had run from the town of Catskill on the Hudson River, linking that river valley with the valley of the Susquehanna.

The Catskill Turnpike went into decline as the iron horse began its ascendancy—and the towns along the turnpike declined with the road. The road's revival and the alterations of its path came when vacationists discovered the by-then tamed and passive beauty of the road's mountain wilderness. Summer hotels appeared where cabins once stood, and motor cars moved where lone horsemen or coaches once passed.

About six miles before we reached the turnpike, now Route 23, we turned off on Route 23A. The road runs east out of Lexington, a town I remembered from an earlier trip.

I had been off by myself that time, driving back roads, and I arrived in Lexington early in the spring of the year, but late enough in the day for the sky to have turned dark. The town had a hotel that seemed bigger in the darkness than it did the following morning. The man who showed me upstairs thought I was in town for the fishing. Most of the hotel's rooms were vacant. I remembered its dim corridors and my stark room, and the river flowing by outside my window. The bare essentials for someone who wanted shelter. It was a place that hadn't changed since the 1920s.

Before going to bed, I took a walk around town. The main street was dimly lit. I dropped into the general store, the one store in town that was open. I wandered about looking over the merchandise. There were only a couple of other customers.

I bought a candy bar and went outside and strolled up the road through a fine rain that had just begun to fall. I crossed the bridge over the river and turned back, walking slowly.

I didn't sleep well. I was restless with a halfway-there feeling, though I had no destination. There was only this aged, nearly forgotten turnpike I wanted to follow to see where it led. About five o'clock I swung out of bed and dressed.

I paid my bill at the desk, went outside, and settled behind the wheel of the car. A streetlamp was burning back what was left of the night.

There was a misty haze in the air, and the mountains beyond town were barely visible. Last night's rain had turned to a fine snow that was beginning to powder the early spring lawns up and down the main street.

Going out of town I passed a yellow frame house where a black and white cat sat between the window glass and a dark green shade, staring out at the road and me. The two of us shared the morning. Now flakes of snow were falling, and the air over Lexington was milky and in motion.

That had been when I saw Lexington last. Seeing it now, I didn't think it had changed much over the years. The hotel looked the same. The sun was shining; no snow lay on the ground. There seemed to be fewer houses in town than I remembered.

Mermer Blakesley knows about old houses, keeps track of those about her, dies a little as they die. She lives in the Catskill Mountains with her son Hansen in a small house she's made attractive. It's at the end of a country road, fields on one side, woods on the other. She was born in this area, learned to ski here as a child, became an expert, and traveled with the U.S. Ski Team. She's blond; curls cross her forehead and curve above her ears. She's a ski instructor, a photographer of old houses, and also a young writer, which was how I got to know her.

Peggy and I had dropped by, taking her up on an invitation to see some of the old houses she was doing her best to protect. We were sitting in her kitchen. Her boyfriend, Eliot, was sitting on a stump in the front yard, whittling a new point on Hansen's broken arrow. Hansen stood and watched, branch-stick bow in hand.

I'd just asked her how she got into this preservation of the past in the first place. Mermer was saying, "The reason I got into it was I had written a letter, gotten a petition signed, about the architecture and integrity of this place, Windham. Windham was a really beautiful town, but the ski people moved in with all their ski stuff, and now it's become real ritzy and everything is a real estate office. A lot of this has happened over the last ten years. . . . The fronts of a lot of beautiful houses have warts on them, additions . . . so I was doing a petition for architectural integrity, and it got in the paper.

"Anyway, I got a whole bunch of people together for a meeting. The place was packed. I'd gotten the ball rolling. There was this woman, she runs a grant center, who was trying to get Windham on the National Register, and she said, 'Why don't you start taking pictures for me?' I did. I started traveling all over the place, photographing any house that was historic.

"I had a lot of anger in me. That's how I started. so I'm photographing all through here now, photographing in little towns, the kind you're looking for.

"There's a place called West Kill that's pretty intact from the early 1800s. The thing about West Kill is that I never see anybody entering or leaving their houses or tending their lawns. I know some people who lived in West Kill for a lot of their life, they live there now, and they still don't see anybody. And every house is perfectly tended, looks freshly painted, the lawns are mowed, and you never see it done. It's so strange."

I asked Mermer if she'd run across any haunted houses.

"There's this place," she said, "not far from here we called haunted when I was growing up. The Hardenburgh Manor House. An old, old place. Queen Anne gave the land to the Hardenburghs in 1708, and the house was built in 1780. A ghost is supposed to haunt it, called Agnes. Agnes lived and died there. She weighed, I've heard, over three hundred pounds; and she never married.

"When I was growing up, the big thrill was to drive by the place. You could never tell if anyone was living there. It's always looked ghostly. I'll show you where it is."

We got into two cars. Mermer came with us, and Eliot and Hansen followed. The house was on the slope of a hill along a country road on the outskirts of Prattsville. It seemed to be built in two parts, the front part stone, the rear wood, both sections so old I couldn't tell which was built first.

Mermer went up and knocked on the door that faced the sideyard. In a while a man in his forties, wearing a striped shirt and cutoff jeans, came out. Mermer introduced us to Livingston Baker, a professor at the Seton Hall Law School. He owned the house, but he and his wife lived elsewhere.

Inside we were shown the morning room, an empty room with wide, hard pine planks for flooring, the planks alternately green and white. "Those boards," he said, "go back to the eighteenth century." The kitchen was being remodeled. "I'm working here myself," he said, "working at it whenever I get a chance. There's a lot to be done."

There were two stairs to the second floor, one of them narrow and enclosed. We went up the main stairway and looked around. "There's little furniture here," he said. "Nothing of value. I don't want anything of value in the house. Break-ins are a problem, quite common in this area. I've got the original front door for the house, a Dutch door, but I can't put it in yet. Not until I get the house more livable."

We went back down the stairs, all six of us, Hansen bringing up the rear. "Does your ghost ever put in an appearance?"

He laughed and didn't look as if Agnes was ever a problem. "Sometimes there are strange sounds, the kind old houses make at night."

"Someone walking around?"

"No. None of that. If I heard anybody walking around, I wouldn't think it was Agnes. This house stood empty for so long before I bought it that a lot of people felt they had an owner's interest in the place. People who'd been coming here years before I bought it."

We went outdoors again. Baker walked us toward our cars. On the way he patted the flank of a huge stump. "An elm," he said. "It was eighteen feet in circumference when elm disease got it. I did everything I could but I couldn't save it, I couldn't save it. I suffered real grief when that tree died. The older a tree is, the harder the disease hits it. I tell you I grieved."

"Do you think," I asked Hansen, who was striding along beside us, "dead trees have ghosts?"

"There aren't ghosts," he said with conviction.

If there are ghosts, what family gatherings could be held in the stagecoach taverns still in use. And if the departed great-great-grandparents and great-great-aunts and uncles hadn't looked in on Earth in a long time, what consternation and confusion there'd be over unfamiliar things, what comfort in anything familiar: an old inkwell, a clay mug, a fireplace . . . a quilt.

Everyone's family tree entangles with everyone else's, everyone's a cousin once or twice removed from everyone on earth. Branches cross branches. Here was a place the Tristram Coffins touched, here the Adamses, the Williams, the Frinks, the Aldens. In the boughs of family histories is the history of the land. Peggy's kin lived through the battles of Rhode Island and Bunker Hill, Monmouth, Saratoga. Behind her, like a forest covering the world, were the trees of all the families on earth—out of which we all came, bridge builders, shoemakers, state representatives, farmers, barn builders, tollgate keepers, butchers, bakers, and so forth— mostly farmers. Because I had so little family as a child, I've adopted Peggy's, as well as all unmarked graves. When I toddled down the street in Mancelona, Michigan, long ago, how could I have known the trees of ancestry stretched beyond the edge of town?

Connecticut

As we drove down the main street of Salisbury, Connecticut, Peggy said that Ethan Allen and some of her ancestors had lived here at the same time. She wondered if they might have known one another. In 1807 an ancestor of hers had acquired the land on which the Salisbury School now stands.

We drove out to the school. It was Saturday. Cars were parked in the driveway near the tennis courts, near the four white pillars that rose some thirty feet from the ground in front of the school's entrance. The land and the house had been sold to the school in the early 1900s.

Peggy gazed at the house, under the spell of past glory relinquished. "Any man," she said, "who built a house that size must have had a good opinion of himself."

"Are the relatives who owned that place in your direct line?"

"No. Oh no. I think we're in the 'Never made a dime' line."

In 1767, Ethan Allen left his family behind in Salisbury and headed alone into the wilderness of Vermont, then known as the New Hampshire Grants. It was winter. He took a good long look at the pine forests trimmed with snow and, returning, came down the middle of the Grants by way of the Connecticut River, through Deerfield, to Northampton, Massachusetts. From there he took the Mohawk Trail home and told his family to pack up, they were moving. His eyes had seen the coming of his glory.

They moved to Bennington, Vermont, the only settlement of any size in the Grants. Thirty-one townships had already been granted by New Hampshire in territory contested by the State of New York, and Allen moved straight into the conflict. He liked conflict, he and his Green Mountain Boys. He took on New York, and, later, the British as well.

We picked up Route 41 out of Salisbury, a beautiful stretch of road in the northwest corner of the state. I was driving. Peggy was checking Salisbury in our 1930s *American Guide* for Connecticut. "Listen to this," she said. "Until recently, town was without street lights. When movement was started to install electricity on Main Street a woman of the opposition said: 'Seems to me that if I was being chased by a stranger, I'd rather it were dark.' "

Between Salisbury, Connecticut, and Great Barrington, Massachusetts, Route 41 is a stretch of country road I now have circled on my map the way I circle timeless towns. It's special—a stretch of rustic beauty, not spectacular, just pastoral, out of old times.

Along this road we came to a place called Stagecoach Hill. The afternoon was ending and we pulled into the inn's parking lot. The people who would shortly be eating dinner there were in the taproom, all the bar stools taken: We sat near the bar at a small pine tavern table. There were bench seats near us with high backs that looked a lot like those we'd seen in a Quaker Meeting House near Pawling, New York. Peggy wondered if they'd found their way here willingly. "Could be," I said. "The Puritans were not opposed to a drink or two."

The beer on tap was British. It was served only mildly cooled, British style, in pint and half-pint mugs. The posts that stretched as supports between the bare floor and the ceiling were hand-hewn. Most of the people at the bar and at the tables were young, the men in jackets. This was a sophisticated, cheerful place. It was pleasant sitting there drinking beer that tasted as British as British beer should; we felt so pleasantly British Colonial that we didn't leave for more than an hour.

Then, still on Route 41, we drove to Pittsfield, Massachusetts, where we switched to Route 7, traveling a stretch of paved highway through mountainous countryside in the dusk of the day. We were following the path of an old Indian trail—by 1764 a toll-free road, the Mohawk Trail.

The following day, doubling back, we found ourselves in Norfolk, Connecticut, an old town, founded in 1758; a twilight zone of a place.

That's true, of course, of all time-kept towns. Sometimes the only differ-ence between the discovered and the undiscovered timeless town is the number of visitors wandering the streets.

Norfolk's village green has a handsome grouping of houses. A foun-tain at one end of the green flows in honor of a local storekeeper; at the other end stands a road sign. In a frame in the air, like a small window, there's a running rabbit, along with the distances to Canaan, Great Barrington, and Pittsfield. A breeze moved the leaves in the trees, but no wind ever moved in the rabbit's world, rabbit-world grass under its paws; there were two village greens under that rabbit, one as timeless as the paint that created it. The rabbit had fixed one eye on us for the first time years ago on another spring afternoon, and now fixed the same eye on us again.

Few travelers pass through the town we were about to see, hidden as it is from summer and winter traffic. A couple of miles out of Torring-ton we turned left on a side road. It was a cloudy day, a light rain had begun to fall, heavier than a mist, short of a shower.

We pulled into Winchester Center, a tiny place made up mostly of a few old frame houses. We drove slowly around the green, more of a shared triangular lawn than anything else, and our windshield wipers swung back and forth as if clearing a sunken vision. White houses coasted by, lapstreak wood appearing more sharply, less sharply, more sharply . . .

We pulled to the edge of the road and stopped. The rain came down a little harder. I turned off the engine. Our wipers made one more sweep and quit. Rain plinked on the hood. A heavy gray light hung over the houses, part of the day's silence. The town's Colonial aura came from shutters, from firewood piled beside a front door, from a great tree ahead of us with limbs as large as most tree trunks, and from the solitude. Out from between two houses came a short-haired brown and white dog. He cut across the green looking preoccupied, heading somewhere at a steady trot.

As we drove down the road beyond Winchester Center, the rain slacked off. Damp slate gleamed on a barn roof.

We came to Colebrook, a small Colonial town strung out beside the road, and drove past a triangular green, past a 1795 Congregational church, past white fences. Grass embankments rose on each side of the road. We parked across from a house where five or six cars were pulled over. Some of the people from those cars had crossed the road and were going through the gate of a white fence, most of the people smiling, as if they hadn't seen one another in some time, as if they were gathering this damp Saturday afternoon for some rather formal party—not a lawn party, it was too wet for that—for a visit, perhaps, by some famous lecturer or guest.

We walked back to the green for a look at the church. I tried its door, but the door was locked. All the church doors are, these days, but I keep on trying them, an old habit.

Walking back, we came to a car that had pulled up behind us. I saw the driver unlock the trunk and raise the lid, and I thought I'd ask what was going on.

"What is it, a party of some kind?"

He hauled a king-size umbrella out of the trunk, gave me a mild look, and didn't seem to know how to answer. He opened the umbrella. It bloomed with bold black and white stripes. He said, smiling, "It's a funeral." Then he crossed the road toward the gate and the people who had reached the front door and who were stepping thoughtfully inside.

We often rambled as we drove, coming to a country road crossing and turning right or left at random. Sometimes this led us into major highways, and sometimes we followed back roads all day long with little more than an occasional look at the 1980s.

On a mountain-gliding road through woods with emerging green leaves, we came to Riverton, Connecticut, and parked in the lot beside the old Ives Tavern, now called the Riverton Inn. We had dinner at a table beside a bay window, looking out at a bridge over a river and the brick walls of the Hitchcock Chair Company on the far bank.

Riverton is on the old Hartford-Albany stage route, and the inn (built in 1796) was a coach stop. Time, since those days, has made some alterations. The inn has been remodeled. The wooden dam that crossed the river is gone. Hitchcock's factory has been enlarged, but it is still turning out copies of its original rush-bottomed chair.

After dinner we walked across the bridge. Below us flowed clear water. We could see clean river bottom from bank to bank.

We settled that night at the Riverton Inn. The room was nestled in the ages the town itself had known. We had a low four-poster bed with a white tufted bedspread, at the foot of the bed a yellow Victorian settee. The room was wallpapered. There was a fireplace, but it was boarded up and papered over, just its wooden mantel showing. There were white curtains at the windows that faced the river and the chair factory. A pull chain dangled from a ceiling light fixture.

The next morning, sitting on the side of the bed, looking out a window at the river and factory, I had the feeling a stagecoach we were waiting for had come and gone. Peggy was still asleep. The sun hadn't yet come up, and the morning was gray. Our stage, I felt, had rattled by.

— ⁓ ⁓

The road that John Adams took from Boston to the Continental Congress carried him for eighteen days. Along that road, along all old roads the colonists traveled, especially the roads now bypassed by thruways, there are glimpses of those times. It's like looking through a window tiny as a pinprick into a world within a shell, thinking, That's great. How is it done?

These are the times the crossovers into the past happen and sometimes offer more than a glimpse of another world. I'll see a village and its streets, and around the village fields and forests. The leaves on the trees are moving, turning. I think I feel a wind. My eye seems to glide in on the village. I come in so close I can see the grain in the wood of a table inside a house; then, my eye gliding back, I see no one is walking any of the village streets. Just as I decide no one lives there anymore, I hear the sound of an ax cutting wood. The wind that moves in the trees among the houses, soft as it blows, for all its gentleness has fragrance. And I'm standing in that world.

Brooklyn, Connecticut, appeared quite suddenly, a crossroads village in the eighteenth century, still a crossroads village today. Israel Putnam was a twenty-year-old farmer when he arrived in Brooklyn with his bride. He moved to a house beside the village green. He ran his home as a tavern. He helped build the village church. He rang its bell.

A man on horseback came by beating a drum, spreading the news of the British-American battle at Lexington and Concord. Putnam dropped his plow and rode off to Boston to become a general.

In time his generalship earned the wrath of Washington, but Putnam's hometown put up a monument to him. There he sits today, a figure in stone astride a mount. He faces the road, reins in his left hand, pointing his finger at those who drive by. A sturdy figure in a three-cornered hat, long-tailed jacket, and boots, he observes his left with confidence and points straight ahead, commandant of a timeless town.

Under the monument, below the decorative wolf's head, he lies at rest. Once there were two wolf's heads, now there is only one. They were cast and put in place on the pediment to commemorate Putman's greatest local exploit.

A she-wolf was killing sheep on the farms around Brooklyn. On a December day in 1742 when a light snow had fallen, the farmers got together and tracked the wolf to her den. They built a fire at the rocky entrance and tried smoking her out. They threw sulfur on the flames. They waited and pondered, Putnam among them. Time dragged on. Night arrived.

The den was a hole that ran back under a rock ledge on the side of a hill. The opening was narrow and low. It was ten o'clock when young Putnam said, "Clear away the fire. I'm going in."

He sat down and tied a rope around his ankle. He took off his coat and vest, grabbed a rifle and a torch, and went in. The den narrowed as it ran under the hillside. He crawled until he saw the reflections of his torch in the wolf's eyes. He kicked the rope. The men holding the rope hauled him out.

In the dark wintry air he tucked in his shirt, took the torch and rifle, and crawled back. This time when the wolf's eyes appeared in the bouldered darkness, he took aim. The blast in that cramped space knocked Putnam senseless. They hauled him out, and he crept in for a third time; when they hauled him out, he brought the wolf with him, holding her by the ears. He had lost, it's claimed, seventy sheep to the wolf, the last wolf in the state.

"Some hero," Peggy said.

"Well . . . that took hatred and determination, and maybe that was the Spirit of 'Seventy-six."

The general's son married Lucy, one of the fourth-generation girls in Peggy's history. Who rang the bell that day in the tower of the church?

Over at the post office, in a building close to Putnam's monument, I asked about the missing wolf's head. It was vandalism, said the woman behind the counter. A Hallowe'en prank just a couple of years ago. She had the longest face, as she spoke. The town was still in shock.

Stiles Tavern in Thompson, Connecticut, is a long, low, white building. It faces the green where the local militia assembled as the Revolution began. This early nineteenth-century inn has rooms that are no longer used for guests, but its restaurant is still in operation. The place has the atmosphere of an early stagecoach stop back when the Middle Post Road was still a principal American highway. Stiles, who gave the tavern his name, in addition to serving travelers had a business on the side of marrying eloping couples. Today the inn and the town are arrested in time along a forgotten highway.

It was along this forgotten highway, the Middle Post Road, that John Adams rode horseback from Boston to Washington. The highway is gone, but I knew it entered Connecticut north of Thompson and went south and west through Pomfret, Windham, Colchester, and Durham on its way to New Haven. An ancestor of Peggy's once had a tavern in Windham. We wondered if Adams stopped there. We'd seen the place, now a private home. Had Adams and the tavern's owner known one another? I thought about John Adams a lot, this tenuously related kin of my father's.

Adams was a Puritan, and self-interest to him was one of man's greatest sins, self-interest of any kind. At the Continental Congress, he was a holy man from the North—incorruptible, staunch, merciful, and wise. In the mind of at least one delegate at the Congress, Adams was the Atlas of American independence.

As a boy he had wanted to be a farmer like his father, but his father thought being a farmer wasn't enough. His father, Adams once said, was the most honest man he ever knew, and he wanted to be a man like him. John was sent to Harvard, where he graduated fifteenth in a class of twenty-four.

John was a lawyer when he and Abigail married in 1764. Ten years later he rode south to the Continental Congress, and from then until 1801, when he retired from government service, Abigail had to share him with his country.

He was never a man of wealth. He couldn't afford to bring his family to Philadelphia. He worked hard. His eyes gave him trouble. He bought spectacles. He wrote his wife, "I must assume the appearance of wisdom, age, and gravity, and put on spectacles to walk about the street." He wrote her constantly.

Abigail spent nights without sleep—lonely. She wondered if she might not, somewhere, find some tea. Tea would help her headaches. Adams wanted and needed tea himself. He found a canister of tea and sent it to her.

She was the right woman for him, one of the great women so often found beside great men, a perfect complement. They shared the same cause. "We possess a spirit that will not be conquered," she wrote him. "If our men are all drawn off and we should be attacked, you will find a race of Amazons in America."

Less than half of their first thirteen years of married life was spent together. He suffered periodic depressions. He worried about his children's education.

My god, how he missed his home, his wife, his children. He wrote, "Posterity! you will never know how much it cost the present generation to preserve your freedom! I hope you will make good use of it. If you do not, I shall repent in heaven that I ever took half the pains to preserve it."

He worried about the morals of his fellow Americans, about the corruption he knew lived in their hearts, but he trusted it would never get the upper hand.

When he went to France as a diplomat, he took with him a dozen clay pipes, thirty weights of brown sugar, and six chickens to keep him and his son supplied with fresh eggs. There were also six dozen small barrels of cider. Abigail got his supplies together.

He played captain for the crossing, or the captain took orders from him. He saw that the crew's filthy quarters were cleaned. He objected to the cursing of the crew and was pleased to see them turn out humbly for Sunday service. He and his young son endured pitching seas and encounters with the British with stately steadiness.

He was a moralist. He knew how everyone should properly think and feel—a housekeeper to the world, ring of keys at his apron, Plymouth Rock in his soul.

He was never known for his humor.

Benjamin Franklin, who acquired a thorough knowledge of Adams while he and Adams and Jefferson were serving as diplomats in Paris, thought Adams had a streak of madness. He confided as much to Jefferson. It was Adams's proposal, Jefferson later recalled, that the title of the first president be "Most Highness."

Rhode Island

*P*eace Dale. That's a name I like. Sounds restful. It's a company town, a mill town, its machinery spinning out clothing for the same family owners, generation after generation, 1829 to 1917. They made the shawl that Lincoln often wore. The Hazard family were the mill's owners, and they put up stone buildings all around the middle of town. Now the factory, where the highway turns, has been converted into office space. Another stone building, the town library, has an enormous corner lawn. On the lawn, leaning against the trunk of a tree, was a hand-printed sign that said:

FANTASY II

A KID'S CABARET

No day or time was given.

Farther up the lawn, between two wings of the library, is a Hazard family memorial called *The Weaver,* created by Daniel Chester French. Violet rhododendrons grow around it. On the span of the monument's surface are sculpted figures. A young man sits at a loom, two women behind him; one holds the skein he weaves. Above the three figures are these words: GOD DESIGNED THE FABRIC OF THE STUFF HE LEAVES TO MEN OF NOBLE MIND.

Long before the Hazards came, this had been Indian land, land the Indians sold in 1685 in the Pettaquamscutt Purchase. Before the Hazards came, horses were bred and raced here. The horses were called Narragansett racers, and Paul Revere, some say, mounted one of these racers for his midnight ride.

We heard about Peace Dale from our friend Kitty Barnes, who owns a house in town. Shingle-sided, built in 1860. She and Chuck bought the place nine years ago. He's an artist, she's a freelance writer and editor, a new breed of people moving into the small towns of the countryside to try to make a living. They weren't in town now. Things hadn't worked out. She was renting the house, holding on to a place in a town that Stewart Holbrook in *The Old Post Road* (1962) called "one of the most appealing hamlets in New England."

"What's that? Kingston Inn?" Peggy said.

A sign hung at the corner of a house we'd passed, and we turned around and drove back. In the parking lot beside the inn, or what we thought was an inn, I got out to check the place. "I'll go get the lowdown," I said. But the lowdown was coming toward me: a stocky young man with a ruddy face wearing a T-shirt. "You looking for someone?"

We stood in the bright sunlight beside the house where I knew we weren't going to stay. "The sign out front says inn," I said. "Is this an inn?"

He stared at me as if he were trying to grasp what I was talking about. "The sign out front says 'Kingston Inn,'" I said.

"No more." He shook his head. "It hasn't been an inn for years. This was a boarding house until it got converted into one-room efficiency apartments. That's what it is now. And they're all taken."

"With fireplaces?" I don't know why I asked that. I just wanted to know what we couldn't have.

"Microwave ovens," he said.

Outside of Jamestown we came to a windmill with four arms in silhouette against the sky. It stood on a hill beside the road at the edge of a field. I had to walk to reach it. The arms weren't turning, and a red door in the base of the mill was locked, as if the wheels, if they ever turned, were a spectacle reserved for special occasions. A few of these windmills still stand along our northern coastline.

A child came across the field behind me. He came hurriedly, eyes on the windmill, followed by his father.

At the mill they tried the door, then walked all around the base of the shingled tower under the still blades.

I made my way over to them, and the father said to me, "I wish we could get in there. I brought my boy here for a look at it."

"Whose is it?"

"It's being preserved by the local historical society. It's a very old mill."

"Dutch, is it?"

"I don't think so. I think it's English. I've read about it, but I forget."

"The only one I know of like it is out on Long Island, and I think that's Dutch."

"Very few people around here," he said, "know anything about this windmill. I just happened to run across it while I was out driving. It had shingles put on it about three years ago. I was glad to see that done. They don't build them like this anymore. They can't build them like this one. They come in now to build using all kinds of instruments. This was built without using instruments."

I saw he wanted to put his son in touch with an age when men were more versatile, an age that had vanished but still rode with us in our blood. He wanted his son to see what men, without calculators and modern instruments of measurement, were capable of building.

The boy, blond like his father, raised his arms and began to slowly whirl around.

On, then, to Bristol on Narragansett Bay, settled in 1672, one of the five most important ports on the Atlantic coast during the eighteenth century. It was a Colonial city trading in rum, molasses, and slaves. The British burned and looted Bristol during the Revolution, so most of the houses and mansions in town are post-Revolutionary. Fortunes were made here.

Privateers made Bristol a headquarters during the War of 1812, but recession hit when piracy and the slave trade were outlawed. There were other fortunes to be made, banked by shipbuilders.

Bristol has always been known for the ships it made and launched. They set sail out of Narragansett Bay for all over the world. Bristol went on building ship after ship until the middle of the nineteenth century, when the demand for sailing ships fell off.

The Herreshoff House, built around 1800, was the home of boat builders. A house nearby has a room with yacht models designed by John Herreshoff, who was blind. He dictated the specifications for his boats from memory, then took the models in his hands to make sure his specifications had been followed.

Old as Bristol is, the town doesn't seem to be trying to attract tourists with boutiques, antique shops, restaurants, or inns. Few people were on the streets. We'd hoped to stay there for the night, but the hotel we found on the main street had a desk clerk who took a look at us and said we wouldn't like the place; we thought he was probably right. It seemed to be a single-room-occupancy hotel that might have seen better days, but those days were long forgotten. We found a motel.

Mary and Mike, Kitty's friends, live in Warren, Rhode Island. They were expecting us, and we drove around Warren trying to find their house. After we gave up and pulled into a gas station to call them, Mike drove out to lead us to their house. He is tall with a short-cropped black beard.

We'd met Mike once before, briefly, in New York. After the theater, several of us, with Kitty, had walked down the street to a restaurant. He joined us, and I said I'd heard he lived in Rhode Island. I wondered what he knew about Rhode Island's small towns, in particular those that are relatively untouched by time. It turned out he took a special interest in them.

Later, in the restaurant, he drew a map on a piece of paper and marked several places he said I should be sure to visit. "These are twilight towns," he said. "Every time I see them, a little more and a little more of what they used to be has gone. The towns that are holding onto themselves best are on the eastern side of Narrangansett Bay."

He and Mary live in a brown-shingled house at the edge of a river that flows in and out with the ocean's tide. Mike is a doctor, and his wife, Mary, a slender redhead, is a professor in the psychology department at Boston College. They'd come to Rhode Island from Minnesota.

They'd felt at once, he told me in New York, the depth of history in Rhode Island. "It's different, a different quality. There's a sense of another time dimension."

Mary said, as we sat at dinner that evening, "One of the things that amazed us about Rhode Island, coming from Minnesota, was how quickly we could reach any place in the state." And then she spoke of a writer whose theory is that people's interest in the past is a longing for the lost Garden of Eden.

Little Compton, on the western, more bypassed side of Rhode Island, had no road signs that directed us to it, but it was one of the towns

Mike had marked for us to see. Little Compton doesn't give a damn whether you find it or not. It is sufficient unto itself.

Even when we reached Little Compton, there was no sign at the edge of town telling us where we were. I had to get out of the car and go into the local grocery and ask. It was Little Compton; we had found it.

Once found, it's an easy town to identify. It has one of the most unusual greens in New England. This green, from end to end, is a grave-yard; the town is built around the graves. In that green is the grave of the woman who links Peggy to Priscilla and John Alden. Peggy's Great-Great-Grandmother Lydia was eight generations removed from Priscilla and her shy suitor. Elizabeth Alden Pabodie, the Aldens' offspring, the first white child born in New England, is buried on the green. A marble memorial has been set up to her. Heritage is a thicket of names, not a tree.

Massachusetts

*B*oston, cradle of the Revolution, is famous, among other things, as the starting place for the Boston Post Road. When I think of the Boston Post Road, I see Benjamin Franklin, in a three-cornered hat and tight jacket. He's riding out of Boston ahead of the wagons that carried the weighty milestones for the new coastal Boston-New York highway.

In 1751, when Franklin, along with William Hunter, was appointed one of the "Joint Deputy Postmasters and Managers of his Majesty's Provinces and Dominions on the Continent of North America," he was a man in his mid-forties, highly regarded by his fellow colonists as well as by the Crown. Philadelphia was the base from which he assumed responsibility for the colonies to the North. Hunter was responsible for the Southern colonies.

A postal dispute took Franklin back to Boston, his first home. Because mail carriers were paid by the mile, there was squabbling about the precise distance their routes covered. Measurement of the miles became necessary. But who was to be trusted with the measuring? How were they to measure? Finally, the miles were measured with an odometer that some think Franklin himself invented. There's no doubt who placed the milestones along the Post Road: Franklin rode ahead of a wagonload of milestones and saw they were placed precisely a mile apart.

It goes without saying Franklin wouldn't know the Boston Post Road today, nor Boston or Philadelphia, for that matter. Early Boston taverns, like King's Tavern, the Lion, the Lamb, and other gathering places for early Americans have had to make way for new midtown buildings. In addition, famous hotels are gone: the Tremont House, Adams House, Revere House. Only a few eighteenth-century landmarks are left. Paul Revere's home, a seventeenth-century cantilevered house, still stands, along with a number of buildings associated with the Revolution. The Boston Common lives on, hale and hearty, as green as ever.

This is a park with a long history, still the size it always has been, forty-eight acres. Only the town around it keeps assuming new dimensions and shapes. We walked across the common slowly.

Violence lurks in the bark of its tranquil trees. This violence came early. Thirty Indians were hanged on the common in 1676; nine were executed with lead shot in 1678. The common also accommodated pirates, strung up for banditry on the high seas. A woman was hanged in the late 1700s for stealing; it was only another woman's bonnet she snatched, but up the rope she went. The common had a whipping post when whipping posts were popular. And duelists used the park. During the Revolution, the British put up 1,750 of their soldiers on the common; garrisoned them on the same land that Ralph Waldo Emerson, in his youth, later used when he drove his cow to pasture. Cows had the use of the park until 1830. In 1872, the common became a refuge for those driven from their homes during Boston's great fire.

Beyond the common we climbed Beacon Hill. Residents here dig in their heels against change. On our last visit to Beacon Hill, in '65, I had taken a picture of the entrance to a mansion, and this trip I found it essentially the same.

Though much has been reshaped by man between Beacon Hill and the sea, the ghost in the bay—the mysterious lights—may still be out there, waiting to rise again. It's a curious story, one set during the years witchcraft was at work, or thought to be, in New England.

Town records assembled by a Boston historian, Samuel G. Drake, note that on January 18, 1664, around midnight, three men in a boat entering Boston's harbor saw lights in the form of a man rise from the water; before vanishing, the lights moved about the surface for fifteen minutes or so. About a week later a similar frightening sight was seen and reported by a number of "godly" people. Then, at another time, double moons rose from the bay, came together, parted, and rejoined several times before sailing up a hill and off toward the stars. On still another night, a doleful voice was heard between Boston and Dorchester, a "voice most dreadful." It shifted around on the dark water some twenty times, and at least once was heard from a great distance.

Out of Boston we followed the old Mohawk Trail, moving west toward the Connecticut River Valley and Deerfield. We kept close to old Route 2 (now 2A). Our first stop was Cambridge, Massachusetts, called New Towne by its Puritan founders.

Cambridge is the home of Harvard University, which was founded in 1636 for the purpose, initially, of educating Puritan ministers, and the Bible was the most important book the earliest students studied. They led a monastic life.

By the middle of the eighteenth century, Cambridge had become a wealthy village of aristocratic families. Washington took command of his troops in Cambridge on July 3, 1775, and Cambridge became headquarters for the first American army.

There were many in the South who felt the Revolution was a Massachusetts war, who would not have armed themselves against the British if Washington, a Southerner, hadn't led the American forces. But they joined up. Behind Washington when he assumed command was an army of 15,000 to 20,000 men.

In the nineteenth century, Cambridge became famous for its literati, who included Longfellow, Margaret Fuller, and Emerson. It's now famous, as well, for their homes. Cambridge was where Emerson lived when the cow-tending days of his youth were well behind him and he hadn't yet taken himself to Concord.

Harvard College, in the meantime, was evolving from its strict and ministerial beginnings into the great university that includes Radcliffe College, many graduate divisions, and the famed Fogg Museum of Art.

Much has changed in Cambridge since last we were here. The streets around Harvard Yard are crowded with young people. Traffic has become congested. Shops and restaurants are jammed. A few seemingly homeless people wander about begging.

In the evening members of rock bands can be seen, and heard, sitting in doorways, their electric guitars, drums, synthesizers, and amplifiers at work. Rock tunes rip the lamplight, fill the streets, the ears.

But the buildings in Harvard Yard are the same, and, close by, so is the common.

I remembered Lincoln, Massachusetts, for its black eagle cast in iron, wings spread as if just landing; an eagle as arrested in the daily drift of life as the town itself. Lincoln's a blip of the past between Boston and

Concord, escaping the flux and flow of tourism that have made Boston and Concord and their historic sites and houses into minimuseums. Lincoln, settled in 1650, saw its full share of history, but reaps no special attention.

Paul Revere rode a little to the north past Lincoln in the night, riding his Narragansett pacer (some say a stout workhorse), and it was near this North Road that Revere's ride was ended by a British patrol. The two other men riding with him, unsung heroes to all of us who read Longfellow's version of the ride, escaped. Revere was escorted back to Lexington and let go about his business—which he took up at once with Adams and Hancock. Revolutionary business.

Other events in the vicinity of Lincoln were unfolding. On the Concord road, the first blood of the Revolution was drawn. A Lincoln Minuteman by the name of Josiah Nelson, a Rambo of his time, took on the marching Redcoats single-handed. He got a sword cut across his head for his trouble. Binding his wound, off he went to Bedford to sound, like Revere, his warning, *The Redcoats are coming!*

Joseph Plumb Martin was a soldier in the Revolution, and he's left us a record of what life in the army then was like. He wrote of awakening in the morning on the ground, hoarfrost around each man, most of the men without a blanket to cover them. They turned in their sleep all night, rotating against the small place on the earth they'd made warm. Rain was always a problem. When the rain came down, they crouched and put the locks of their muskets between their thighs to keep them dry.

There wasn't much to eat in camp. Said the hungry and thirsty soldier, "You can drink at the brook, but you can't bite at the bank."

It was worth it for a man to volunteer for a scouting expedition. There was a chance that the houses in the countryside had food, and most of the men were more worried about starving than about getting shot.

When there was food, when they'd been issued beef and flour, they stuck the beef on a stick and roasted it in a fire. The flour they spread on a flat rock in the hot sun, mixed it with cold water, and let it cook by the rock's heat.

One day, hunting for food, Martin said he went into the kitchen of a house and came across a cat mounted on a big hock of fresh beef cooking in an iron pot over a fire. While the old cat tore at the beef, flames and smoke and steam rose about her, "wreathing her head one way and the other, and twisting the beef into her face as fast as possible, winking and blinking in the steam and smoke like a toad in a shower." There is brotherhood in hunger shared by animals and men, and he didn't disturb the cat as he helped himself.

"We this night," he wrote, "turned into a new ploughed field, and

I laid down between two furrows and slept as sweet as though I had laid upon a bed of down."

We turned north, heading for Boxford, to take a look at a town one of my ancestors lived in back in the eighteenth century. Sometimes those old houses almost bring a kind of inherited memory into focus.

We drove through Boxford, but there was nothing my buried memory seemed to recognize. I couldn't get it working, but Boxford is one beautiful town, a town of undiscovered charm with a number of eighteenth-century houses. I had no idea which one the Adams in my line had lived in. The homes had no identification signs. There were no clues.

Peggy thought the local library might have a book that identified the town's historic houses. Some of these small town libraries do. But the library, when we got there, was closed.

We got the name of the librarian from a couple of women walking by. They told us where the librarian lived and said she wouldn't mind at all opening the library for us; she often did.

We drove out to her place, one of the town's older houses. The windows that faced the street rose from ground level all the way to the first-floor ceiling. I walked through silent air to a front door that faced a sideyard. I rang. I knocked. No one was home. Not even a dog inside the house answered.

It was lunchtime when we reached West Boxford, and there wasn't a restaurant around. But West Boxford's village store had a counter at the rear, and a microwave oven. We bought a couple of spinach pies and took them out on the store's back porch to eat, then went to West Boxford's library. It was open. No one was in it but the young woman librarian. She found us several books to look through, but nothing the library had identified Boxford's Adams house.

West Boxford was another town whose streets and yards seemed mysteriously empty of inhabitants. It made us think of West Kill, New York, the village of well-kept lawns and houses where no one seemed to live. We asked the librarian where the people were.

"Everyone," she said, "commutes these days. The children are in school, and their parents are away at work. Everyone living in small towns is a commuter. It's just thirty-five minutes from Boxford to Boston. I'm a commuter myself."

Village after beautiful village, deserted by day, coming alive each evening.

The Spalding factory in Townsend Harbor, Massachusetts, an enormous barn of a place the other side of railroad tracks, loomed up beside our car. The factory seemed big enough to spread over a city block, and it looked as if it had been shut down for a long time, maybe twenty-five years. We pulled over and gazed at all that wood, no bricks I could see in it anywhere. A square tower gave the place a spooky dignity.

Large entry doors on the front of the factory were open when we passed. I'd seen a couple of men inside, like caretakers, resident guardians of an industry long dead, an industry halted in midstride.

Peggy, looking at our guidebook, said, "It closed in 1952."

"Does the book say what they made?"

"No."

I walked back along the road. When I got to the entryway, I could see the men were working on a car. It was an auto body shop. One of the men came over. I asked him what the factory made before it closed.

"Fabric wastebaskets," he said, "and other fabric products."

His beard came down from his sideburns and over his chin. No mustache. He was tall and lean with a thick head of dark hair and a direct, honest gaze.

When I got back to the car, Peggy said, "Who were they?"

"The one I talked to," I said, "I think was Abraham Lincoln."

We were on a route labeled on the map as scenic, passing century-old and older houses. It was the stagecoach road that ran between Boston and Keene, New Hampshire. A few recent cottages were mixed in with the venerable, some of the older houses connected by sheds to a barn. Then we were on a winding, wooded part of the road.

We stopped in Ashby beside the common and got out and walked through the graveyard behind the First Parish Church. The tombstones closest to the church, their backs scored, had been cut long ago from slate. Sunlight shadowed the edges of the cuts. Near the church was a faded yellow building. Its wide porch had sunk in the middle. It was approaching dilapidation. A railing ran along the porch roof, and it was sagging, too. All the windows of the place were curtainless, dusty, and blank.

The building, whatever it was, seemed too large to have once been anyone's home. "It must," I said, "have been an inn."

"Hard to say now," Peggy said.

"Certainly a big place. Do you think it's haunted?"

"Didn't Mermer's son tell you, there aren't any haunted houses?"

"That's just what his mother told him. She doesn't want him worried."

"Or us!"

When we got to Deerfield, we found ourselves on a street as timeless as anything we'd seen in America. The main street is a mile long, and most of the houses on each side of the street are Georgian Colonial. Some, those painted brown, look even earlier. They're wood frame houses, big places. Their doors have fanlights. Deerfield Academy is in among them. Though it predates the Revolution, Deerfield gives no sense of being a reconstructed town. The houses appear so new a visitor seems to have gone back to the eighteenth century, as if by time machine.

A man and a girl who might have been his daughter were walking along the street, the only people in sight. They were strolling the way sightseers do, but they weren't stopping from time to time to gaze around. They seemed, instead, to belong in Deerfield, this town so ancient, so otherwise uninhabited. The man wore a blue blazer. He was bareheaded. The girl wore shorts. Though they walked the streets like apparitions, they weren't dressed like ghosts of the past, or like guides. They were more like ghosts of Deerfield's future: strolling on an overcast day in 1776.

Vermont

As we cross the border from Massachusetts into Vermont near the lower edge of New Hampshire, Vermont seems much less prosperous than the state we've left behind, as if the struggle to survive was and still is greater in this land of high hills and dense pines. Trailers begin to appear among the houses. The yards of farms are a little less tidy. The houses aren't as freshly painted. But small towns, reminiscent of the days of horses, cows, and winter sleds, are more numerous now.

In the early days of Ethan Allen's residency, the New Hampshire Grants marked the edge of the earth, or at least the edge of the civilized world. It was a wilderness limbo that extended south from Canada to Massachusetts and west from the Connecticut River into disputed ground along the Hudson River. Perhaps four hundred people lived in the Grants.

In the two decades that followed the Revolution, Vermont's population jumped from 85,425 to 217,895. Allen got in early on a good thing. In those days farms were largely self-sufficient. Then trade grew. Exports included marble, grain, beef, and wool. Dairy farming began to bankroll the state after the Civil War; then, at about the turn of the century, tourism put its money into the coffer. These days, Vermont depends heavily on the outsiders its landscape and towns attract. For the winter months of the year, that landscape lies under snow, a blessing to all skiers. In summer, the weather is usually dry and cool, an attraction to vacationers sweltering to the south of the old Grants' border.

Beyond Brattleboro we moved north beside the Connecticut River; big rocks lay in the stream, like the calcified bodies of pigs and cattle, the specters of lost farms.

Newfane, founded in 1787, was first settled on a hill, now known as Newfane Hill, an early strategic location. It helped the townspeople defend themselves against Indians. In time there was a need to move closer to a river to garner water for power. The town moved down the hill in 1825 to its present location.

Its grocery is an authentic country store, but the townspeople are keeping up with the times. On one of the shelves was a row of VCR tapes, black packages of evening nourishment lined up with other foods.

Then through South Newfane, a well-preserved and handsome village a little out of the way for the highway traveler, and on to Williamsville, a lovely and, to our eyes at least, undiscovered village. A stream runs through Williamsville and, in the middle of town, takes a drop over a falls. The post office is in a Victorian house. On the other side of town we drove through a covered bridge, a dusky passage to forest and hilly, winding roads.

In the struggle with the State of New York over who would control the western area of the Grants, Ethan Allen was an invincible wild man. He had his headquarters on the main street of Bennington, not today's Bennington, but the Old Bennington that is now a street on a hillside above the Bennington of today. The Catamount Tavern where Allen had his headquarters is gone. Its site is marked. Up and down that street called Monument Avenue are eighteenth-century houses. The First Congregational Church, built in 1806, stands beside a green. Men and women who knew Ethan Allen lie in the graveyard beside the church.

Old Bennington, when we came to it, was quiet. Spring was well underway. As I walked to an old hotel, the limbs of trees shaded my feet.

It had been so long since the hotel was painted that it seemed, at first, to be abandoned. On the other hand, there were curtains on the windows. The last time I'd been through Old Bennington I'd decided the hotel was empty, a ruin without guests, ready to fall in on itself.

A driveway and a walk ran up to the front door. I followed the driveway and at the door peered into the lobby. I could see a stairway to a second floor and chairs and rugs. A pillar beside the stairway had been recently painted. I wanted to go up that staircase with our luggage and check into one of the old rooms. What I figured I had before my eyes was the closest thing I'd found to a haunted hotel since Fort Gaines, Georgia. Once more I faced a locked door and a mighty silence that pressed against the door from the inside and ran up my arm.

When I turned away, I saw a car parked in the sideyard. Two women were standing beside it, talking. They didn't seem to have noticed me. The dark-haired woman, wearing a sweater, was face to face with a police-woman who didn't seem to be on duty. She was hatless, her blouse was unbuttoned, and she was smoking a cigarette.

I walked over. They turned their heads with surprise to watch me approach, and I said, "Is the hotel open?"

The dark-haired woman shook her head.

"When will it open?"

"Get off my property," she said. Her eyes looked hard and storm-laden, rage building there.

"I was just asking," I said, "because I'd like to stay here."

"Did you hear me?" She was yelling now, eyes bulging. "Get off my property!"

The policewoman, a neutral force, took a drag on her cigarette. Since I could see that further explanations were going to get me nowhere, I left.

There it was, though, a perfect hotel out of the past, not a guest in any of its rooms, a place that might have been in absolute touch with the past, a place, perhaps, the past might never have left. If so, I can tell you this: the past is guarded by a dark-haired woman in a sweater and a policewoman who stands at her side.

In the Catskill Mountains east of Prattsville, New York. A bridge that reminds us of a time before automobiles, when you had to make your own wobbly way over a chasm.

Norfolk, Connecticut.

Hardenburgh House, built in the eighteenth century in the Catskills near Prattsville, New York—one of the ghostly places. Kids would drive past, looking at it from the road, and they could never tell if anyone was living there or not. Now occupied.

Jamestown, Rhode Island. A surviving windmill to celebrate,
one of the few that's left.

In Deerfield, Massachusetts, we found ourselves among streets and houses as timeless as anything we'd seen in America.

This Model-T Ford with a 1925 Cretors steam-operated popcorn machine was still in business on a street where I had seen it twenty years ago. Cambridge, New York.

North of Salem, New York, it's red-barn country.

Newfane, Vermont.

Harrisville, New Hampshire.

Harrisville, New Hampshire. The community notice board.

Nelson,
New Ham

Here at Townsend, Massachusetts, was a bandstand such as my great-grandfather stood in when he led his small-town band.

The old factory looked haunted, and it may have been. Townsend Harbor, Massachusetts.

Lincoln, Massachusetts.

Yarmouth, Maine. A street little changed since we first
saw it twenty years ago.

Penley's Corner, south of Auburn, Maine.

One more steady
place out of the living
past. Mt. Desert,
Maine.

Steps to the Truth. The Holy Ghost and Us Society, Shiloh, Maine.

The Elijah Kellogg Congregational Church (1843) in Harpswell Center, Maine.
Sometimes the glass in a window is so old its imperfections enhance the
illusion of timelessness. Standing inside looking out was like looking back on
the year the church was built.

Old roads like this abandoned highway in northern Maine seem to lead the way to the men and women, and the days and the years, left in the past.

New York Again

*F*rom Old Bennington, it's not far to the New York border, and not so far from there to the rural towns of Cambridge, Shushan, and Salem. I used to visit that area fairly frequently to see a couple I knew, city folks escaped to a country setting. They lived near Shushan then, but not anymore.

When we got to Cambridge, a few miles from Shushan, we saw something that hadn't been carried away by time. It was the Model-T Ford with the 1925 Cretors steam-operated popcorn machine, still in business. Inside the car's glass enclosure, a woman with hair as white as her popcorn was handing out hot dogs to several children.

"I'll take a couple of those," I said.

Behind her, two little round balls, a part of the antique machine, whirled.

"Didn't I first see this car some thirty years ago?" I said.

"My father," she answered, "owned it before me, so yes, you did. He bought it forty-one years ago."

"How do you get spare parts?"

"They're around. I can get them."

"Forty-one years is a long time ago."

"A long time," she said.

Cambridge, like Shushan and Salem, I remembered with pleasure. These were towns I liked coming back to. They had atmosphere, and nothing about the atmosphere was concocted. With the exception of Cambridge, there were no hotels. Even the Cambridge Hotel, a three-story place with outdoor pillars, was so empty that no one stood behind the desk in the deserted lobby. It had gone out of the business of renting rooms, a waitress told me, but rumor had it the hotel might soon open again under new management. A bar was still in operation, and meals were served, but that was all.

The people in the bar wore denim jackets and pants and old felt hats. Their shoes were heavy-soled. I took those men with weathered faces for farmers still working their land.

Shushan looks as if years had passed over or through it. There are several abandoned buildings on the main street, and weeds grow high in empty lots. There are people in Shushan who still hang out their laundry in the backyard to dry in the sun. This was a town in farming country, big red barn country. Shushan was early twentieth-century, slumbering. The house that my friends owned was nearby. It slumbers, too, behind locked doors.

Salem has a spacious look about the buildings on its Main Street. That's because a good part of the town was burned within recent memory. The man sitting next to us at the counter, wasn't sure just when. His shirt collar was open, and one end of a tie hung out of his jacket pocket. He didn't live in town, but he came here often on business. He was trying to remember: "This town has had its share of sorrows. I recall the merchants were cutting down all the maple trees along Main Street before the fire. That was back in the early fifties."

"Was there a tree blight?"

"No. Fear of falling limbs was all. Never did make any sense, cutting down those trees. People around here were pretty mad about it. And it was a great loss to all the dogs in town. Fire came after that. The pajama factory burned. That and the bargains it used to have was another loss."

When he heard we were traveling back roads because we enjoyed it, he thought we were in town to look at Salem's Revolutionary cemetery. "It's the best in Washington County," he said. "A thing of real beauty. A hundred or more men, Revolutionary soldiers from the county and vicinity, are buried there. A few of the stones are a little marred up. I understand some women, way back, trying to get into the DAR, did it."

"Changing dates?"

"Something like that. Maybe names."

Driving the upper New York State countryside, I thought of old proverbs I'd heard as a kid, all but forgotten now because of changing times, times that were already changing fast as I grew up.

You can never tell the depth of a well from the length of the handle on the pump.

You can't judge a horse by its harness.

Broad as a Dutch barn.

Busy as a fiddler's elbow.

Common as pig's tracks.

Cold as a corncrib.

Drier than a covered bridge.

Tough as bull beef at a penny a pound.

Makes more noise than a wagonload of calves.

She's got a disposition like a cross-cut saw.

Her face was long enough to eat oats out of a churn.

He's poor potatoes and few in a hill.

That horse is old enough to have been born in Adam's stable.

It rained so hard the water stood ten feet out of the well.

I could eat a horse and chase its rider.

I'm so poor that if steamboats were selling at ten cents apiece, I couldn't buy a gangplank.

I wouldn't trust him any farther than I can throw the chicken house.

Most of my ancestors on my father's and mother's side, going back to America's earliest days, were tillers of the soil. Until the industrial age came along, the country was full of farmers, and those proverbs came out of their way of life. It was an occupation that, in my lifetime, faded. My grandmother, on my mother's side, grew up on a farm. When I remember her best, she was living in a bungalow on ten acres of land north of Grand Rapids, keeping a cow and milking it herself. She didn't need to, it was a nostalgia trip, a sentimental exercise in a barn shrunk to the size of a two-car garage.

Farmers, small farmers, are dropping out every day. I have an older cousin who, shortly after he got out of college, married and moved to a farm in Vermont. He had a herd of dairy cows and a sugar bush to work, and he worked the farm and brought up three kids. When he had time, he exercised his talents, writing plays and acting in local productions. He wasn't what you'd call a gentleman farmer. He slipped around in cowshit, milked his cows, and cut his own hay. He milked so many cows twice a day that he believed he could crush people's knuckles, if he wasn't careful, when he shook their hands.

We had swung east and were heading toward the Vermont border again, toward Londonderry where Cousin Dick and his wife Millie live. Dick doesn't farm anymore—it got so it simply wasn't profitable—but he and Millie still live on the home place.

Vermont Again

*E*than Allen followed up his triumph at Ticonderoga with a fiasco outside Montreal. It may not have been his fault. He was leading a detachment of men from the American forces when the British caught him without support, pinned him down, then captured him. It wasn't a bloody surrender, which might have got him points. He said after the fight, "Never have I seen so much shooting with so little damage." Following his spell of captivity, it was to his wife and home in Sunderland, Vermont, that he returned.

We tried our best to find Sunderland. I went into a small country store to get some help. I stood at its wood counter waiting. Someone came out of the back, a woman. She came through the doorway behind the counter, smiling pleasantly, and in answer to my question said, "No, there isn't any other Sunderland. This is it."

"It's my understanding," I said, "Ethan Allen once lived in Sunderland, but we can't find any town. Where was his house?"

"Oh, I see what you mean. Sunderland is this area. It's all around here. The Allen boys had houses over on what's now Highway 7. But you know who you should talk to if you want to know about the Allens? You should see Mr. Thompson."

I went outside and cut around behind the store over a sideyard lawn toward a lean man in a red sweatshirt. He stood erect and square-shoul-dered. Taking a guess, I thought he'd have been born around the turn of the century. He was yard-tending, burning trash in a wire incinerator.

Thompson, I'd learned at the store, had lived in Sunderland all his life, so I asked him where the narrow road near us went. That road, he told me, went nowhere. "It just runs back to an old marble quarry."

Under the red sweatshirt, he wore a blue shirt buttoned to the collar; no tie. The bristles on his cheeks and chin glistened in the bright sun like grains of sugar.

"The Allens, yes. Oh, yes, they lived here." He pointed off to where I'd find their homes, homes that had been used for many generations, but not by Allens anymore. We should, he told us, turn around, follow the road back, and take the turn that went over to Route 7 between a church and a graveyard. It was called the Allen graveyard, not because the Allens were buried there, but because the land had come from the Allens as a gift.

He had their whole history. "Ethan's wife died here," he said, "and after she died, Ethan got married again. He got along better with his second wife. You know, that first wife couldn't have cared much for the way he drank and carried on. He and his second wife lived up north on his Onion River land. That was another of his real estate deals. He died up there. That's where he's buried. A lot of people like you come through here wondering if he's buried in the cemetery across from his old house. No, he's buried north of here."

Just before he died, Thompson told me, Allen, who had been away from home on a trip, came down sick. "It was winter, and he came home on a sled and went straight to bed. A preacher was sent for. He looked down at Allen and he said, 'General, the angels are waiting for you,' and Allen, never a pious man, said 'Goddamn 'em, let 'em wait!' "

Bed-and-breakfast places, it's time to speak of bed-and-breakfast places. In the last few years they've proliferated throughout the country, in cities and in small towns, as if pre–World War II tourist homes have returned, reborn, bigger, older, more handsome, some as old as eigh-teenth- and nineteenth-century creations. A few years ago, if these road-side houses, too big for today's families, weren't converted into restaurants or funeral parlors, they were bulldozed to the ground. Back from the edge of perdition they've come. Their resurrection has begun. Wherever we have historically interesting areas, minimansions are being polished, painted, and refitted for a traveling public that likes having the atmosphere of the past around them as they slip into sleep.

When we checked out a B&B, we looked mainly for the atmosphere of another age. If floors were wide-board, good. If they sagged with time, even better. If the tubs in bathrooms had claw feet, great. We wanted a working fireplace if that was possible, and we preferred armoires to closets.

A sound period house, like a sound antique table, can be ruined by a refinishing that wipes out its sense of age along with its patina. Character is important. So what if the table has a few nicks and cuts? It's carrying its history in its wood.

Sometimes in the B&Bs we saw, antiquity struggled with comfort, and flawless reproductions of antiques were set about on wall-to-wall-carpeting, a TV set hidden behind cabinet doors. That's when I'd tell myself again that antiques were once modern. The illusion! The illusion! It's only the illusion we're after. Comfort, along with beauty, is important, too. When the sense of the past is in a room, it breathes on everything. That's what matters.

In Weston, one of those perfect small Vermont towns, there are three B&Bs. The latest of these, the Wilder Homestead Inn, is owned by Roy Varner. It's an 1820 house on the National Register of Historic Places, and it faces the back road that goes to Peru, Vermont. We parked and went inside. Varner put down a jack plane he was holding and said he'd be glad to show us around the place. When I asked him why B&Bs are burgeoning around the countryside, he said it's because of village zoning restrictions. Villages, even cities, don't want any more motels. In Vermont, he said, local people are being asked, during the fall and the skiing season, to open their homes to visitors. "So that's why," he explained, "more and more houses every year are accepting guests on a paying basis."

He was a tall man with a black beard just beginning to turn gray, a T-shirt under his plaid cotton shirt. He had come to Vermont from Philadelphia with the idea of opening an inn. He was a builder by profession, so restoring the house to the way it looked early in its history was right up his line. He'd opened for business last September, he said, but he was still working to get the house into the shape he wanted it in.

Some of the doors on the second floor were unfinished. In one of the upstairs rooms he was preserving a wall stenciled by Moses Eaton. When I found Varner, he'd been at work on the dining room. He looked like a man who enjoyed his work, a majordomo of restoration.

"Another reason," he said, "bed-and-breakfast places are appearing all over the country is that a great many people, as opposed to twenty or thirty years ago, have been to Europe, where they got used to staying in homes. Now they're looking for homes to stay in in this country. And another thing: staying in a B&B is a completely different experience from staying in a motel. In a motel, in essence, you travel all day and then stay in the same room night after night; but in a bed-and-breakfast, the house and the room are always different."

"Do any of your guests ever complain because there's no TV in the room?"

He shook his head. "Those people stay in motels. Most B&Bs have a TV in the common room for anything guests want to watch. Our guests are here for something else. There's a growing interest in seeing and staying in the small towns of America, and in exploring the American past outside of our museums and museum villages. People coming through are looking for towns to stay in where an atmosphere of times gone by has been preserved, or in the case of this house, where it's been returned."

There's a small waterfall on the outskirts of Weston. Just beyond it the unnumbered highway swings left and rises, curving through shade and trees and stretches of sunlight. In a little while we came to a Colonial house on our right, then another. After that we didn't pass many houses, and the road became narrow and graveled.

Shortly after we passed the Village Inn, a cluster of red buildings with white windows, the road turned right and we were in North Landgrove. Over to our left was a barnyard with a brown horse frisking about. North Landgrove has a sprinkling of houses: a leafy place in an idyllic setting. The road plunged back into woods. Down, down then. A fieldstone wall turned up on our left and in a little while we came to Peru.

Peru has no more than a dozen houses, a church, and a grocery store. Two of those houses provide bed and breakfast, but we have not been in either of them. Peru used to have a hotel. It burned. A great loss. It had wall-to-wall, floor-to-ceiling atmosphere, genuine tavern tables in the bar, stairways to mysterious time levels. But it got too old. Aged electrical wiring, we heard, did the hotel in. But the town didn't burn, and it's a living early Vermont village, close to my Cousin Dick's farm.

Houses in Vermont are often built along roads with views of fields and distant mountains. Dick and Millie's place is no exception. They've had hard times, but they live in an area where millionaires in second homes have become their neighbors and friends.

Their horses are gone, sold along with the cows. A Jeep has replaced the horses. The road to their house from Londonderry is long and steep and, in the winter, slippery with ice and snow. Dick once used his Jeep to haul our car out of a ditch because we couldn't make it.

When the farm went bust and one more dairyman was out of business, the financial blow was softened by Millie's going to work as a schoolteacher. Dick had his training as an architect to fall back on, and occasional jobs came his way. He even put in a subsidized period coauthoring a play with Blanche Yurka.

He'd been coming to New York on visits, or I'd been driving up to see him, for most of my adult life. Dick is a member of an extensive family into which I'd been adopted, back when my name changed from Adams to Humphreys. It was a closely knit family with many cousins and aunts and uncles and a powerful grandmother.

Dick (we have the same name, and he liked to call me "little Dick") was someone I'd greatly admired since high school days. Now he is all that's left for me of the Humphreys family. After Grandmother Humphreys died, after the aunts and uncles succumbed, the cousins splintered and drifted out of communication. But I knew whenever I went to see Big Dick, I could step back into a time when I felt a family around me, like a city with many streets and towers and courts to which I, by chance, had a key.

Dick, in spite of his troubles, has lived a good life, but he was complaining now about the traffic that went up and down the country road past his farm. "Too damn much of it," he said. It was ski people in the winter, and in summer the traffic was almost as bad.

Dick had grown a goatee since I'd seen him last. Bald as he was, he looked like Uncle Wiggly's nemesis, Farmer Brown. But I don't think he ever shot a rabbit, or shot at one, in his life. He is a man with a tender heart—although he once accidentally killed a cow in anger. The cow, a mean one who liked to crowd him into the side of the stall while he was milking her, crowded him once too often. Dick carried a knife with a broken point in a sheath at his waist, and he pulled it out, meaning to give the cow a jab that would teach her a lesson. But the knife didn't bounce off the cow's thick hide. It sank in. Come next milking time he had one less cow in his herd. There was nothing he could do but butcher her. Knowing Dick, I know it must have been a scene of horror, an ordeal replete with guilt and regret. When he went down to the village, he talked about it with his usual lack of reserve and glints of humor. The humor was there as comic relief, and he had them laughing, but in short order, he was up on charges of inhumane slaughter.

Dick's farming methods seemed strange to his neighbors anyway. During, I suppose, his years in the theater, he had developed the habit of sleeping late, and his cows were milked around noon and again around midnight.

Once, after he gave up farming, he came to New York for several months to take in the current theater, and we hung out together. He began to sleep later and later every day until he was finally rising and shaving early in the evening, well on his way to rising in the wee hours of the morning, the earliest he'd ever been up in his life.

"When you and Millie came to Vermont," Peggy asked, "were there ski lifts near you then?" It was a blur in my own mind, their first years on the farm.

"Oh, just personal skiing hills. On the farm. I guess there was a slope over at Bromley."

"Did you keep skis here? Back then?"

"Oh, yeah, we had skis."

"Where'd you use them?"

Dick's voice came out of his chest, his consonants crisp. His vowels could roll when he wanted them to. Watching him, even as he sat slightly slumped in his easy chair, was like watching a controlled, nerveless performance. "Any hill. Down a hill out here and over a stone wall. Land in a heap."

"Anybody ever get hurt?"

"Oh, yes, our neighbor got hurt once. Turned his ankle and broke it, or something. But he was able to stand up." Dick paused to cough. He was suffering from emphysema, but it couldn't have been too severe because when he'd finished coughing, he went on talking with more breath support than I thought he could muster.

Dick reached over to a table beside his chair, got one hand on a pipe, and lit it. He puffed a while, short puffs, nothing inhaled.

"What made you decide to go into farming after you got out of Yale Drama School?"

"I didn't. I bought the farm with some money I'd inherited and came here to write plays. I never meant to farm the place. It was all unintentional."

"Then how'd you get into it?"

"One cow at a time. I named the first cow Clementine after Grandmother Noble. And, ah, Clementine was always jumping the fence to get in with the neighbor's cows and his bull. So he lent me a heifer, she'd been bred, to keep Clementine company. Pretty soon I had two cows and two calves, and I hate to butcher. They just multiplied until I was milking eleven, not counting the bull. He was number twelve. You knew," he said, "I was in a movie, didn't you?"

"I knew you had a line or two in a movie they were shooting around here called *Baby Boom*, and you're billed as "A Vermont Character." That the one?"

"That's it."

"Why did you give up farming?" Peggy asked.

"Millie wanted me to. And my aunt gave us some money. I don't remember all why. It was two fools on a farm."

"Millie told me once she had her children on the kitchen floor," I said. "Did she?"

"You mean she gave birth to them there?"

"That's what I thought she said."

"She was exaggerating. She had her first one right here, though, in the house. Judy was born in Springfield Hospital. Prudy was very premature and only weighed a pound and a half when she was born. She needed hospital care and attention. They all grew up helping on the farm, cutting hay and bringing it in, milking. We've watched gradual change in the town and countryside. It hasn't been sudden, this change from farming to tourism and summer people. Developers moved in. There's a development called Western Heights above us, so many new houses around we haven't begun to see them all. Styles of some of them have little if anything to do with Vermont. They're chalets, big places. All kinds, actually."

Millie, who had been in the kitchen, came into the room. She is a trim woman whose voice, like Dick's, was honed in the theater. "Ask him," she laughed, "if he likes what's happened around here."

"Hell, no," Dick said. "People drive over our hill outside at sixty miles an hour. And they can't see what's over the hill. I take my life in my hands every time I back out of our garage, which, as you know, is right on the edge of the road. I play it by ear. Sometimes it's a couple or three motorcycle boys coming along the road trying to make as much noise as possible.

"I don't know what the people around here think. Most of them own homes someplace else and stay only part of the time. But I don't like what's happened, and neither does Millie."

"I love to get out of doors," Millie said. "It's winter that gets me down. I don't look forward to winter, but where the hell am I going to go except here? I'll be here, come winter, if I'm still alive."

Dick said, "Another movie's in the works. I've just written to the producer asking him for the name of the casting director for Warner Bros. He lives in New York. Millie wants to be in this one."

Some of the furniture in their house is a part of my childhood. The long table in their dining room came from the family home in Van Wert, Ohio. The Humphreys family gathered around it each Christmas. Grandmother Humphreys sat at the head of the table, a pious woman who did not approve of Dick's wit and language. As the Christmas dinner began, she said a prayer for all of us, sixteen or more people. There were no toasts. I don't remember that wine ever got into any of the goblets.

The kitchen, in my memory, seemed as big as the dining room in most restaurants. All the rooms in the house could signal the kitchen by pull cord.

Most of the older people who sat around that table are gone. The long table has made its way to Vermont. Now I sat at it again.

Heading north, we came to Cuttingsville, Vermont, and found the mausoleum in the graveyard beside the highway where the figure of the father kneels outside the door to the tomb. Inside are his wife and daughters. It hasn't changed. Someone has stuck a rose in his outstretched hand, that's recent. It's a real rose and seems appropriate. Across the road is a white frame mansion of a house, like the Van Wert home before it was torn down. There's a sign in front of it: HAUNTED MANSION BOOKSHOP.

It's the northern part of Vermont that's the most untouched by time, and we moved there swiftly. Roads in the north wind through mountains and farmland. Small white towns turn up that seem from the past. There are split-rail fences along the road and fences of fieldstone. We were on our way to Peacham and a section of a Revolutionary road I wanted to find again: the Bailey-Hazen Military Road, built for the singular purpose of invading Canada, but never used—except by pioneer settlers.

We'd found the road years ago, but we'd had trouble finding it even then, and we were having trouble again. Where was Elkins Tavern? The tavern, dating back to 1787, seemed gone, along with stretches of the old Bailey-Hazen Road. Peacham is north of Barre, over toward the Connecticut River. My notes said that just beyond Peacham, on the way to Danville, the Bailey-Hazen Road cut to the left, a gravel road. We had followed it the other time until woods and limbs closed in around our car and we could go no farther. And now I was wondering: Where had the old cutoff been?

Back we went to Peacham, where we'd seen a man in his yard clipping his hedge. He had on a blue windbreaker and khaki pants and looked old enough to be retired, which he was. He'd moved to Peacham from Delaware when his mother died. The year 1802 appeared on the front of his house. Across the road was an 1803 house. "You go on down the hill along this road," he said, "until you come to the schoolhouse, and you'll see the old road cutting off to your left. Follow that road and you'll come to the tavern. It's a dirt road in there for a little ways."

When I got back in the car, Peggy said, "What was he telling you about the road? Why was he laughing?"

"He said the Americans built the road to invade Canada without thinking that the British could use the road to invade us."

"That's war for you."

"He says a governor lived in his house for a while. And he said—he wasn't laughing anymore—developers are moving in, even here, buying up huge tracts of land, buying it from farmers. He wished things could stay the way they are. He wished, he said, there was some way to keep things as they are."

We found the cutoff section, a tree-shaded avenue that led to what had been Elkins Tavern. The old tavern was getting the attention from its new owners that age requires. The foundation was under repair and one of the doors as well. The road ran on to rejoin the one that goes into town, but even now, turning back, I couldn't find the cutoff that had led me into underbrush and left me staring into rain and darkness.

A lost road is a lot like a magic garden.

We drove on, moving north over gravel that I was pretty sure was the Bailey-Hazen attack trail; still, I wasn't certain. We pulled over beside a house with two parked pickup trucks and a couple of barking dogs. I crossed a yard where a tricycle lay in the weeds near a truck tire that served as a border for a dozen or so flowers. The house itself was old and unpainted. Some of the porch boards were rotting, but the front door had a shiny brass knocker. I knocked. When the door opened, the man facing me wore a work shirt and an orange cap. He was about thirty-five.

"Yes," he said, "you're on the Bailey-Hazen Road, all right." I could see he wondered why I cared. The two dogs followed me back to the car, barking all the way.

Following the road again, we came to a cemetery, then passed a beautiful old house that had been abandoned, and another house with boarded-up windows, then a barn with a collapsed roof, then twenty or so black-and-white dairy cows.

There is a monument to the Bailey-Hazen Road in East Hardwick. The monument says: 1795. MILITARY ROAD RAN TWO MILES NORTH TO CASPIAN LAKE. But this was as far as the present road would take us, this town with its cluster of aging houses, some with sagging shutters, others rejuvenated by fresh paint. A former tavern that dates back to 1789 lives on in East Hardwick, with a secret room, Peggy read, behind its chimney. We heard a lonesome train whistle but couldn't tell where it was coming from.

New Hampshire

*D*ropping south along the Connecticut River, as Ethan Allen at one time must have done, we came, near Plainfield, New Hampshire, to the former home of the sculptor Augustus Saint-Gaudens (1848-1907), now a museum of his work.

The eyes in his statues are human and piercing. The eyes of Sherman burn with the sight of the hell Sherman said war is. These figures, sometimes only a head, include Admiral Farragut, General Sherman, Robert Louis Stevenson, and Abraham Lincoln.

The first thing we see when we walk into the building called the Gallery is the towering figure of *The Puritan*. It is Deacon Samuel Chapin staring straight at us: a square-jawed man in a wide-brimmed, high-crowned hat, stern but not grim, carrying in one hand a Bible, in the other a heavy walking stick. His short coat hangs open, his vest tight, half the buttons released for comfort. The knickers that come to his knees are baggy. Bulging calves, square-toed shoes. An immense presence, a man not to fool around with. Five Chapins had married into Peggy's family, the earliest in 1782. We stood face to face with, who knows, a family judge. I felt accountable, not at all sure we had his approval.

The route we followed took us along the river for a while, with glimpses of Vermont across the way, houses and factories, and then we cut southwest into Cheshire County, following Route 12. We were heading for Harrisville, a town we'd read hadn't changed in the last hundred years.

Along the way we turned aside for a look at Park Hill, said to have one of the most beautiful churches in New England. Built in 1762, it was moved, board by board, by oxcart and wagon, to its present site, and there it has remained, above a sloping village green. It is a beautiful church, but there are so many beautiful churches in New England that it's hard to say one is more beautiful than another.

"Over there," said Peggy, "is the Iron Kettle Spring." We slowed and I coasted in beside an iron kettle sunk into the ground, spring water flowing into it from an iron pipe in a log jutting from the hillside. "Time," she said, "we got away from city water." She took the thermos and left the car. I watched her pour water from the thermos onto the ground, then refill the thermos from the pipe. When she came back, we poured the fresh water into cups and drank. From where we sat I could see the kettle was slightly tilted and the overflow of water ran off one side.

"Who sank the kettle in the ground?" I asked.

"The book doesn't say. It just says it's been there over a hundred years. It's a potash kettle. Maybe potash kettles don't rust. In the old days," she said, "back when there were horses, horses drank from it. They raised a fuss, the book says, if they weren't allowed to stop and drink."

"I can understand that," I said. "I would raise all kinds of fuss myself. That's good water."

Up the line, along the side of the road, high in the air, the enormous head of a grinning cat gazed down at us. It was the Cheshire Cat. "Look," Peggy said. "We've come to Wonderland."

This was the sign for the Cheshire County Classy Cat Cafe. We pulled over, went inside, and had a coffee while we studied our map. It was a small place for a truck stop, but that's what it was. Drivers sat at the short counter, their semis parked outside.

Harrisville is well hidden from major highways, tucked away in what seems to be a wilderness. Hills rise around it. A river flows by its side. Its streets slope. Brick factories stand beside the road that splits the town, the bricks so old they're turning pink. The stone steps that lead to houses are crumbling. Yet the place seems as if it had always been where it is and always will be, its streets quiet. But the silence was nothing new to the small towns we'd been seeing.

Harrisville's mill began to fail in 1970. Anyone who wanted a mill town lost in the wilds could have bought up the whole place for $750,000. Then the mill went broke. In came new owners who, obeying the historic zone restrictions, pulled the town together. Harrisville lives on, a place where time sat down and did not get up again because it liked it where it was.

This long-established New England factory town (population 500) has its own church, library, blacksmith shop, general store, mill buildings, and houses. Surrounded by the forests of New Hampshire, Harrisville was for a long time so self-sufficient that some of the adults, with factory, church, and store at hand, never bothered to get a driver's license. Its boarding house has been in operation for 125 years. The town is now a designated historic district.

We saw no tourists. There's one B&B, outside of town. There's a grocery store for the hungry; there are no restaurants.

We stayed that night in Fitzwilliam, New Hampshire, at the Fitzwilliam Inn. It's an inn we return to, in a town almost as perfectly out of the past as Harrisville. The town is small, arranged around an oval green enclosed by a white fence. The inn faces the green and a row of early New England houses.

We have stayed at the inn a number of times at Christmas because of the setting, and because it always gives me the feeling of being back in time as far as my childhood. No, farther back than that. A number of Adamses are buried in the church cemetery at Rindge, a tiny town only a few miles from Fitzwilliam, near the Massachusetts border. Israel Adams, great-grandson of the first Adams immigrant, lies buried there, a man who took his mother's last name.

Sitting in the bar at the inn with Peggy, leaning at the small table over my coffee, I said, "Here's what amazes me. Sarah's child was born in her hometown where the first Adams settled. During her child's early years, she called the kid by the biblical name Benoni, 'my sorrow.' Her father did not disown her; he even left her well provided for in his will."

Sarah married, after a time, John Hutchinson, and moved to his hometown, Andover, Massachusetts, bringing young Israel along. She lived out her life with Hutchinson, and she's buried in Andover.

The next morning we drove on to Rindge, where there are twenty-two Adams graves under the shade of three large trees, most of the graves marked by headstones of slate with rounded tops. The DAR has decorated the grave of one David Adams with a flag. His wife Phoebe is buried beside him. He died in 1831. Next to him is another David Adams, who died in August 1852; buried beside this David is a wife whose name was Silence.

Israel Adams, whose father is a mystery, served in the French and Indian Wars and was a cordwainer and farmer. That was all I knew about him except what his tombstone told me. His tombstone said he lived to be eighty-two. His wife, I read, died in 1802 at the age of ninety-seven.

"It's so hard to know what any of them were like," I said. "You can't say they were good, simple people. They must have been as complicated as any of us are today. Maybe, like my cousin, Israel had a short temper and hated farming and couldn't keep his mouth shut when he had a secret."

Going back to the car we passed a space on the ground, a place where a fallen tombstone had lain for a long time, for so long the grass was yellow and flattened. The tombstone was gone and the grass looked like a trap door in the ground.

We were walking toward the parish church, a building of simple Colonial lines. Until 1819 all the residents of the town and countryside were considered members of the parish, regardless of denomination or belief. So you could say the Adamses made the membership list easily. When the meeting house went up in 1796, the Adamses had been around for fourteen years, whoever they were, whatever they were like. I'm small-boned and narrow-shouldered. I'm tall and lean. Could any of them have been like me? And what would they have made of an Adams whose name changed to Humphreys?

There's not much to the town of Rindge: a country store, a library, a few houses, a church, and a graveyard. But what there is is unspoiled. I can't imagine it's changed much since David Adams's time. May it rest in peace.

Maine

Maine: the largest state in New England, also the most remote, the least settled, its population scattered along a jagged Atlantic coastline. There isn't much to support that population except fishing, potatoes, and, to some extent, tourism; but one of the first things we hear as we cross into Maine is that its inland towns and islands are resisting the tourist industry. The reasoning seems to be that the people of Maine like Maine the way it is and don't want to see developers moving in.

Monhegan Island, one of the state's earliest settlements, has by will and determination held off change. Mount Desert's Bar Harbor is gradually changing from old to new, but not like the historic parts of coastal cities and towns from Portsmouth, New Hampshire, all the way to Key West, Florida. Portland is at work recapturing its past, reviving old buildings and doing a handsome job of it. Yarmouth, too, seems to have decided it needs summer people, and it has doubled in size in the last twenty years. But these changes have been comparatively light. Maine is still an underpopulated state, a semiwild region.

Wars barely touched Maine, except for Portland, the state's largest city, which was bombarded and burned by the British during the Revolution, leaving two thousand homeless. The town, quickly rebuilt, by 1800 had a population of almost four thousand, a large city for that time.

American history blends into Portland's streets and buildings, stands in the shadows, leans in stairways.

By 1822 progress was underway in Maine. Portland had a paddle-wheel ferry in its harbor called the *Kennebec*, nicknamed "the ground hog." It sometimes broke down in the middle of the bay; when it did, the passengers got out and pushed. What they got out on were the paddles, who knows how many people, a dozen, two dozen? And they walked the paddles into the water of the bay, getting their feet wet, I suppose, falling in, climbing back up on the paddles again. I wish I could have seen it, I wish I could have been there.

I wish I could have known MacDonald Clark, one of Maine's poets, a man with a touch of madness. Not read at all today, he was supported in his time by friends. He lived a poet's life, which is to say a life of poverty, and died a poet's death. Death came to him, brilliant and eccentric to the end, on Blackwell's Island in his prison cell. He drowned in the water that flowed from the cell's open faucet. It was 1842 when he went, let's hope, to a poet's heaven. I would like to go back in time and meet him. Shortly before the poet died, he said, "Four things I am sure there will be in Heaven—music, little children, flowers, and fresh air."

Wandering now, north of Portland, west of Brunswick, near Lisbon Falls, we saw that the Holy Ghost and Us Society Church at Shiloh was still with us. We saw its golden tower from the Lisbon Falls road and turned in the long driveway that leads to that imposing wood structure. No one was around. Not a soul anywhere. Wide steps rise to the porch of the church, so white in the sunlight it could have been carved from a hill of snow.

Reverend Frank W. Sandford was the man who founded the church, who gathered his flock around him early in the 1900s and said to them, "I have just spoken to God and God has told me the world is coming to an end. We must go to the tower of our church and wait for the end of everything, praying as we wait. Come, let us go." And up to the high tower under the golden dome they went, and there they prayed and prayed and waited. But the world went on, the sun rose and set, and finally they gave up; back to their homes and farms they went. Some of them must have been relieved.

Sandford was a man of energy, full of ideas, and he shortly said to his congregation that he had been in communication with God again. God wanted him to rig out a ship and set sail to find heathen and convert them.

Once more he had his followers convinced he was on track. They helped him outfit a 150-ton sailing ship, and out of Portland's harbor they sailed. It is reported that Sandford stood at the bow of his ship in a purple robe, a Bible under his arm, a sailor's hat on his head, white beard flowing in the sea breeze.

He sailed on and on, not making any converts to speak of. Finally, after eight members of his crew died of scurvy, his congregation had enough. They sailed for home. Two years of neglect back at the church with the golden dome left Sandford powerless. He drifted away into obscurity, one more dreamer hooked to a dream, dragged from sight. His church went on without him.

Another religious group in the Portland-Auburn vicinity is still holding on, barely. These are the Shakers of Sabbathday Village. Their population ran as high as 1,866 in 1937, then began to die off. There were no children. They didn't go in for making them, didn't believe in it. They danced and shook instead and adopted children, or others, when they could.

Their society was formed in England in the middle of the eighteenth century, comprised of spiritualists and Quakers. Mother Ann Lee brought a group to America in 1774 and set up a colony near Albany, New York. In 1793 the Shakers, as they came to be known, settled Sabbathday Village in Maine.

Shake they did. They danced and shook their bodies, heads, and hands. They danced to shake off sin, and as they shook it away, goodness, they believed, descended upon them from above, falling into their upturned palms. They believed in the purification of confession and felt the Quaker abhorrence of war and violence. They also believed in ghosts.

They came to America to escape persecution. They came to America and shook as they danced and practiced celibacy to their hearts' content—counting on adoption to keep their colonies going. Now, sticking to their principles, the Shakers are disappearing, along with many another Early American institution.

Driving along the road above their buildings we slowed down and out of curiosity turned in. We'd seen a man and a woman sitting on a bench beside a brick building. The man wore a broad-brimmed hat, the woman a full skirt. They were like two figures out of the nineteenth century.

When we got below and parked, the man and woman were gone. Painters, working on the outside of one of the houses, were the only people around. They had a radio on a windowsill blaring away. Rock music.

I went into the vestibule of the brick building and rang a bell. Outdoor clothing, jackets and raincoats, hung on wooden pegs on each side of the vestibule. A dog inside the building began to bark. And then a stocky young man came to the door.

"I just wondered," I said, "if it's all right to take a look around."

"There's no one," he said, "to show you anything right now, and the shop up on the road is closed until summer, but go ahead, take a look."

The place appeared prosperous. The white buildings had been recently painted. Lawns were cut. The Shakers, I decided, small in number as they are, do well for themselves.

I'd heard that the ages of the eight Shakers who are carrying on run from the twenties to the nineties, and that the men and women live separately. Some of the Shakers who died and departed lie in a graveyard beside the highway above.

As we left Sabbathday Village, we stopped beside their cemetery. There were no tombstones to read, and only thirty or so graves lay within the graveyard's wrought-iron fence. The fence is decorated with a series of spearheads painted white, and so are the graves. A shaft with a spearhead marks each grave, as if the people below were buried standing up, a spear in their hands. There are no names on the graves. And no spear is larger or higher than another.

We headed north the next day and stayed that night in a motel. I'd wanted to call a friend who'd invited us to her house on Mt. Desert to tell her we were on our way; but few motels in Maine provide room telephones, and I couldn't call.

I have sleepless spells. At four in the morning I lay watching, with the sound off, an old Western movie starring Ken Maynard. In the flickering light, soundlessly, I saw justice done. At the climax of the picture Maynard and the villain were alone in a ranch house. Maynard, in a white hat, had just beaten the black-hatted man to the draw and shot a pistol from his hand. Then Maynard dropped his gun and gunbelt and they went at it. It was tiring to watch. The fuse on five sticks of dynamite was burning. When I was a kid, this was great stuff. Time has killed my gullibility. In my sleeplessness, watching that old-timer as if I were ten years old again, I felt out of joint with reality, as if I'd sat in the theater and watched this movie 100,000 times without going home.

I doubt that anyone reads about the exploits of Frank Merriwell anymore, collegiate hero of boys' books. If they do, they must have come across him as I did, on an attic bookshelf.

I was eight or nine when I found these books that had belonged to my mother's younger brother. In his day Merriwell had been known in every household in the nation.

Merriwell was a superb athlete. Like my idol Ken Maynard, he did not smoke or drink or chase girls; did not tell lies, never cheated, did not take lip from bullies. He hewed close to the ten commandments followed, according to Gene Autry, by cowboys. Among those commandments: fair play, truthfulness, patriotism, cleanliness of thought, and cleanliness of speech. Like Maynard, Merriwell was a two-fisted young man. He blazed through every trial. He went to Yale. And God-a-mighty, he was admired by every boy who read about him.

Burt L. Standish, who sent him to Yale, who came up with this paragon, was born in Corinna, Maine, in 1866. Standish was a pseudonym. The man behind the name was Gilbert Patten, one of the most successful and prolific writers of his time. At least 125 million copies of his Merriwell stories were circulated. In serialized form, the stories ran for 986 consecutive weeks.

We decided to find where Standish had lived, but it wasn't easy. In Corinna, we pulled up beside a couple of young men who were examining a tire in the sunlight, looking for a nailhead. They were in their early thirties, pot bellied, hair hanging in their faces, tattoos on their arms. I approached them cautiously.

"Is this," I asked, "the center of town? There aren't any stores in sight, and that's why I'm asking."

They both nodded. One of them said, "You're there."

"I'm looking for the former house of someone, Burt L. Standish he called himself. He was a writer."

They looked at one another and shrugged.

"Ever heard of Frank Merriwell?"

"No."

"Patten?"

One of the guys, the one in the blue T-shirt, went inside the house to speak to someone, then came out shaking his head. "You sure," he said, "you got the right town? There's nobody in this town we heard of got those names."

Leaving them in their yard, we followed Pleasant Street out of Corinna and came to a church just letting out. It was Sunday. Service was over, and the minister was out front shaking the hands of his departing congregation.

I stood around waiting to speak to the minister, a slim man with dark hair and gray sideburns, his hair so dark above the sideburns it looked like a wig. He was still bidding good-bye to the people filing out of his church, shaking hands, kissing a baby; a congenial man. Beyond him, on the wall of the vestibule, hung a picture of a city on the edge of a chasm. The city was in flames, as if Sherman had been there and gone. A gigantic cross, wide as a six-lane highway, stretched from one edge of the chasm to the other, forming a bridge to the beautiful city on the far side. Masses of people were in flight from their flaming streets, crowding the cross in their stampede to salvation.

When his congregation was gone, I asked the minister about Frank Merriwell. He'd never heard of him, but he wanted me to speak to his wife, who might be of some help. She was the town librarian.

As we walked through the church, I saw an antique chandelier over the center aisle, a kind I'd never seen before, wrought-iron, electrified, quite large. I asked him about it.

He'd found it in the church's attic, he said, after he'd been appointed to the church. A man in the congregation had restored and hung it for him. He, too, admired it.

We went into a corridor where he opened a window and, raising his voice, said to someone in a car, "Come inside. I want to speak to you."

Then he led me down some steps, and his wife met us at the back door, a gray-haired woman.

When I asked about Burt L. Standish, she hesitated, then shook her head, but when I said "Frank Merriwell," she looked up with recognition. "Oh, yes," she said. "We have his books in the library." But she didn't know where his former house was, and seemed surprised to hear he was born in town.

There was someone, however, she was sure would know where his house had been, a Mr. Byrd. He lived just down the road and three houses up the next block.

We found the house. Mr. Byrd himself came to the door.

When I asked about Merriwell, a smile beamed toward me as if crossing a lifetime, a smile of pleasure. He knew the house I wanted. It was a brown house, three houses over from the state road, practically across from the yard with the young men with the tire.

We left then, came to the state road, turned, and passed the place where I'd talked to the ruffians—they smoked cigarettes, which alone would have made them Merriwell's enemies—and came to the house. It was brown with white window trim. A boy about five years old was applying mud to the white trim with a stick. The foundation of the house, I decided, was old enough to have been standing when Patten lived there.

The front door faced the sideyard. I walked around, went up to the door, knocked, and stood looking at the yellow barn behind the house. A bearded man in a blue visored cap came to the door. He was obviously puzzled when I asked, "Is this the house where Burt L. Standish, who wrote the Frank Merriwell series, lived?"

"Never heard of the guy," he said.

It was the only brown house around.

I went back and got in the car and said, "It's the house, all right."

We cut east over Route 95, then southeast along Alternate Route 1 to the coast and Mt. Desert. The older I get, the more it seems to me my past hangs in the distance like the dim edge of the vision of an underwater swimmer. As I swim along in the clear water of time, the deepening haze of my past moves along with me.

Until I was twenty-eight years old, I thought I could remember every detail of my life; only the details I'd been let in on of my parents' and grandparents' lives, which were imaginary to begin with, took on a blur. Then, as if memory could hold only so much of my gathering past, a blurring of my own life began. Every new experience seemed to crowd some sharply outlined memory into the blurred distance, into the haze of grandfather-and-grandmother-land—where what I thought I remembered was half-imagined. The older I get, the more my life becomes creative in its own right. I become, to some degree, an imaginary person in a real world.

The haze, however, has clear places, and it was still easy to remember that twenty years ago we'd spent a few days at Lenore's cottage on Birch Island off the Maine coast. It had been like an elaborate game, trying to reach her insular retreat. She had no telephone or electricity. She got her supplies by running a motorboat to the mainland and back. In order for us to reach the island, she had had to come over in her boat and haul us there. She'd left a message with instructions for us at general delivery in the Brunswick post office.

I remember reaching under a bush and finding the sheet, where she'd told us it would be; then Peggy and I unfolded it and spread it on the slope of the hill that faced her house across the water. The sheet lay heavily on the ground, gray with the water of a recent rain.

We sat and waited.

Lenore, a widow, had been the wife of a college president; she spent her summers in Maine and the rest of the year in New York City. She had a large family who often joined her on the island, and she had friends who came on visits. The sheet was a signal she'd devised. Within minutes after she spotted the sheet spread out on the ground, she was in her boat, a tiny gray-haired woman, steering her way toward us.

She had three cabins behind her shingle cottage. They had been built originally for a boys' camp on her end of the island. Only her house was standing before the cabins came. Mr. Johnson, she said, had hauled them to her cottage in the winter, across snow and ice, with horses and sleds.

One of Lenore's sons was there when we were. The island is about half a mile from the mainland, and halfway over we could see Mac and his wife Dot descending the long flight of steps cut into the cliff's edge that led down from Lenore's yard.

We docked and climbed, carrying luggage. Mac led us over a path behind the house, through woods, to one of the cabins.

Lenore baked her own bread. After the bread was baked and we'd all had a highball, she and I went off to fill gallon jugs with springwater. Mac split kindling for the lobster feast that night.

The spring was at the end of the island, a boat ride away. We climbed a path with the empty jugs to get there. Shaded by pine trees, the spring rose from a plank box sunk in the earth. I carried the full jugs one by one to the boat, grains of earth between my wet hands and the cold glass.

I carried the jugs into the cottage, into the oven odor of fresh-baked bread. Dinner was started just before the kerosene lamps in the house were lit. Mac had balanced a washtub of seawater on an oval arrangement of stones and lit a fire under it, and we sat around the tub. By the time the lobsters were in the brine and steam was rising between the planks laid across the tub, it was dark enough to need the firelight to see one another.

The fire lit the side of the old lobsterman's shack that Lenore came to each summer with her children and their wives and children. There was firelight for dinner, and after dinner there was light from kerosene lamps with bright Aladdin wicks. When we turned in, we carried a lantern down a path between evergreen and birch trees, and we slept that night in forest with board walls and screened windows around us.

In the nineteenth century, people were living on the island. There was even a school. What emptied them out was the discovery of gold in California, the same glittering news that separated my Great-Grandfather Beam from my great-grandmother. Lenore herself lives in California now, in a retirement community near Carmel.

Her house and the cabins are still on the island, and her son Mac-Gregor goes there summers. A sheet is probably still spread out on the ground to signal for the boat, and Mac, nearly as old now as his mother was then, goes over to bring his visitors back to the steps that rise along the side of a cliff to a place where the past hangs on.

Our friend Elena, who lives on Mt. Desert, where we were headed, is a friend of my cousin Dick's. She is one of the original members of the Group Theater. We had never seen her away from New York.

A narrow bridge reaches from the mainland to Mt. Desert, and a road on the far side runs along the shore to Bar Harbor. Bar Harbor is where the stores and hotels and restaurants are, a shopping center. The shops were just beginning to open for summer.

The island, one of the oldest summer centers in New England, picked up popularity after the Civil War. Many houses and acres of forest and land were destroyed by fire in 1947, but we never saw the island until the sixties; by then it had recovered and seemed as beautiful as it was said to have been before the holocaust. (I thought of a great cross stretching from the island to the mainland and thousands of islanders fleeing flames.) The roads are paved and narrow; no thoroughfares cut from one side of the island to the other.

A few miles from Elena's, forsythia in bloom, we drove through Somesville, past frame houses, decidedly old but still in good shape. Somesville is out of the sunken past, a clearing in the mist of time, but so small a town we had only a glimpse of it in transit.

Mt. Desert belonged to the French early on. Credit goes to Champlain for discovering it in 1604. Cadillac, who founded Detroit, has the island's mountain named after him to remind us of the island's French settlers. His granddaughter is buried at Hull's Cove.

Elena has three small houses in a line between the road and the shore, on an inlet where the tide carries ocean to her and then takes it away, leaving behind a mud flat: a calm ocean at times is below her windows, then it's gone.

The fence along the road in front of her property opens at a gate. The small parking spot beyond is surrounded by evergreens. A path leads to the back of the middle house, tan-shingled with gray trim around the doors and windows. Elena was fixing up one of the flanking houses for rental and had a couple of interior decorators helping her. Two men. The older of the pair, the boss, an ex-colonel in the marines, was an actor friend of Elena's.

They helped us get our luggage in, and Elena took us upstairs, where we had a single-bed situation in each of two small rooms; my view was of tree-edged ocean bay. The house is small. The upstairs toilet was in my room, in a former closet with a door that didn't quite close on my knees when I sat inside. A washbasin stood outside the closet door.

Everyone pitched in on the cooking. We ate one night in the kitchen and the next night in the living room. It was a place to be relaxed and cheerful, a place with no need to ask the time.

Elena's living room, where we sat mostly, has a screened porch facing the water, knotty pine-paneled walls, and a brick fireplace. Over the wooden fireplace mantel hangs a muzzle-loading rifle with a missing rod. The stock is hand-carved.

On the mantel, framed, there's a photograph of someone long dead, a man. An old boyfriend, a man who once owned all three houses before Elena bought them. Now there he was on the mantel, like a spirit still in the house. Elena believes in ghosts, and she has reason to.

Her father, a fierce old man, living alone, died in his New York City apartment. To let his daughter know he'd died, he appeared, she believes, at her country place outside New York in the body of a fox. Her husband, John, was alive then, and they both heard the fox screaming out by the stable. John, a stocky, tough executive, did not put up with screaming. Even so he didn't go out to look for the fox.

"It was," Elena told us that night, "an absolutely unearthly scream. I'd never heard anything like it. John hadn't either. It was terrifying. I went out on the porch. I saw the fox. It had come out from behind some bushes and was staring at me. Then it screamed again, and I said, 'I know! I know!' And I knew it was my father. I went into town at once. I went to his apartment and found him. Dead. I don't know for how long."

"Did the fox ever appear again?"

"No, never again."

I'd taken a picture nearly twenty years ago of a Mt. Desert dock piled with lobster traps, and Peggy and I kept driving along the shoreline looking for it. I'd about decided it was gone, or so changed I wouldn't know it when I caught a glimpse of the dock between a couple of buildings. We drove down. I got out, the old picture in one hand for comparison. There'd been some change in the arrangement of the lobster pots, but not much. Here was another patch of the past.

There was still another patch at Eastport, Maine. Maine itself continues north beyond Eastport, but Eastport is where the coast of the United States and the Atlantic Ocean part company. The place they part is off the Bay of Fundy, across from Nova Scotia. People who go to Eastport can see the largest whirlpool in the Western Hemisphere.

The road to the ledge of land where the whirlpool can be seen is paved, but full of potholes. At the end of the road we circled around through a mudwallow and stopped. No one has paved this piece of land, this perch above the whirlpool, nor set up telescopes for twenty-five cents a look. We were the only car around.

I got out and limped about, looking. I had only the slightest limp now, but I was walking carefully. Cool ocean air held me. I couldn't see any whirlpool.

We drove back to town past the road that went down to the shore, another patch of the past I'd photographed earlier. It was unchanged, this high framework of a dock with a cliff and a house in the background, all of them in the same spatial arrangement.

Eastport senses approaching tourism. Many more of its houses were painted this visit. The town looked more like the historic village and seaport it is.

Rain was falling when we parked the car on the main drag and ran for the coffee shop across the street. The shop had a counter and a few tables. We took a table near a window that faced out over docks, and ordered lunch.

I asked a man at a table beside us if the whirlpool was something someone could see from town, and he assured me it was. He looked like a local businessman, knocking off for lunch.

"Sure," he said, "it can be seen from that point you were at. Two currents come together below there and the water swirls."

"Is the whirlpool big enough to be dangerous?"

"It's big enough," he said, "big enough so you wouldn't want to sail a small boat through it. That would be dangerous. At least I wouldn't want to try it myself. A while back a man in a rowboat got caught in the whirlpool. It caught him up and whirled him around and around and finally threw him up on shore."

"I thought," Peggy said, "whirlpools whirled you around and pulled you under."

"Sometimes. Way back in the past, I understand, the whirlpool caught a five-masted schooner and pulled it under, crew and all."

We sat in silence, in tribute to the mysterious and whimsical forces of nature.

The way in and out of Eastport is along causeways, a series of them, past shores without inhabitants, like the shoreline of the Everglades . . . as if our trip were ending the way it had started, water on each side of us like a long river, woods coming down to the water's edge. With this difference: the woods now were evergreens without the spidery legs of mangroves; and the voices coming over the car radio were French instead of Spanish. But the islands off in the haze reminded us of the Everglades, the emptiness of the Everglades and their solitude.

Beyond the causeways, we passed through the Moosehorn Wildlife Preserve. We came to logs piled beside the road and knew we were in lumbering country.

We moved north through a land of Christmas trees, all the perfect height for a living room. Then the trees got taller and were no longer aligned. We drove for miles and miles, the forest packed in on each side. The next day, through various landscapes, including hilly scenic countryside, we came to Houlton, a place from the past I recognized, that felt familiar. It was Norman Rockwell country, the country of my boyhood, carried intact to northern Maine.

Houlton is full of houses with big white porches on each side of clean streets. Some of the houses are enormous. The trees along the streets are of moderate ambition, and throughout the town there is a sense of modest prosperity and peace, the good life.

This town, for me, went back to the early forties or thirties, perhaps even the twenties. The side lawns of the houses are often deeper than the front yards. There are few sidewalks, just paths through grass along the streets. The town has tourist homes, instead of bed-and-breakfasts. We even passed a sign advertising the playing of beano—not bingo. I hadn't come across the beano lure since the Great Depression.

Houlton has a historic business district. In it are twenty-eight architecturally significant structures that date from 1885 to 1910. In 1910, the town's population was 6,000, and that's about what it is today.

We had breakfast the next morning in the Elm Tree Diner. The townspeople around us looked like Rockwell's small-town characters; they seemed, that is, idealized, alert, well-scrubbed, friendly, cheerful . . . assorted ages, men in blue jeans, some in overalls, men old enough to have been my Grandfather Beam, wearing slacks and V-neck sweaters and jogging shoes; a mix in the diner of working class and middle class; all of them, it seemed, content to be who they were and where they were. The odor that hung in the air was the same as at Lenore's, the odor of homemade bread.

The girls waiting tables wore white outfits with blue aprons, and they were smiling. Their cheeks were rouged, and lipstick reddened their lips. Northern Maine had become uncommonly strange though thoroughly familiar.

Farther north, across the St. John River, the French-Canadian border came into sight, and we passed a Canadian town called *Rivière Verte*.

There are still towns in northern Maine where French is heard on the streets, and it sounds as natural there as, say, a Brooklyn accent does in Manhattan.

In Madawaska, Maine, a few miles down the road, there are children of children of settlers who chopped out homes when the place was called Acadia; descendants of French settlers. The French and the English fought over this land until the English, before the Revolution, kicked most of the French out. Like an outraged landowner shaking a title, the English shook the 1773 Treaty of Utrecht before the Acadians. When the French refused to evacuate, 4,000 or more of them were herded onto ships and hauled away.

That mass eviction moved Longfellow years later to stanzas of poetic compassion—too late to help the Acadians. Some of the dispossessed Frenchmen made their way back to Acadia, and there their French descendants are today: French-speaking Americans, but New Englanders

nonetheless. That's what I'd read, only to discover that the latest generation is breaking with tradition.

"Only the older folks still speak French," our waitress told us. We'd
stopped for lunch in Madawaska before heading south. "I don't speak it
myself any more." She might have been fifteen years old.

I said, "Except at home?"

"Yeah, only there."

We were in a countryside now of enormous barns. Several had caved
in, their roofs buckling, we imagined, under too many winters of heavy
snow. Wood, cut and stacked beside houses, was now a familiar sight.
"We're in a foreign land," said Peggy. "Doesn't it feel that way?"

"It's as if we'd crossed a time belt," I said, "and might not ever
return."

"Don't say that."

"Where those who were once ghosts have now become the living."

Route 11 is a long road south out of Fort Kent. It ran homeward for
us from the Canadian border, a road through wilderness like the wilderness of an earlier age.

We came to the crest of a hill. In the distance, spread out over at
least twenty miles, or as far as we could see, was forest, a mist in the near
distance blurring the trees the way memory blurs the past.

Yes, the past is rapidly disappearing. We're stardust in an expanding
universe—but not everything is gone, not all the old houses and inns, or
all the horses and carriages. There are barrooms with sawdust on their
floors, and hotels with brass beds, and restaurants where meals are served
family-style. Fireflies flash in field grass. Some farmers still wear homespun
clothing, plow their fields with horse-drawn plows, and ride in horse-
drawn buggies. The country store is not a fable, nor are millponds and
courthouse benches. There are villages from Maine to Florida that carry
their history openly and simply, with elms and uncurbed streets and brick
and clapboard homes that were standing when Lafayette traveled the land
from end to end.

The past is with us, some of the past always will be and always has
been, falling as Walt Whitman said, "into niches and corners before the
procession of souls along the grand roads of the universe."

Appendix:
Towns and Inns

I haven't included in the text all the timeless towns through which we passed, nor have I mentioned all the interesting inns and restaurants where we stayed or ate, and so what follows, to make up for that omission, is a more complete record, or an elaboration, of the timeless towns and inns we encountered. Every inn is one we either stayed at or scouted for the future. The list is only a sample (limited by our sometimes whimsical choice of roads) of the East Coast's historic and undiscovered towns and inns that are making a stand, whether deliberately or not, against shopping malls, fast-food joints, and motel clusters.

Time is constantly at work making its alterations, however minor. This is especially true of inns. Prices change. Owners and managers change. Hotels go in and out of business. Call ahead.

When you're traveling the untraveled road where the past is scattered, there's always the chance night might fall, as it did in the old days, before you have a place to stay or eat. Let that risk remain for as long as possible. Nothing risked, nothing to get excited about.

Alabama

EUFAULA   Originally called Irwinton, Eufaula is on the west bank of the Chattahoochee River, over a bridge from Georgetown, Georgia. Eufaula ("beech tree") is the name of a branch of the Creek Confederacy. Population was 5,208 in 1941; is now 12,097. Many large Victorian and Greek Revival houses; annual azalea festival.

Connecticut

BROOKLYN   Incorporated in 1786, Brooklyn now has a population of 900; it had 2,250 residents in 1938. A bronze plaque on a boulder across from the handsome crossroads green marks the site of the General Wolfe Tavern. It later became the farm and hostelry of General Israel Putnam. Putnam's vandalized statue stands nearby. An undiscovered town.

COLEBROOK   On a small country road at the top of a hill stands Colebrook, the last town to be settled in Connecticut. According to a sign in front of its town hall, it is the best-preserved example of a post-Revolutionary village center that has survived in the state. The white wooden Methodist Episcopal church of 1833 has a two-story tower. The Colebrook Store of 1812, a federally registered historic building, is Greek Revival; described as deserted in 1938, it appears to be thriving.

GUILFORD   Guilford is a found town, but a well-preserved one, with a large green dominated by giant elms and a Greek Revival church. Many beautiful old houses throughout the town.
Accommodations and restaurants.

HAMPTON   A cutoff town on old Route 6 and on Route 97, Hampton was founded in 1786. Its population, 511 in 1938, seems about the same now. Wide lawns and large white houses, a general store, and a quiet air.

NORFOLK   Incorporated in 1758, Norfolk has been a cultural center since the turn of this century. Many large summer homes were built here. In 1938 there were 1,298 residents; now there are 1,500. Yale holds its Summer School of Music and Art in Norfolk. The Joseph Battell Memorial Fountain, designed by Saint-Gaudens and executed by Stanford White, stands at the southern corner of the spacious green. An interesting old signboard shows distances to other towns.
Accommodations, restaurants.

ORANGE   Just off the turnpike, the historical area in Orange is a sudden surprise. Its Congregational church dates to 1810. A number of notable houses.
Accommodations, restaurants.

POMFRET   Pomfret, at the crest of a hill, has the Pomfret Academy, a boys' prep school, and a columned Congregational church built in 1832. There were formerly two inns; now there are none. Substantial, well-cared-for homes.
No accommodations, no restaurants.

RIVERTON   The Hitchcock Chair Company was founded here on the Farmington River in 1818. Known as Hitchcockville until 1866, the town is once again producing its famous chairs. Riverton has interesting houses and churches.

Accommodations and restaurant: *Riverton Inn*, P.O. Box 6, Riverton, CT 06065, (203) 379-8678. A 1796 inn, once a stagecoach stop called Ives Tavern; ten rooms, ten baths, one suite with fireplace, some rooms with antiques and fourposter beds; antique doll's house feeling. Moderate. Excellent restaurant.

THOMPSON   Settled in 1693, Thompson was not incorporated until 1785. Its common is surrounded by white homes with porches. A crossroads town on Routes 193 and 200, the town and its Vernon Stiles Tavern were on the Boston-to-Hartford and the Providence-to-Springfield "pikes." Stiles, the tavern's owner, was also a justice of the peace, and eloping couples made this their first stop. No longer open as an inn, the tavern still serves meals.

Delaware

DOVER   Although William Penn in 1683 gave orders that a county seat named Dover be laid out along the King's Highway, the town was not platted until 1717. It became the state capital in 1777. Dover's historic green, serene on a Sunday afternoon, is surrounded by old buildings, most of them eighteenth-century brick. Christ Church (1734) has white pews with gates at each end. Many old houses can be seen along State Street, with Victorian homes appearing on the route out of town. The Dover Heritage Trail can be followed either with a guide or with a self-guiding brochure.
    Accommodations available.
    Restaurant: *Blue Coat Inn*, 800 North State Street, Dover, DE 19901, (302) 674-1776. Early American atmosphere in a restaurant that overlooks Silver Lake. Moderate.

KENTON   Colonial houses, sideyard gardens, and barns appear in this un-found town lying in the midst of farming country. Once named Grogtown, it was a stopping place for travelers.

NEW CASTLE   Oldest town in the Delaware Valley, New Castle was already settled in 1651 when Peter Stuyvesant arrived. Before William Penn came in 1682, the town had undergone five changes of sovereignty. New Castle has not been renovated or restored; it stands as it was, houses of the seventeenth, eighteenth, and early nineteenth centuries, essentially unchanged, lining the brick streets.
    Accommodations: *Janvier-Black House*, 17 The Strand, New Castle, DE 19720, (302) 328-1339. An 1825 house with one guestroom, virtually a three-room apartment; antiques. Formal garden behind the house, which faces the river. No outside sign reveals the accommodations within.
    Restaurant: *Newcastle Inn*, Market Street, New Castle, DE 19720, (302) 328-1798. An inn since 1980, the building was an arsenal in 1812. Cobblestone street in front, with grass growing between the cobbles. Candlelight, fresh flowers, authentic antiques, and excellent food. Moderate.
    New Castle has a number of inns and restaurants.

ODESSA   Once known as Cantwell's Bridge, Odessa took its current name in 1855. Its finest houses are located on Main Street, formerly the King's Highway, the main thoroughfare through town. The street is now bypassed by Route 13, but the old houses have been preserved. A highway grocery store and an auto dealership do not intrude.

Accommodations: Bed-and-breakfast in town; motels along Route 13. Restaurants on Route 13.

SMYRNA   Like Odessa (above), Smyrna was also a port that grew up along the King's Highway, and its main thoroughfare and historic houses have been bypassed by more recent, larger roads. But its handsome eighteenth-century houses are being kept and cared for, and its population, 1,958 in 1938, is now 4,750.

No accommodations. Restaurants on Route 13.

Florida

CEDAR KEY   Pretty much a ghost town until 1970; reminded me of Key West in the 1950s. Good selection of inns and restaurants.

Accommodations and restaurants: *Cedar Cove Motel and Marina*, P.O. Box 508, Cedar Key, FL 32625, (904) 543-5332. Thirty-four rooms, eight townhouse units, all with bath. Bar, restaurant, docking facilities, pool, fully equipped kitchens. Built 1981; modern cape. Moderate.

Island Hotel, P.O. Box 460, Cedar Key, FL 32625, (904) 543-5111. Built 1849, Jamaican architecture, ten rooms, six with bath. Restaurant; bar next door. Upright piano in lobby, coalstove, two ceiling fans, atmosphere is early Hemingway. Excellent food. Moderate.

COPELAND   Restaurant: *Jane's*, Route 29, Copeland, FL 33926, (813) 695-4323. Near Everglades City. Black-eyed peas, homemade chowder, jukebox. Popular. Inexpensive.

EVERGLADES CITY   In the 1870s, an Indian trading post at the mouth of the Barron River. It was briefly the county seat of Collier County; now known as the western water gateway to Everglades National Park. Excellent accommodations and restaurants. Mosquitoes in season, April–November.

Accommodations and restaurant: *Rod and Gun Club*, Everglades City, FL 33929, (813) 695-2101. Built by the founder of Everglades City on foundation of the first house on the south bank of the Barron River. Became a private club where several U.S. presidents and other dignitaries have been guests. Inn since 1960. Cottages on grounds, small rooms in inn. Bar, restaurant, airstrip. Inexpensive.

INVERNESS   Has the appearance of a prosperous 1930s town. Founded 1868. Population now 4,095; was 1,000 in 1939. Lakes around town; yellow brick house with white columns; big yards; many trees.

Accommodations and restaurant: *Crown Hotel*, 109 North Seminole Avenue, Inverness, FL 32650, (904) 344-5555. Once a one-story general store, has been a sizable Victorian inn for ninety years; thirty-four rooms, all with bath, one suite. Brass beds, velvet chairs, tasseled draperies in rooms. Fireplace, crystal chandeliers in lobby, hand-rubbed wood on spiral staircase. Bar with tin ceiling. Restaurant. Some convention business. One hour north of Tampa, inland. Rooms moderate; meals inexpensive.

KEY WEST   Southernmost city in U.S.; no longer a lazy fishing village. Old-time atmosphere still exists if you can find it among the hotels, restaurants, boutiques, hustlers, and conglomeration of tourists. Hemingway house worth a visit.

Accommodations: *Duval House,* 815 Duval Street, Key West, FL 33040, (305) 294-1666. Two Victorian houses built in 1880s. Twenty-one rooms, eighteen with private bath. Paddle fans, white wicker furniture, tropical trees, pool. Continental breakfast. Moderate.

Other accommodations, restaurants all over the place.

LA BELLE   Founded 1870; population 2,287. Dense with palm and live oak trees. Few cattle ranches now, but cowboys still ride into town wearing Western hats. Rapidly becoming citrus-growing area because of many bad seasons farther north.

Accommodations, restaurants.

ST. AUGUSTINE   Oldest permanent European settlement in North America. Work began on the stone fort, Castillo de San Marcos, in 1672. Tourists and tourism have taken a toll on St. Augustine, but there is still much that is interesting to see here.

Accommodations: *Victorian House Bed & Breakfast,* 11 Cadiz Street, St. Augustine, FL 32084, (904) 824-5214. Built 1860–90; inn since 1983; seven rooms, five with private bath, one with fireplace; Victorian decor; hand-woven coverlets and quilts; stenciled floors; hand-hooked rugs; some canopy beds, some four-posters. No bar or restaurant. Inexpensive.

St. Augustine has many other inns and restaurants.

WAKULLA SPRINGS   Accommodations and restaurant: *Wakulla Springs Lodge and Conference Center,* 1 Spring Drive, Wakulla Springs, FL 32305, (904) 640-7011. At junction of Routes 267 and 61, eleven miles south of Tallahassee, in Wakulla Springs State Park. Built as an inn in 1937; stone fireplace in lobby; Tennessee marble floors; Moorish archways. Twenty-seven rooms with bath; Honeymoon Room, Heritage Room, Edward Ball Suite. Restaurant, no bar. Glass-bottom boat trips. Once had a pole-vaulting fish called Henry. "Old Joe," two-hundred-year-old alligator, now stuffed, is encased in the lobby. Movie starring Johnny Weissmuller filmed here. Moderate.

Georgia

CUTHBERT   Founded 1834; population now 3,635. Antebellum and Victorian houses. Population has changed little in forty years. Birds sing. Has thirty homes on National Historic Register.

DAWSON   Greek Revival town; population 4,774. In pecan country; signs on stores say: WE BUY, WE SELL PECANS. No tourists, no town square with Confederate soldier.
Restaurants include catfish takeout shop.

FORT GAINES   Founded early 1800s; population now 1,260, just 12 less than in 1940. Greek Revival homes on Washington Street. Site of a log fort during Jackson's war against the Indians.
Food available.

MACON   Founded 1822; population 122,000. Modern, with Old Town area; houses on College, Georgia, and Jefferson streets are large, white, and impressive.
Accommodations and restaurant: *1842 Inn*, 353 College Street, Macon, GA 31201, (912) 741-1842. Greek Revival antebellum house built 1842; inn since 1984. Twenty-two rooms, all with bath, eight with fireplace. High ceilings with ceiling fans, crystal chandeliers, oriental rugs, TV in armoire. Bar, restaurant. Moderate.

MADISON   Founded 1809. Population now 2,890, was 1,966 in the thirties. Block after block of old white Greek Revival and Victorian houses, serene, no one moving—a movie set. Many white pillars. Mentioned to us by many people as a "must-see." This town seems a climax to a journey.

MILLEDGEVILLE   Founded 1803; population now 12,176. Antebellum and Victorian homes. The only historic area is east of Georgia State College, though there are Victorian houses all over town. Brick storefronts downtown.

SAVANNAH   Historic area extends over two and a half square miles with spacious squares, many Victorian and earlier buildings. Parks, boulevards, live oak and pine trees. Said to be the first planned city in America. Population 141,000.
Accommodations: *The Gastonian*, 220 East Gaston Street, Savannah, GA 31401, (912) 232-2869. Built 1868; inn since 1986. Ten rooms with bath, one with fireplace; three suites, all with fireplace. Regency decor. Oriental rugs. No bar, no restaurant. Guests served full Southern-style breakfast in parlor, or continental breakfast in room or courtyard. Sundeck with hot tub. Moderate to expensive.
Magnolia Place Inn, 503 Whitaker Street, Savannah, GA 31401, (912) 236-7674 or (800) 238-7674. Built 1878; inn since 1983. Thirteen rooms, twelve with gas fireplace, all with bath. Victorian with grand staircase, English Georgian antiques, pencil-post beds, armoires. Faces Forsyth Park. Full breakfast served to guests in bedrooms, parlor, courtyard, or on porch. Moderate to expensive.
River Street Place, Factor's Walk, 115 East River Street, Savannah, Georgia 31401, (912) 234-6400 or (800) A-LEGACY. Became an inn in 1987, formerly a cotton warehouse. Large and atmospheric. Forty-four rooms on five floors, eighteen with gas fireplace, all with bath. Two restaurants, bar. Original wood; most rooms have river view. Antique reproductions, four-poster beds. Moderate to expensive.

17 Hundred 90 Inn, 307 East President Street, Savannah, GA 31401, (912) 236-7122. Built 1790, inn for ten years. Fourteen rooms, twelve with gas fireplace, two suites, all with bath. Federal period. Brass beds, antiques, complimentary bottle of wine, continental breakfast. Restaurant highly praised. Moderate to expensive. Reservations required.

Restaurant: *Elizabeth on 37th*, 105 East 37th Street, Savannah, GA 31401, (912) 236-5547. Built 1900, restaurant since 1981. Two gas fireplaces. Lunch, dinner; closed Mon., Tues. Dim lighting, excellent service, good wine list, fresh ingredients. Moderate.

Savannah has many fine inns and restaurants.

WASHINGTON   Founded 1780; population is now 18,842; 3,158 in 1940. Greek Revival and Victorian houses. Once the most important town north of Augusta. Big trees everywhere, big lawns, old homes. Robert Augustus Toombs, 1810–1885, local resident, opposed building a hotel in town after Civil War. He is reported to have said, "If a respectable man comes to town, he can stay at my house. If he isn't respectable, we don't want him here at all."

Maine

CHERRYFIELD   On the very rocky Narraguagus River, which offers excellent Atlantic salmon fishing, Cherryfield is an untouched village with deep, deep lawns, no sidewalks on its side streets, shutters on most windows. The heart of blueberry country.

Accommodations: *Ricker House*, (207) 546-2780, bed-and-breakfast inn. Restaurant in area.

DOVER-FOXCROFT   These two towns, on either side of the Piscataquis River, were founded in the early 1800s, united in 1915. A placid town with a turn-of-the-century mood.

Accommodations: *The Foxcroft Bed & Breakfast*, (207) 564-7720.

Restaurant: *Thistle's on Monument Square*, (207) 583-4037.

EASTPORT   Easternmost city in the United States, settled in 1780; captured by the British in the War of 1812. Smuggling, at that time, an important part of its history. Once a center for fishermen as well as farmers. Lots of early houses still around getting prettied up, like a girl who senses suitors approaching. A good walking town.

Accommodations include bed-and-breakfasts in houses on the National Register of Historic Places. Restaurants.

EAST SUMNER   Lost in time, East Sumner is north of Auburn. Large, many-windowed houses, big fields.

FREEPORT/DURHAM   Accommodations: *Bagley House*, RR 3, Box 269C, Freeport, ME 04032, (207) 353-6372. A 1770 house recently made into a country bed-and-breakfast. A blue sleigh stands in the yard. No one was home; I peered through windows into an atmosphere of luxury out of the past. The card of proprietress Deborah Burns indicated the house has original architecture and period furnishings. Worth investigating.

Restaurants in Freeport, a far-from-unfound town.

HOULTON   A Norman Rockwell–type town, Houlton was settled in 1805. Once a lumbering center, its chief business today is the Maine potato, something special when prepared here. The former Ricker Classical Institute of 1847 is now Ricker College. An unusual cast-iron drinking fountain in Pierce Park is of a boy examining a leaking boot.

Accommodations. Restaurants.

MACHIAS AND EAST MACHIAS   A trading post was established in Machias in 1633, but the first permanent settlers did not arrive until 1763. An early pirate stronghold, the town became a major shipbuilding center during the nineteenth century. In spite of an unappealing Main Street, this is an attractive old town. The Machias River runs through a gorge behind Main Street. Burnham Tavern, now a museum, dates back to 1770. In East Machias, four miles away, are a number of historic houses.

Accommodations: Bed-and-breakfasts in East Machias. Restaurants.

NORTHEAST HARBOR   A summer colony town, Northeast Harbor still retains an undiscovered feeling and an early 1900's air. Roads that run along the shore have great views of water and islands. Large, beautiful homes.

Accommodations. Restaurants.

PARIS HILL   Chartered in 1793, this is a cutoff town of beautiful homes and much history. Its old jail is now a library, the exterior unchanged, the interior cells removed to make room for books. An early nineteenth-century church on the green has four fluted pillars and a clock tower. One of Maine's most beautiful and timeless towns.

PITTSFIELD   On Bates Street in Pittsfield, there is a roll of the past—big trees, no sidewalks, frame houses with small porches, a movie theater still in operation. Three governors were born here. At the Maine Central Institute, founded 1866, trees border a U-shaped drive. Its first class had one student.

PORTLAND   In spite of having been twice destroyed, once by the British, once by fire, Portland, Maine's largest city, still has some fine old buildings and a strong feeling of the past. Its Old Port has been reconstructed, and a few old mansions are still standing. The Portland History Trail can be followed on a self-guided walking tour.

Plentiful accommodations, restaurants.

QUODDY VILLAGE   This village was to have been the center of the Passamaquoddy Project to harness the tides for hydroelectric power. When Congress cut off funds for the project in 1937, the village lost its population. For a time it was the home of a National Youth Administration experiment in which 250 boys were housed here in 120 temporary cottages. Most of the buildings are still standing and some are occupied, but the temporary feeling remains. Two roads run through this hidden town.

SOMESVILLE   Oldest town in Maine, Somesville's widely separated white houses on one of Mt. Desert's roads form just enough of a cluster to make an unfound village.

SOUTHWEST HARBOR   Inn: *Moorings Inn*, P.O. Box 744, Southwest Harbor, ME 04679, (207) 244-5523 or 244-3210. Built in 1784; became an inn in 1916. Nineteen rooms with bath, four with fireplace. Suites and cottages also available. Enclosed on three sides by boatyards, the inn faces the bay. Boatpeople predominate here. Sunny and pleasant. Moderate.
   Restaurant: *The Restaurant*, (207) 244-7070. Adjoins the Moorings Inn but is under separate management. Dining indoors or on an open deck at water's edge.

WAYNE   Located on a millpond that leads into Androscoggin Lake. An old mill can be seen from a small bridge in town. Picturesque and undiscovered.

Maryland

ANNAPOLIS   First named Anne Arundel Town and settled by Puritans in 1648, Annapolis was the first peacetime capital of the United States. Streets here radiate from State Circle, and they are lined with perhaps the highest concentration of Colonial buildings in the nation. Annapolis was a social center with racing, dancing, and gambling early in the eighteenth century, the period to which most of the houses date. The Naval Academy was established in 1845 at what had been the army's Fort Severn. St. John's College, in the center of town, was chartered in 1784, successor to King William's School, established in 1696. Shaded streets and beautiful homes.
   Accommodations: *Historic Inns of Annapolis* (formerly the Maryland Inn), 16 Church Circle, Annapolis, MD 21401, (301) 263-2641 or (800) 847-8882; in Maryland (800) 638-8902. Now one of a complex of five separate inns (others are the Governor Calvert House, State House Inn, Robert Johnson House, and Reynolds Tavern) in the heart of Annapolis, the Maryland Inn is a pie-shaped building of 1704 with a fourth-story mansard roof. Forty-four rooms with bath. Many rooms have antique furnishings, nine have nonworking fireplaces. Continental breakfast included. Moderate.
   Restaurant: *King of France Tavern*, adjacent to the Maryland Inn. Time-forgotten atmosphere. Popular bar. Fine food.

CHESAPEAKE CITY   Accommodations: *Inn at the Canal*, 104 Bohemia Avenue, Chesapeake City, MD 21915, (301) 885-5995. Known locally as the Brady-Rees House, it was built in 1867 and became an inn in 1987. Six rooms with bath, high ceilings, view of Chesapeake & Delaware Canal from two rooms. The canal, opened in 1829, is the town's chief attraction and source of business.

An important link in the Inland Waterway, it also serves as a water shortcut between Baltimore and Philadelphia. A lively town on summer weekends. Inn's rates include full breakfast. Moderate.

Restaurants.

FREDERICK   Founded in 1745, Frederick had earlier been known as Tasker's Chance. Its settlers were Palatine Germans from Pennsylvania, and its oldest houses are reminders of houses in Pennsylvania towns. Many antique shops. Walking tours.

Accommodations, restaurants.

WILLIAMSPORT   Washington came to Williamsport in 1790 and considered making it the capital of the country. It had long been a junction point for important early trails. Eighteenth- and nineteenth-century houses of brick and stone, many of them two-story.

Accommodations, restaurants.

Massachusetts

ASHBY   On Ashby's green, the First Parish Church of 1809 is shaded by elms and pines. The church has triple doors, black shutters, and a belfry tower. Behind it is an old cemetery with slate tombstones, their backs scored when cut from the earth long ago. Incorporated in 1767, Ashby was on the stage road from Boston to Keene, New Hampshire. Its population in 1937 was 957; probably about the same today.

BOLTON   Highway 85 goes into the past as it runs through Bolton. An early industrial town, it was still manufacturing handmade ostrich-feather dusters in 1937. The Country Manor was its hotel at that time. Now a community of private homes.

BOXFORD   Settled in 1645. In an unspoiled area of rolling hills, unpaved country roads, woods, and large lakes, Boxford has a white Congregational church close to its green. John Adams, before he became president, once served as an attorney for the defense in a murder trial here.

CHESTERFIELD   Settled about 1760, Chesterfield was first called New Hingham, and later renamed for the Earl of Chesterfield. Its population was 445 in 1937, and is probably unchanged.

DEERFIELD   Old Deerfield Street is a mile-long walk past ancient and beautiful houses, most of them Colonial. There are no shops, and the street is arched by elms. The characteristic two-leaf front doors of the Connecticut Valley, rare elsewhere in New England, are on many of these houses. Deerfield Academy is one of the oldest boarding schools in the country.

Accommodations and restaurant at *Deerfield Inn*, (413) 774-5587.

FALL RIVER   Fascinating old three-story frame houses and big Victorian mansions on the hills above the city contrast with gray stone factories below that sometimes extend for blocks. Called the "Spindle City," Fall River boomed in the late 1800s when it became a leading textile producer, with more than 120 mills in operation. There were still 236 industrial plants in 1936. The Quequechan River runs through the city and provided power for the mills. Manufacturers of finished clothing now occupy the warehouses.
  Accommodations. Restaurants.

HAYDENVILLE   A stream flows through this town, which has a couple of big Greek Revival houses, one of them Hayden House, built about 1800, the home of Governor Hayden. A busy highway is nearby. Cloth-covered buttons were first manufactured by machinery here, but today there are no industries.
  Accommodations available in Williamsburg. Restaurant.

LANCASTER   Incorporated in 1653, the town was destroyed during King Philip's War. Luther Burbank was born here in 1840. Facing the green is the First Church of Christ, designed by Charles Bulfinch in 1816, called the finest of his many churches. It reflects the beginning of Greek influence on American architecture.

LINCOLN   Named for Lincoln, England, and settled in 1650. Many beautiful houses, including the home of Walter Gropius, great architectural innovator. The house blends New England tradition with modern expression.
  No accommodations. No restaurants.

SHEFFIELD   Accommodations and restaurant: *Stagecoach Hill*, Route 41, Sheffield, MA 01257, (413) 229-8585. A country pub that was an 1800s stagecoach stop on a winding road in the Berkshires. Fourteen rooms with bath. English beer on draft. A rosy fire on the hearth in winter.

TOWNSEND   Settled in 1676, Townsend had gristmills and sawmills by 1733; these later became cooperage plants. An octagonal brick house stands on Main Street. Black-and-white frame houses appear around the green. West Townsend was a stagecoach stop.
  Accommodations. Restaurant.

WORTHINGTON CENTER   Big lawns, wide yards between houses, big trees in this unfound town. The town hall has a Greek Revival entrance with two columns.
  Accommodations: *Worthington Inn at Four Corners Farm*, Old North Road, Route 143, Worthington, MA 01098, (413) 238-4441. Built in 1780; became an inn in 1986. A registered historic landmark; on fifteen acres. Building rather secluded on a country road. Wide pine floorboards, English and American antiques, oriental rugs, comfortable sofas. Five rooms with bath, five fireplaces. Canoeing, cross-country skiing. Restaurants nearby.

New Hampshire

CHARLESTOWN   Twelve-family population in 1744. Their historic fort where seven hundred French and Indians were driven off in 1747 has been reconstructed. Wide lawns and streets on both sides of the road, some houses early nineteenth-century.

No accommodations. Restaurant.

CORNISH   Cornish became a major New England art colony in the early part of this century when Augustus Saint-Gaudens, the sculptor, opened his studio here in a former country tavern on the Connecticut River. A covered bridge, one of the longest in the country, connects New Hampshire to Vermont two miles south of Cornish.

Accommodations: *Chase House*, Chase Street, RR 2, Box 909, Cornish, NH 03745, (603) 675-5391. Recently remodeled Federal-style house, the birthplace of S. P. Chase, founder of the Republican party. Six rooms, four with private bath or shower. Canopy beds, wingback chairs; three tables by fireplace.

FITZWILLIAM   Accommodations and restaurant: *Fitzwilliam Inn*, Fitzwilliam, NH 03447, (603) 585-9000. An inn since 1796, twenty-five rooms, ten baths, some rooms in annex. Faces the village green. Tilting wide floorboards, fireplace in the bar/pub, tole lamps. Men's room has a rocking chair. Inexpensive.

Inn's restaurant serves traditional New England meals with home-baked breads and desserts.

HANCOCK   Accommodations and restaurant: *John Hancock Inn*, Main Street, Hancock, NH 03449, (603) 525-3318. Former stagecoach stop, an inn since 1789; ten rooms with bath. Canopy beds, four-posters, braided and hooked rugs, rockers, wingback chairs. Once had ballrooms. Bar has tables made from old bellows with padded buggy seats on either side. In the Mural Room is an 1825 pastoral scene by an itinerant artist, Rufus Porter. Moderate.

Inn has excellent restaurant.

HANOVER   Accommodations and restaurant: *Hanover Inn*, P.O. Box 151, Hanover, NH 03755, (603) 643-4300. Completely rebuilt in the 1890s after a fire, frequently renovated since then, the rambling five-story inn has a wide porch that faces the green of Dartmouth College. The campus includes notable Colonial buildings. Inn has Colonial-style rooms or suites. Ninety-four doubles, 1 single, 6 suites, all with bath. Four dining areas. Expensive.

HARRISVILLE   A factory town that has sustained its factories without growing ugly. Recognized as a National Historic District, a nineteenth-century textile village in its original form. Although settled in 1786, the town was not incorporated until 1870. Most of its public buildings are around Harrisville Pond. A blackboard in front of the post office provides a central message center. Harrisville is the Timeless Town in its essence.

Accommodations: *Squires' Inn*, P.O. Box 19, Harrisville, NH 03450, (603) 827-3925. A country house made into a bed-and-breakfast; four rooms, two with private bath. Breakfast included, served in country kitchen or dining room. Inexpensive.

HAVERHILL   Near the white fence-enclosed green is Haverhill Academy, founded in 1816. A mixture of white frame and red brick houses can be seen throughout town. The first frame building was used as a blockhouse during the Revolution. Court Street is part of the Old Coos Turnpike from Plymouth, New Hampshire, to Concord. A stone marks the turnpike. A stagecoach stop.
    Accommodations: bed-and-breakfasts.

NELSON   On a hilltop on a small country road, Nelson has the Olivia Rodman Memorial Library, a 1787 town hall, and a brick building (1846) with tower-and-fish weathervane. Two flags on bowl staffs are planted in grass in front of town hall. Rows of mailboxes line the crossroad.

ORFORD   Samuel Morley built and operated a steamboat here in 1793. Has handsome, big houses with long, sloping lawns that reach to the highway; enclosed by white fences. Orford is built on a ridge facing west. A peaceful, pleasing place.

PARK HILL   Park Hill Meeting House, built in 1762, was moved to its hilltop here in 1779. A cut-off, hard-to-find village of few homes, no shops. No signs point the way.

PLAINFIELD   Small Colonial town of white buildings on Route 12A. No shops.

PORTSMOUTH   Much work has been done on Portsmouth's Strawberry Banke historic area (named for the sweet berries that grew on the banks of the Piscataqua River), but there are also many old houses outside the area. Construction for restoration can be seen all over town. Until the Revolution, Portsmouth was the most fashionable and probably the wealthiest city in all of New England. There were more private carriages and liveried servants than in any other New England town. Prosperity declined, but the houses were kept fairly intact. Structures of every period since 1664 can be seen. Walking tours available.
    Portsmouth has many inns and restaurants.

WALPOLE   A half mile above the Connecticut River, Walpole was once called Bellowstown after the Bellows family. Some houses have Greek Revival pillars, some are Federal, some Victorian. There is a cement horse trough.
    Accommodations: *The Homestead,* (603) 756-3320, bed-and-breakfast inn.
    Restaurant: *Major Leonard Keep Restaurant,* (603) 399-4474.

New Jersey

CALIFON   An early twentieth-century town at the bottom of a hill; many backyard sheds and barns. Has a railroad station built in 1875; its railroad and railroad tracks are now gone.

CAPE MAY   Named for Captain Cornelius Mey, who explored the coast in 1620, Cape May has been a summer resort since the early 1800s. Much of the town has been designated a Historic District, and there are nearly three hundred carefully preserved Victorian buildings, many of them built after the fire of 1878, but carefully modeled, with gingerbread additions, on their predecessors. A good walking town.

Large number of Victorian bed-and-breakfasts as well as motels and hotels. Many restaurants.

COKESBURY   Once had two churches; one now seems to be a home. Its few houses are strung out along a sigmoid curve. Woods.

GREENWICH   In 1701, Greenwich (pronounced as spelled) was one of New Jersey's three ports of entry for international shipping. It had its version of the Boston Tea Party in 1774 when young patriots disguised as Indians took the tea from the cellar of the Tory who had hidden it; they burned it on the town square. A monument naming the tea burners marks the site. Old houses, widely spaced, include the Nicholas Gibbon House of 1730. Old Stone Tavern, also known as Pirate House (1734), is said to be haunted by the pirate who once lived there.

LONG VALLEY   Known as German Valley for more than two hundred years; name changed after U.S. entered World War I. Still shows the influence of eighteenth- and nineteenth-century German settlers. Has an old stone mill and houses of stucco. Washington and his staff are said to have stayed in this town.

Restaurant: *Long Valley Inn*, (201) 876-3216, built in 1787, serves lunch and dinner.

MT. HOLLY   Settled by Quakers before 1700 and named for a 183-foot-high holly-covered hill. Many old homes and buildings along High Street. Shuttered white bay windows emerge from brick walls. Mill Street is another street of brick and frame houses, some with slender posts on their front porches. Patterned brick sidewalks in front of many buildings; some square structures. Occupied by British troops during the Revolution; the Friends meeting house, still standing, was their commissary. The Burlington County Courthouse, built in 1796, is a good example of Colonial architecture.

Accommodations. Restaurants.

MOUNTAINVILLE   Cutoff town with antique shop and a pond full of ducks. A live deer on one lawn watches us pass. An old Model-A Ford comes toward us and passes into history.

OLDWICK   Known as Smithfield in Colonial days, then as New Germantown, Oldwick has Victorian houses, with wide front and side lawns and a general store. Has an early-twentieth-century look. Its Zion Lutheran Church, built 1750, is the oldest Lutheran church in continuous use in New Jersey.

Restaurant.

New York

ASHLAND   Victorian town; once had two inns, one still standing with five square-post pillars. Footbridge nearby.

BARRYVILLE   Restaurant: *Reber's*, Barryville, NY 12719, (914) 557-6223. Animal heads, moose, African fox, along with bear in window are decorative accents. Three dining rooms, filled to capacity in season. Tops in German food. Bratwurst, sauerbraten, dumplings.
    Accommodations in nearby motel only.

CAMBRIDGE   A Victorian town, founded in 1835. It had the feel of a place about to be rediscovered. The railroad station was locked up, deserted. The Cambridge Hotel's rooms were without guests, only its bar and restaurant open. An inn for 104 years, now a National Historic Site about to be remodeled.

GOSHEN   With houses shaded by big trees on wide streets, Goshen is most interesting for its harness racing; the track claims to be the oldest trotting track in the world and was the sporting world's first National Historic Landmark. Its first half-miler was held in 1911. Self-guiding tours of the barn and blacksmith shop.
    Restaurant: *Orange Inn*, Main Street, Goshen, NY 10924, (914) 294-5144. Near the track, this three-story hotel dating to 1797 serves meals but makes no concession to eighteenth- or nineteenth-century timelessness; it looks just as it did some twenty years ago, with a small lobby and plain dining tables. No rooms available. Inexpensive.

HIGH FALLS   Restaurant: *DePuy Canal House*, High Falls, NY 12440, (914) 687-7700. A top-rated restaurant since it opened in 1969. Gray stone one-time tavern with weathered shutters, built in 1797 beside the Delaware & Hudson Canal; the canal was abandoned in 1899. Fireplace. Worn floor sills, moss on the roof, an odor of woodsmoke. American nouvelle cuisine. Expensive.

HURLEY   The sign says, WELCOME TO HISTORIC HURLEY, and we find a town of original stone houses, privately owned, with sloping roofs that come down to first-floor windows. In one house General Washington was given a public reception in 1782. Called Nieuw Dorp (Dutch for new village) in 1661, it was renamed in 1669. The Van Deusen House, which has a secret room, was the capital of New York for a month in 1777. Stone House Day is held each July.

JEWETT   Jewett is like a New England village of the 1800s with white houses, a church, a big barn. It has no visible post office or store.

KINGSTON   After having been a Dutch trading post from 1614, Kingston became a permanent settlement in 1652. The oldest stone houses are near the town center; they escaped the British burning of Kingston during the Revolution. The stone courthouse was built in 1815. The Old Dutch church and cemetery on Main Street were established in the mid-1600s. In the lower town are narrow streets and slate sidewalks edged with bricks. Between John and Front streets, storefronts are shaded by covered walkways, unique to Kingston. In the upper town are limestone houses from Revolutionary times. A good walking town; self-guiding tours are available.

Accommodations and restaurants.

LEXINGTON   The main road through Lexington crosses an iron bridge over the Schoharie Creek; an art center is on one side; near the bridge is a hotel. Lexington also has a Victorian house, a Methodist church, backyard sheds, and a big white frame building on Main Street.

Accommodations: *Lexington Hotel*, Lexington, NY 12452, (518) 989-9797. An inn for over one hundred years. Five stories; showers at end of hall. Authentic 1920s atmosphere. Iron beds for hard-core timelessness. Inexpensive.

Restaurant in the hotel.

NEW PALTZ   Established by the French Huguenots in 1677, Huguenot Street is now a National Historic Landmark. It has six stone dwellings from about 1700, four practically unaltered. Several fieldstone houses have steep shingle roofs over single-story front windows and door. An American flag beside one door, green shutters on the windows.

Accommodations available.

Restaurant: *Du Bois Fort Restaurant*, 81 Huguenot Street, New Paltz, NY 12561, (914) 255-1771. This house, whose first story was built in 1705 on the site of a stone fortress, perhaps with some of the fortress stones, became a restaurant in 1934. Wide floorboards, carpets, fireplace. Chef owner. Inexpensive.

PRATTSVILLE   Zadock Pratt built one hundred houses here on Schoharie Creek in 1825. He operated the largest tannery in the mountains, a grist mill, and a hat factory. Still a living town, it has houses facing the riverfront; the Reformed Dutch church of 1804 still stands. An old hotel has closed. The Zadock Pratt Museum is in Pratt's 1828 house; original and period furnishings.

SALEM   A spacious, timeless town. The Fort Salem Theater is in an old brick church with columns. There are big maples; ivy on bricks; a picket fence. The bank is in a 1790s house; in the Victorian era this building was remodeled to give it a Victorian appearance. Nearby is Gallows Hill; public executions, holiday and picnic occasions, were held here until 1808.

Restaurant: *Bobbie's Bakery*. A good bacon, lettuce, and tomato sandwich cost us $1.35.

SHANDAKEN   Accommodations and restaurant: *Auberge des 4 Saisons*, Route 42, Shandaken, NY 12480, (914) 688-2223. Chalet motel beside a trout stream; an inn for over thirty years. Rooms available in the inn or chalet. Pet rabbit on the grounds, swimming pool, tennis court, etc. Modified American plan. Excellent French Provincial food and a good wine list. Moderate.

SHUSHAN   An unfound town on old State Road 22. Several empty buildings on Main Street; the post office has moved to the old railroad station.

STONE RIDGE   First known as Butterfields, Stone Ridge is on the Old Mine Road. Court was held in the Tack House after the burning of Kingston by the British. Has a number of stone houses.

WADHAMS   A turn-of-the-century farm village with early houses, mostly Victorian. Small and unfound.

WEST KILL   West Kill is at the edge of a New York State forest preserve, and everything is white here—the post office, the houses, the community hall, the Baptist church. The cemetery beside the church has a white picket fence; old tombstones behind the church, they're white too. No stores.

No accommodations. No restaurants. Keep going.

WESTPORT   Late nineteenth-century homes on a natural terrace face Lake Champlain. Wide lawns, gardens.

Accommodations and restaurant: *The Inn on the Library Lawn*, P.O. Box 381, Westport, NY 12993, (518) 962-8666. A country inn since the 1860s. Twenty rooms with bath. Individually decorated rooms have high ceilings and tasteful color combinations. The ceiling in our room was so high I thought I'd shrunk. Moderate.

Dining room has wide floorboards, fireplace; faces the lake across Main Street. Cheerful service.

North Carolina

BATH   Founded 1705, oldest town in North Carolina, Bath has water on three sides and seems at times like an island. An unfound town, it has always been important to seafarers, among them Blackbeard, who lived on a nearby island. Ballast stones were used in walls and foundations of many buildings. Swindell's Store, a general store, has been in operation since the late nineteenth century. St. Thomas Church, oldest in North Carolina and on the National Register of Historic Places, dates to 1701 and has two-foot-thick solid brick walls. An annual production of an outdoor drama, *Blackbeard, Knight of the Black Flag*, takes place in Blackbeard Amphitheater. Walking tours.

Accommodations: *Bath Guest House*, South Main Street, Bath, NC 27808, (919) 923-6811. A bed-and-breakfast; rear of house faces the Pamlico River; boats and bicycles available to guests. White house with red shutters; long porch; brick sidewalk. Southern breakfast served. Inexpensive.

BEAUFORT   Settled in 1709 and first called Fishtown, Beaufort (pronounced Bo-fort) is a seacoast town. Captured by Spanish pirates in 1747; they were driven out a few days later. Today Front Street has restaurants and boutiques, but the old eighteenth-century homes are being preserved. Many have narrow front porches and no eaves. This is a found town, yet old, well-cared-for, attractive.

Accommodations: *Langdon House,* 135 Craven Street, Beaufort, NC 28516, (919) 728-5499. Handsomely restored house dating to 1732; bed and breakfast inn since 1984. Three rooms with queen-size beds, private bath and/or shower. Bicycles available.

Beaufort has a number of larger inns on the waterfront.

EDENTON   The Chowan County Courthouse of 1767, Georgian Colonial, is on the site of an early church of 1719. Its green extends all the way to Edenton Bay, in front of town. There are proud houses along the waterfront. Court Street is particularly handsome. Rewarding walking tour.

Accommodations, restaurants.

HALIFAX   A river port on the Roanoke River, Halifax was founded in 1760 and is trying to preserve its old buildings with a program called Historic Halifax. Main Street consists mostly of antique shops. Bypassed by the railroad as a major stop in the 1830s. Federal- and Georgian-style houses. Tourist center and guided tours.

MURFREESBORO   An unfound town that is fast being found. Murfreesboro is making an attempt to save and restore its ninety old brick and frame structures with the help of an active historical association. A port on the Meherrin River, it was incorporated in 1787, named for William Murfree, who donated ninety-seven acres of land. Dr. Walter Reed, who found a cure for yellow fever, spent several of his childhood years in Murfreesboro and returned to marry his childhood sweetheart. William Hill Brown, the first American novelist, died here September 2, 1793.

Accommodations, restaurants.

NEW BERN   New Bern, named after Bern, Switzerland, when founded in 1710, became a thriving Colonial seaport and social center. In 1774 it was made the capital of the Province of North Carolina. Tryon Palace, one of the most beautiful buildings in Colonial America, built in 1770 and destroyed by fire in 1798, was fully restored to original design in 1959, as were its formal palace gardens. Home of Royal Governor William Tryon and later of the first constitutional governor, Richard Caswell. Renovation is continuing throughout New Bern. A town for walking.

Accommodations: *King's Arms,* 212 Pollock Street, New Bern, NC 28560, (919) 638-4409. Built in 1848, much remodeled, has been a bed-and-breakfast since 1980. Eight rooms with bath, each room with fireplace (nonworking) and antiques. Canopied, four-poster, and brass beds. Full breakfast with freshly baked breads served in rooms. Moderate.

Restaurant: *Henderson House,* 216 Pollock Street, New Bern, NC 28560, (919) 637-4784. Red brick house with green shutters. Serves lunch Tuesday through Saturday, 11–2; dinner Thursday, Friday, Saturday, 6–9. Moderate.

WILMINGTON   Wilmington was captured by Cornwallis, and the Burgwin-Wright House (restored) was British headquarters during the winter of 1781. Its basement was made into a dungeon. St. James Church, across the street, was used as a stable. Historic houses are scattered through the downtown area, mingled with Victorian and modern buildings. Costin House, 1849, has a herringbone brick walk. The Customs House, 1916, is of stone with a fountain in front, an esplanade with a beautiful view of Cape Fear River. At the Cotton Exchange there is an Old Wilmington restoration. Whistler's mother was born here, and Woodrow Wilson had a home in town.

Accommodations and restaurants.

Pennsylvania

BETHLEHEM   A community settled in 1741 by Moravians. The Germanic architectural tradition of the eighteenth century was followed by Federal architecture in the nineteenth; later came Victoriana. The railroad station is one of the finest examples of Victorian architecture in the country. There are Colonial houses of stone and brick around and below the cemetery, called God's Acre. There is even a log house of 1826 still standing. Bethlehem has been a music center since its settlement; its annual Bach festival is called the Musikfest, and it crowds the town with music-lovers.

Accommodations and restaurant: *Hotel Bethlehem*, 437 Main Street, Bethlehem, PA 18018, (215) 867-3711. A 1920 inn in the downtown historic area, a short walk from the Moravian Church; 126 rooms with bath. Restaurant in hotel.

CARLISLE   Settled in 1720. Carlisle was Washington's headquarters during the Whiskey Rebellion, and was attacked by J. E. B. Stuart's forces during the Civil War. A number of red brick buildings surround the Public Square on Hanover Street. Many old buildings, with shutters, built close to the streets.

Accommodations and restaurants.

CHAMBERSBURG   Burned during the Civil War, Chambersburg has an attractive town center, a circle with a high cast-iron fountain in the shape of a Christmas tree. Figures around the base include a Civil War soldier. A towering, needle-pointed steeple rises above one church, at least as high again as the church itself. Other old houses on adjoining streets. John Brown's house was on King Street; he lived here while he made preparations for the Harpers Ferry raid.

Accommodations, restaurants.

DICKINSON   A string of white frame Victorian houses along the highway, among them a red brick Colonial with breasted chimneys; more old brick farms and homes.

FISHER'S FERRY   Stopping place: *Penn's Tavern*, also called Penn House or Stone Tavern. A two-and-one-half-story, pre-Revolutionary stone inn, below road level on Route 147, across the railroad tracks. The ferry, over the Susquehanna, no longer operates. No rooms, but the bar serves sandwiches; dinner for a large crowd from neighboring towns on Saturday nights. Small dining area with a two-hearth, wood-burning stone fireplace. The tavern is recently remodeled, quite expertly. Inexpensive.

Accommodations: Bed-and-breakfast in Selinsgrove.

GREENCASTLE   South Washington Street has a spectacular line of houses on both sides of the street; pillared porches; brick sidewalk. Most houses in this Civil War town, undiscovered, have short lawns.

Accommodations, restaurants.

MILFORD   A good-sized town with a green park, clean, neat yards and lawns. Victorian houses. A Tom Quick monument at Broad and Sarah streets honors a first settler who was killed by Indians in 1755. Tom Quick Inn is near town center.

Accommodations, restaurants.

PHILADELPHIA   This is where the nation was born, and within easy walking distance in older Philadelphia are the buildings where independence was debated and declared, a Revolutionary army raised, the Constitution written, the Bill of Rights adopted. Nearby residential areas have handsome historic houses. The brick arcade in Head House Square dates from 1803. Fine walking town.

Many accommodations, restaurants.

Rhode Island

ADAMSVILLE   In a valley. A 1750 grist mill stands beside a pond. There is a monument to a chicken, the Rhode Island red; also a Spite Tower, built by a wife to keep her husband from looking out the window at his lady friend's house; Adamsville cheese, New York cheddar is aged here.

Restaurant: *Abraham Manchester's Restaurant*, Adamsville, RI 02801, (401) 635-2700. Square pillars support the ceiling of this popular crossroads eating place. Iron sconces around the walls, blue checked tablecloths. Country comfort. Open year-round. Moderate.

KINGSTON   Taking Route 138 into Kingston is like following a road to an earlier century. Originally known as Little Rest, it was settled in 1700. Many old houses remain. The Old Courthouse of 1775 is now the public library; the general assembly met here during the Revolution. Congregational church dates to 1820.

LITTLE COMPTON   This village is built around a common that's an old, old graveyard with historic stones. The white-spired United Congregational Church, 1832, stands next to the cemetery. An unfound town.

Small restaurant beside the Wilbur General Store, an old house itself.

PEACE DALE   One of the state's most interesting corners of the past. A former manufacturing town. Accommodations in nearby Wakefield.

PROVIDENCE   Founded in 1636 by Roger Williams, Providence quickly became a shipping and shipbuilding town. It is now an industrial and commercial port twenty-seven miles from the sea. Nearly all phases of American architecture can be found here—Colonial, Federal, Georgian, and Greek Revival. Renovated commercial buildings that once stored cargoes of rum and molasses now house restaurants, shops, and offices. The Arcade, Greek Revival, on Westminster Street dates from 1828 and is clearly a forerunner of present-day enclosed shopping malls. Benefit Street has been busily restoring its eighteenth-century mansions. On this street is the Providence Athenaeum, one of the country's oldest libraries. The Beneficent Congregational Church, also called the Round Top Church (1810), is an early example of Classical Revival architecture; its interior is patterned after the New England meeting house. Overlooking the city is the state house, designed by McKim, Meade, & White, the first unsupported marble dome built in the nation. It's is the second largest marble dome in the world, after St. Peter's of Rome.

Many accommodations and restaurants.

WAKEFIELD   Accommodations and restaurant: *Larchwood Inn*, 176 Main Street, Wakefield, RI 02879, (401) 783-5454. Three-story inn surrounded by wide, landscaped lawns enclosed in wrought-iron fence. Built in 1831, the estate, called The Larches, became an inn in 1926. Twelve rooms with period furnishings and bath, three with shared bath. Seven rooms across street in Holly House, a Victorian inn. Inexpensive.

The Larchwood Inn has three dining rooms and the Tam O'Shanter Cocktail Lounge.

WICKFORD   Settled in 1707, Wickford has a long street of Colonial houses, more than any other town in New England, according to the townspeople. Colonial worship service is held once each year at St. Paul's, commonly called Old Narragansett Church, using silver chalice and paten (plate for wafers) given to the church by Queen Anne. Gilbert Stuart was baptized here while the church still had its silver baptismal basin, which was unaccountably melted down and made into plates in 1851.

Accommodations, restaurant.

South Carolina

AIKEN   Incorporated 1835; population now 14,000; was 6,000 in 1940. Shady boulevards crisscross through the quiet town. Polo is played here, and horses are held in high regard.

Accommodations and restaurant: *Willcox Inn*, Colleton Avenue at Whiskey Road, Aiken, SC 29801, (803) 649-1377. Built as an inn in 1898. Wood-burning stone fireplaces at either end of lobby. Thirty rooms, including six suites, all with private bath. Queen Anne period, sedate atmosphere. Bar, restaurant. Winston Churchill, the duke and duchess of Windsor, the Vanderbilts have all been guests. On National Registry of Historic Places. Moderate.

Aiken has a number of inns and restaurants.

BEAUFORT   Accommodations: *Bay Street Inn,* 601 Bay Street, Beaufort, SC 29902, (803) 524-7720. Built 1852; inn since 1983. Five rooms with fireplace, bath. Polished wood floors, oriental rugs, fan-footed tubs, river views. No bar or restaurant; evening chocolates, decanter of sherry, fruit basket, full breakfast, and use of bicycles included. Victorian atmosphere in historic zone of town (pronounced Byoo-fort). Moderate.

Accommodations: *Rhett House Inn,* 1009 Craven Street, Beaufort, SC 29902, (803) 524-9030. Five rooms with bath, a sense of the Old South. Two fireplaces, antiques. Pool table, library. Home-baked bread goes with breakfast. Moderate.

Other accommodations, restaurants.

CAMDEN   First settled 1733–34; incorporated 1791. Population now 7,462; was 5,183 in 1941. Greek Revival and Victorian houses. On Lyttleton and Broad streets, an abundance of old homes. Heavy atmosphere of past. Revolutionary battleground.

Accommodations: *The Inn on Broad Bed & Breakfast,* 1308–10 Broad Street, Camden, SC 29020, (803) 425-1806. Built as the McLean house in 1890, has been an inn since 1984. Eleven rooms, two with fireplace, all with bath. Restaurant next door serves dinner, also has rooms. Full breakfast served to guests. Abraham Lincoln's brother-in-law lived here. Fine view from upstairs corner room. Inexpensive.

Restaurant: *Rainbow Shop,* Garden Street at Chestnut, Camden, SC 29020, (803) 432-9180. Open as a restaurant since 1984. Unpretentious. The best of Southern cooking. Crowded. Excellent service. Inexpensive.

CHARLESTON   Charleston's historic area has preserved its antebellum air, with beautiful mansions looking out on manicured gardens and footpaths. Crooked streets and narrow alleys make this a fascinating town for walks, and although tourists throng to see its recent boutiques, Charleston cannot be spoiled by visitors.

Accommodations: *Battery Carriage House,* 20 South Battery, Charleston, SC 29401, (803) 723-9881 or (800) 845-7638. Restored carriage house built 1861, originally belonging to private mansion next door; inn since 1977, Victorian. Ten rooms with bath, wet bar. Glass of wine served in room each day. Breakfast in room or in courtyard. Bicycles provided. Room 29 has canopied bed, view of garden. Expensive.

Indigo Inn, 1 Maiden Lane, Charleston, SC 29401, (803) 577-5900 or (800) 845-7639. Nineteenth-century indigo warehouse, became an inn in 1978; thirty-seven rooms, three suites, all with bath, face central courtyard. Furnished with eighteenth-century antiques and reproductions. Cannonball beds and famous Charleston rice beds in many rooms. Breakfast buffet served to guests in room, courtyard, or lobby. Moderate.

Jasmine House, 64 Hasell Street, Charleston, SC 29401, (803) 577-5900. Greek Revival house built in 1840; same owners as Indigo Inn. Six suites, four with fireplace, furnished with nineteenth-century antiques. Bar, no restaurant. Hunt breakfast served to guests. Expensive.

Planters Inn, 112 North Market Street, Charleston, SC 29401 (803) 722-2345 or (800) 845-7082. Built as drygoods warehouse in 1840, inn since 1984; forty-one rooms, five suites, all with bath, four suites with gas fireplaces. Bar, restaurant. Four-poster beds, chaise longues, folding doors, TV in cabinet; original moldings, flooring, and outside façade preserved. Expensive.

Restaurant: *Baker's Cafe,* 214 King Street, Charleston, SC 29401, (803) 577-2694. Informal, inexpensive. Oilcloth on tables. Liquor license. Breakfast, lunch, dinner. Omelettes, eggs Benedict, flounder amandine, croissants for breakfast.

Charleston has many inns and restaurants.

COLUMBIA   Capital of South Carolina, Columbia has wide, shady streets, dominated by the state house, one of only two buildings on Main Street to survive Sherman's torches. Robert Mills lived in Columbia for ten years beginning in 1820, and many of the oldest houses still standing show his influence.

Accommodations: *Claussen's Inn at Five Points,* 2003 Greene Street, Columbia, SC 29205, (803) 765-0440. Historic bakery, newly designed as an inn; twenty-nine rooms with bath, loft suite with spiral staircase, continental breakfast, turndown service including chocolates and brandy. Four-poster, iron, and brass beds, reproductions or traditional furnishings in a modern building. Moderate.

Columbia has a number of inns and restaurants.

GEORGETOWN   On the ocean highway, sixty miles north of Charleston, Georgetown was first settled in 1526 by the Spaniards. A hurricane and Indian attacks prevented the settlement from becoming permanent. The town was more firmly founded in 1729, named for the Prince of Wales who later became King George II. Pre-Revolutionary structures still stand. Self-guided walking tours through its historic area include the Rice Museum, the first local structure listed in the National Register of Historic Places.

Accommodations: *1790 House,* Georgetown, SC 29440, (803) 546-4821. Built 1790, newly opened as an inn; four rooms with bath. Antebellum atmosphere. No bar or restaurant. Beautifully furnished with antiques. Moderate.

Restaurants available.

Tennessee

CADES COVE   Preserved by the National Park Service as an open-air museum. A trip through Cades Cove is a visit to a community, unchanged and unchanging, where pioneer mountain people lived from 1794 to the 1920s in isolated conditions, cut off by a mountain barrier from the outside world, though not shut off from the rest of humanity. The land here, two thousand acres, is still lived on and farmed, leased to private individuals under specified conditions, because without farming the Cove would return to woodland. A self-guided auto tour over an eleven-mile loop gives a real sense of the rural past.

No accommodations. No restaurants.

GATLINBURG   Accommodations: *Wonderland Hotel,* Route 2, Box 205, Gatlinburg, TN 37738, (615) 436-5490. With rocking chairs on its long porch, this 1912 inn within the Great Smokies National Park has the homey feel of the 1930s. It is seven miles from downtown Gatlinburg. Twenty-seven rustic but not primitive rooms, seventeen baths, a fireplace, a game room, spacious lawns, views of the Smokies, and Little River Gorge just seventy-five yards away. Altitude: 2,400 feet. Old-fashioned square dance on Saturday nights. Swimming hole nearby. Innertubes for guests who want to float on the river. Open from May 2 through October. Inexpensive.

The inn has a restaurant.

JONESBOROUGH (JONESBORO on some maps)   Oldest town in Tennessee, discovered, but sleeping in its past. Modernization has been resisted here for years. Once a part of North Carolina, it later became the state of Franklin and applied for admittance to the Union. Statehood lasted only four years. There are rows of old buildings and many interesting houses. Daniel Boone's trail passed through town. Fine walking tour.

Restaurants.

Vermont

CASTLETON   Houses one hundred years old or over. The brick Federated Church, 1833, designed by Thomas Dake; many Dake-designed houses. In Zadock Remington's Tavern, Ethan Allen and Benedict Arnold planned the attack on Fort Ticonderoga.

Restaurants.

CRAFTSBURY COMMON   On a plateau, Craftsbury Common has big white houses, many with shutters, and the longest picket fences we've seen in the Northeast. A single-railed wood fence surrounds a green that looks more like a fairgrounds. Sweeping vista to the west. Congregational church is from 1820; the Craftsbury Academy, 1829. This was once the county seat of what is called the Northeast Kingdom.

Accommodations: *The Inn on the Common*, Craftsbury Common, VT 05827, (802) 586-9619. Behind one of the picket fences, this inn has three buildings that date from the early nineteenth century and have been restored. Beautiful gardens with many perennials. Woodstoves and fireplaces. Seventeen rooms with bath include antiques, quilts, hooked rugs, and folk art. Modified American plan. Moderate.

Restaurant at the inn has an excellent wine list and fine food.

LANDGROVE (NORTH LANDGROVE on Vermont map)   A cluster of well-cared-for houses on a back road deep in the Vermont woods.

Accommodations. *Village Inn*, RFD Box 215, Landgrove, VT 05148, (802) 824-6673. Red clapboard buildings with white trim. First opened as an inn in 1939; twenty-one rooms, most with private bath, breakfast included. Moderate.

Restaurant at the inn. Vegetables from their garden.

NEWFANE   Noted for its much-photographed buildings around the county courthouse of 1825 and for its common in front of the courthouse, Newfane, founded in 1776, has been well discovered but not spoiled.

Accommodations and restaurant: *Four Columns Inn*, Newfane, VT 05345, (802) 365-7713. Built in 1830, opened as an inn in 1965; twelve rooms with bath, furnished with antiques. Expensive.

Inn has three-star restaurant.

OLD BENNINGTON   Founded in 1749, has long common on boulevard, around it are historic buildings. Old First Congregational Church (1805) and Old Burial Ground are on Monument Avenue. The Bennington Battle Monument towers over all.

Accommodations and restaurants in Bennington.

PAWLET   Crossroads village on the slant of a hill. Flower Brook flows through town. Jesuit mission settlement, about 1755. Community Church with square towers, a 1790 house, a tiny green. Once a thriving mill town.

Restaurant.

PEACHAM   Historic village on crest of hill, site of Peacham Academy of 1795, then called the Caledonia County Grammar School. Congregational church of 1806 has a beautiful clock, black letters on a white face, white hands. Deacon Jonathan Elkins was father of the town; arrived in 1775 and made a settlement the next year. Elkins Tavern still stands. Bailey-Hazen Military Road went through town, a main thoroughfare for pioneer travelers.

Restaurant.

PERU   A cutoff town on a hill. Across the road from the Peru Congregational Church, built 1846, is the J. J. Hapgood Store, a movie-set of a place, as Vermont as Vermont cheddar.

Accommodations: Two bed-and-breakfast inns, restaurants nearby.

WESTON   Many old restored homes in this discovered village; the green, a shallow frog pond before the Civil War, is surrounded by a black iron-pipe railing. Mountains on all sides. Weston Playhouse, an active little theater, is in a reconstructed abandoned church. The Vermont Country Store is a revived 1890 emporium. The handsome Farrar-Mansur House, once a tavern, is now a museum and community house, filled with antiques.

Accommodations: *Wilder Homestead Inn*, RR1, Box 106-D, Weston, VT 05161, (802) 824-8172. Built in 1827, one of only two brick homes built in Weston. On National Register of Historic Places, it has been an inn since 1986. Eight fireplaces, four working; Moses Eaton stenciling on walls of one room. Seven rooms, six with private bath. Country breakfast. Inexpensive.

There are a number of inns and restaurants in Weston.

WILLIAMSVILLE   West of Newfane on the road to South Newfane, this undiscovered early-nineteenth-century town has a river, a falls, and a covered bridge.

Accommodations: One bed-and-breakfast. No restaurants.

Virginia

ALDIE   No more than a dozen houses in the town, but they are houses of another age. Founded in 1758; originally renowned for Mercer's and Cooke's Mill, one of the last dual-wheel-powered grain mills in the U.S. Many Confederate raider maneuvers conducted in this area.

Accommodations: *Little River Inn*, P.O. Box 116, Aldie, VA 22001, (703) 327-6742. Restored to become an inn in 1982, this 1868 house was constructed using bricks of an earlier period. A strong sense of the past here, a feeling for this old-timer of having come home. Immaculate with shining pine floors. Five rooms, one with fireplace, two with private bath; three cottages with fireplaces are also rented. Full breakfast is included. Moderate.

Restaurant five miles away in Middleburg.

FREDERICKSBURG   On the Rappahannock River, the town was a major objective of both sides during the Civil War; it changed hands seven times over the course of four bloody battles. More than 15,000 men who died in that war are buried in the National Military Cemetery, only 3,000 identified.

Accommodations: *Richard Johnston Inn*, 711 Caroline Street, Fredericksburg, VA 22401, (703) 899-7606. Built as a Federal-style townhouse in 1789, has been an inn in the center of the historic district since 1984. High ceilings, pine staircase and floors, antiques, and handmade quilts in rooms. Eleven rooms, including two suites, seven with private bath, seven with working fireplaces; breakfast included. Moderate.

Fredericksburg has a number of inns and restaurants.

LEXINGTON   A large number of nineteenth-century buildings, most of them brick, in the restored downtown area. The Alexander-Withrow House was one of the few that survived the fire of 1796. Lawyers' Row and Court House Square were part of the original 1778 town. Robert E. Lee and Stonewall Jackson are buried here. After the end of the Civil War, Lee became president of what was then Washington Academy; after his death, it became Washington and Lee University, a campus of white colonnaded buildings.

Accommodations: *Historic Country Inns of Lexington*, 11 North Main Street, Lexington, VA 24450, (703) 463-2044. Three inns under one management—the Alexander-Withrow House, Washington Street, and McCampbell Inn, on Main Street, and Maple Hall, an 1850 plantation house six miles north. McCampbell Inn, built in 1809, is half-surrounded by double porches. Fourteen rooms, two suites, decorated with antiques. Breakfast served downstairs in the Great Room. Moderate.

Several restaurants in Lexington.

MIDDLEBURG   Surveyed by George Washington, Middleburg is considered the capital of Virginia's hunt country. Fieldstone walls line the road. It was once an overnight stop on the stagecoach route between Alexandria and Winchester. A discovered town with old stone and brick houses and cottages.

Accommodations: *Red Fox Inn and Tavern,* 2 East Washington Street, Middleburg, VA 22117, (800) 223-1728, or (703) 687-6301. A tavern since 1728; during the Civil War, it served as a hospital. J. E. B. Stuart and John Mosby conferred here, and rooms are named for them. Has thirty-inch-thick stone walls. Also offers rooms in the nearby Stray Fox and the McConnell House. Breakfast included. Seventeen rooms, decorated with antiques, all with private bath and/or shower. Most of the four-posters have canopies; several rooms have their original fireplaces. Pine floors. Fresh flowers. Polished dark tavern tables. Eight rooms in the Stray Fox Inn, five in McConnell House. Expensive.

The Red Fox Inn has seven dining rooms.

MONTEREY   The first battle of Jackson's Valley Campaign fought here; has the aura of a turn-of-the-century town. White frame buildings. The Highland County Courthouse, red brick with white columned portico, was built in 1848.

Accommodations: *Highland Inn,* Main Street, P.O. Box 40, Monterey, VA 24465, (703) 468-2143. Built in 1904, the four-story white building with green-trimmed windows has porches on its first and second floors. A one-time mountain resort, it is on the National Register of Historic Places. Has an outside wooden staircase; twelve double rooms, five suites, all with bath. Inexpensive.

Restaurant in the inn. Local trout a specialty.

PARIS   A cutoff town near Ashby's Gap through the Blue Ridge Mountains. A local hill was used as a signal station by both sides during the Civil War. Frame houses, wide stone chimneys. No sign on the highway indicates the town exists.

Accommodations: Ashby Inn, Route 1, Box 2A, Paris, VA 22130, (703) 592-3900. Built in 1829; four working fireplaces; six rooms, four with private bath. All have antiques. Inexpensive.

Restaurant in the inn.

RICHMOND   Besides the capitol, designed by Thomas Jefferson in 1785, other sights in Richmond include St. John's Church, built in 1741, site of the Revolutionary convention where Patrick Henry gave his famous speech.

Accommodations: *Jefferson Sheraton Hotel,* Franklin and Adams Streets, Richmond, VA 23220, (804) 788-8000 or (800) 325-3535. An 1895 hotel encompassing an entire city block, recently restored. Has statue of Thomas Jefferson in lobby and a grand staircase that legend says was the model for the one in *Gone With the Wind.* Massive, rose-colored pillars around the lobby. The hotel is in the National Register of Historic Places and the Virginia Landmarks Register. There are 276 rooms with bath, 9 with fireplaces. Two presidential suites have grand pianos. Expensive.

Restaurants, several, in hotel.

Richmond has many attractive inns and restaurants.

UPPERVILLE   Has a post office, store, library, and a long Main Street of brick, stone, and frame houses. In the midst of hunt country.

Accommodations: *Gibson Hall Inn,* Box 225, Upperville, VA 22176, (703)

592-3514. Built in 1832; became an inn in 1983. Brass and four-poster beds. Six rooms, four with private bath, five with fireplaces. Expensive.

WILLIAMSBURG   A found town, once the capital of Virginia, with a recon-structed Colonial Williamsburg Historic Area that is a separate entity. The streets of this historic area are black-topped, but no automobiles appear. Traditional Christmas in Williamsburg is an annual event. A tourist center.
     Many accommodations and restaurants.

West Virginia

BERKELEY SPRINGS   Indians were using these mineral spring baths before the white man arrived. Already a popular spa in 1730, its distinguished guest list is long, including Thomas Lord Fairfax and George Washington. The town was officially established as a health resort in 1776 under the name of Bath, which is still its official name.
     Accommodations and restaurant: *Country Inn*, Berkeley Springs, WV 25411, (304) 258-2210. An inn since 1932 on the site of a former hotel that burned in 1898. Adjoins the village green and Berkeley Springs State Park and spa. Thirty-six rooms or suites with bath; thirty-six rooms with shared baths. Inexpensive. Attractive restaurant.

CHARLES TOWN   Named for George Washington's brother, who laid out its streets in 1786; better known as the town where John Brown was tried and hanged for treason. The one-room courthouse of 1833, where Brown was tried, has been incorporated into the present courthouse at George and Washington Streets. A pyramid of three stones on Samuel Street marks the gallows site.
     Accommodations, restaurants.

HARPERS FERRY   There had been ferry service here for thirty years when Harpers Ferry was established in 1763. At the junction of the Potomac and Shenandoah rivers, with a panoramic view. Jefferson wrote, "the scene is worth a voyage across the Atlantic."
     Accommodations and restaurant: *Hilltop House*, P. O. Box 806, Harpers Ferry, WV 25425, (304) 535-6321. Built on the side of a cliff in 1890, now being restored. Changes should probably be expected. Wide porches with view of three states. Woodrow Wilson and Mark Twain were guests. Sixty rooms with bath, fireplace in lobby. Inexpensive. Large dining room can seat three hundred.

LEWISBURG   Historic district includes 236 acres of eighteenth- and nine-teenth-century houses, churches, and commercial buildings, among them the 1837 county courthouse and the Old Stone Church of 1796, still in use.
     Accommodations and restaurant: *General Lewis Inn*, 301 East Washington Street, Lewisburg, WV 24901, (304) 645-2600. A white building of 1834 with 1920 additions, partly brick, with six white pillars. Antique furnishings in lobby and rooms. Raftered ceilings in lobby and lounge. Handmade walnut and pine registration desk. Twenty-seven rooms with bath. Inexpensive. The inn has a restaurant.

LOST RIVER   Accommodations: *The Guest House,* Lost River, WV 26811, (304) 897-5707. Looks out over Lost River Valley, surrounded by four mountain ranges; George Washington National Forest in back. Heated pool, Jacuzzi, indoor hot tub. Has been an inn since 1984, and finishing touches are still being added. Rustic luxury. Full breakfast included. Six rooms with bath. Inexpensive.

Restaurant nearby at Lost River State Park.

MATEWAN   A Hatfield-McCoy shootout took place here. The railroad station is gone, but the underpass remains. The railroad still gets a little use; two sets of track run through town, one rusty, one slightly rusty. Main Street is below the tracks. Old brick buildings.

MOOREFIELD   Town has several eighteenth-century log houses covered with siding. Many interesting buildings in an unfound town that dates back to 1777.

Accommodations: *McMechen House Inn,* 109 North Main Street, Moorefield, WV 26836, (304) 538-2417. Built in 1853, an inn since 1983. Three-story Victorian house filled with antiques, immaculate, decorated with care and affection. Three rooms, three suites, all with bath, each room with a name, such as Margaret Rebecca Room. Full breakfast included. Inexpensive.

Restaurant: *Old Stone Tavern,* 117 South Main Street, Moorefield, WV 26836, (304) 538-2186. Moorefield's oldest standing building, it dates to 1788. On the National Register of Historic Places. Has a fireplace in the old stone section. The frame part of the house was added in the early 1900s. Memorabilia and moodiness upstairs. Inexpensive.

ROMNEY   First known as Pearsall's Flats, Romney was part of Lord Fairfax's holdings; settlers were forced to pay him rent or buy outright. After the Revolution the Fairfax lands were seized. This unfound town changed hands fifty-six times during the Civil War. A log house is standing on Main Street.

Accommodations, restaurants.

SHEPHERDSTOWN   Settled in 1762 and first called Mecklenberg, Shepherdstown resembles some Pennsylvania towns, but it is older than most. German Street holds onto its past, as does an old grist mill built in 1738. Almost every street in town is snagged in the past. Washington is said to have seriously considered making this the national capital. Good town for walking.

Accommodations: *Thomas Shepherd Inn,* P.O. Box 1162, Shepherdstown, WV 25443 (304) 876-3715. A parsonage when it was built in 1868; an inn since 1984. Restored and furnished with Victorian pieces. Six rooms, four with private bath. Rooms have shutters. Full breakfast included. Moderate.

Restaurant: *Yellow Brick Bank and the Little Inn,* 201 German Street, Shepherdstown, WV 25443, (304) 876-2208. Good food in an old bank, which now has yellow striped awnings, stenciled beams, candlelight. Guest rooms to be added.

Index to Towns and Roads

ALABAMA

Eufaula, 73, 183–4

CONNECTICUT

Brooklyn, 134–5, 184
Colchester, 135
Colebrook, 132–3, 184
Guilford, 184
Hampton, 184
Litchfield, 9–10
Durham, 135
Middle Post Road, 135
New Haven, 135
Norfolk, 131–2, 184
Orange, 184
Pomfret, 135, 184
Riverton, 133, 184–5

Salisbury, 130–1
Stonington, 6–8
Thompson, 135, 185
Torrington, 132
Winchester Center, 132
Windham, 135

DELAWARE

Dover, 185
Kenton, 185
King's Highway, 185–6
New Castle, 32–3, 185
Odessa, 185–6
Smyrna, 186

DISTRICT OF COLUMBIA

Washington, 96, 135

FLORIDA

Cedar Key, 66–8, 186
Copeland, 186
Everglades, 57, 180, 186
Everglades City, 61–4, 186
Indian Key, 54–6
Inverness, 186–7
Key West, 53–4, 62, 66–7, 170, 187
La Belle, 65, 187
Lake Weir, 66
Marco Island, 61, 63
St. Augustine, 52–3, 187
Sunniland, 65
Suwannee, 68–9
Wakulla Springs, 69, 187

GEORGIA

Americus, 73
Andersonville, 73
Augusta, 76
Bainbridge, 70–1
Colquitt, 71–2
Cuthbert, 187
Dawson, 188
Eatonton, 75–6
Fort Gaines, 72, 74, 152, 188
Frederica, 49
Georgetown, 183
Greensboro, 76
Macon, 73, 188
Madison, 188
Milledgeville, 74–6, 119, 188
Ocmulgee National Monument, 73–4
Savannah, 48–51, 188–9
Sandersville, 75
Thomasville, 70
Washington, 189

MAINE

Bar Harbor, 170, 177
Birch Island, 176–7
Brunswick, 171, 176

Cherryfield, 189
Corinna, 174–5
Dover-Foxcroft, 189
Eastport, 179–80, 189
East Sumner, 189
Fort Kent, 182
Freeport/Durham, 189–90
Houlton, 180–1, 190
Lisbon Falls, 171
Machias, East Machias, 190
Madawaska, 181–2
Monhegan Island, 170
Mt. Desert Island, 170, 173, 176–9
Northeast Harbor, 190
Oxford, 5
Paris Hill, 190
Pittsfield, 190
Portland, 170–1, 190
Quoddy Village, 190–1
Sabbathday Village, 172–3
Shiloh, 171–2
Somesville, 178, 191
Southwest Harbor, 191
Wayne, 191
Yarmouth, 170

MARYLAND

Annapolis, 97, 191
Chesapeake City, 191–2
Frederick, 192
Oldtown, 106
Princess Anne, 33
Williamsport, 192

MASSACHUSETTS

Andover, 168
Ashby, 148, 192
Bolton, 192
Boston, 106, 134–5, 143–5
Boston Post Road, 143–4, 192
Boxford, 147, 192
Cambridge, 145
Chesterfield, 192
Concord, 134, 145–6

Deerfield, 145, 149, 192
Fall River, 193
Great Barrington, 131
Haydenville, 193
Lancaster, 193
Lexington, 134
Lincoln, 145–6, 193
Mohawk Trail, 131, 145
Pittsfield, 131
Sheffield, 193
Townsend, 193
Townsend Harbor, 147–8
West Boxford, 147
Worthington Center, 193

NEW HAMPSHIRE

Charlestown, 194
Concord, 195
Cornish, 194
Fitzwilliam, 168, 194
Hancock, 194
Hanover, 194
Harrisville, 167–8, 194–5
Haverhill, 195
Keene, 148, 192
Nelson, 195
Old Coos Turnpike, 195
Orford, 195
Park Hill, 167, 195
Percy, 11
Plainfield, 166, 195
Plymouth, 195
Portsmouth, 170, 195
Rindge, 168–9
Walpole, 195

NEW JERSEY

Asbury Park, 28, 30
Atlantic City, 30
Atlantic Highlands, 23
Batsto, 29
Bordentown, 18
Bridgewater, 16
Califon, 123–4, 195

Cape May, 28–30, 196
Cokesbury, 123, 196
Communipaw, 15
Cotsworth, 28
Crosswicks, 5, 16, 19–20
Deal, 25
Elizabeth, 16
Elizabethtown, 16
Greenwich, 196
Imlaystown, 20
Larison's Corner, 16
Lambertville, 16–17
Long Branch, 25–6
Long Valley, 196
Morristown, 16
Mt. Holly, 196
Mountainville, 123, 196
Navesink, 24–6
North Branch, 16
Oldwick, 122–3, 196
Old York Road, 16
Pine Barrens, 27–9
Ringoes, 17
Sea Bright, 26
Titusville, 18
Trenton, 18

NEW YORK

Albany, 172
Ashland, 197
Barryville, 197
Cambridge, 153–4, 197
Catskill Turnpike, 126
Goshen, 197
High Falls, 197
Hurley, 125, 197
Jewett, 197
Kingston, 125–6, 197–8
Lexington, 126–7, 198
Marbletown, 125
New Paltz, 198
New York City, 4, 12–15, 106, 119,
    178–9
Old Mine Road, 14–15, 125, 199
Pawling, 131
Port Jervis, 125

Prattsville, 128, 198
Salem, 153–5, 198
Shandaken, 198
Shushan, 153–4, 199
Stone Ridge, 199
Wadhams, 199
West Kill, 128, 199
Westport, 199
Windham, 127

NORTH CAROLINA

Bath, 89–91, 199
Beaufort, 199–200
Edenton, 91, 200
Halifax, 200
Murfreesboro, 91, 200
New Bern, 89, 200
Washington, 90
Wilmington, 88, 201

PENNSYLVANIA

Bethlehem, 117–19, 201
Carlisle, 115–16, 201
Chambersburg, 201
Dickinson, 201
Fisher's Ferry, 116, 117, 201–2
Greencastle, 202
Intercourse, 117
Lancaster, 34
Milford, 202
New Hope, 16–17
Old York Road, 115
Philadelphia, 16, 26, 31–2, 34, 117, 136, 143–44, 159, 202
Philadelphia-Lancaster Turnpike, 16, 35–8
Selinsgrove, 202

RHODE ISLAND

Adamsville, 202
Bristol, 140
Jamestown, 139–40

Kingston, 139, 202
Little Compton, 141–2, 202
Peace Dale, 138–9, 202
Providence, 203
Wakefield, 203
Warren, 141
Wickford, 203

SOUTH CAROLINA

Aiken, 77–8, 203
Beaufort, 47, 204
Camden, 79–81, 204
Charleston, 43–4, 46–7, 204–5
Columbia, 78, 205
Georgetown, 73, 81–7, 205
Middletown Place, 45
St. George, 43–4
Sandy Island, 84–6

TENNESSEE

Cades Cove, 205
Cumberland Gap, 112–13
Gatlinburg, 205–6
Jonesborough, 112, 206
Morristown, 112
Tazewell, 112

VERMONT

Bailey-Hazen Road, 5–7, 164–5
Barre, 164
Bennington, 131, 151, 207
Brattleboro, 151
Castleton, 206
Craftsbury Common, 206
Cuttingsville, 164
Danville, 6, 164
East Hardwick, 165
Granby, 5
Landgrove, North Landgrove, 160, 206
Londonderry, 156, 160–3
Newfane, 151, 206–7

Newfane Hill, 151
Old Bennington, 151–3, 207
Pawlet, 207
Peacham, 6, 164–5, 207
Peru, 159–60, 207
South Newfane, 151, 208
Sunderland, 157–8
Victory, 5
Weston, 159–60, 207
Williamsville, 151, 208

VIRGINIA

Aldie, 97, 100, 207
Alexandria, 96, 209
Ashland, 96
Blue Ridge Parkway, 114
Fredericksburg, 96, 208
Jamestown, 93
Jermantown, 100
Lexington, 208
Middleburg, 97, 100, 208–9
Monterey, 208
Paris, 101, 209
Richmond, 94–6, 209
Surry, 93

Upperville, 100–1, 209–10
Williamsburg, 32, 93–4, 210
Winchester, 101, 209

WEST VIRGINIA

Beckley, 108
Berkeley Springs, 105–6, 210
Charles Town, 104, 210
Clintonville, 108
Darkesville, 105
Harpers Ferry, 102–3, 201, 210
Inwood, 105
Lewisburg, 210
Logan, 108
Lost River, 107, 211
Lost River State Park, 107, 211
Martinsburg, 105
Matewan, 108–10, 211
Mathias, 107
Moorefield, 211
Romney, 211
Shepherdstown, 103–4, 211
Springfield, 106–7
Upper Tract, 107–8
Williamson, 108

... To Maine

North

Houlton

Maine

Eastport

Corinna

Mt. Desert Island

Stark

Hardwick

Shiloh

Vt.

N.H.

Plainfield

Cambridge Newfane Fitzwilliam Boxford

Bennington Rindge Cambridge

New York Deerfield *Ma.*

R.I.

Prattsville Brooklyn

Riverton Peace Dale

Kingston *Ct.* Stonington

Fisher's Ferry Bethlehem *N.J.* Navesink

New Hope

Pennsylvania Philadelphia

Intercourse Batsto

New Castle

Md.

Oldtown

Annapolis *De.* Cape May

Washington, D.C.

Atlantic Ocean